TRANS FORMERS

All Fall Down

Simon Furman
Andrew Wildman
Stephen Baskerville

TITAN BOOKS

TRANSFORMERS™: ALL FALL DOWN
ISBN 1 84023 300 1
BOTCON EXCLUSIVE EDITION
ISBN 1 84023 378 8

Published by Titan Books,
a division of Titan Publishing Group Ltd.
144 Southwark St,
London SE1 0UP
UK

This book collects issues 69-74 of *Transformers*
(vol 1), originally published in single-issue form
by Marvel Comics, USA.

A CIP catalogue record for this title is available
from the British Library.

First edition: August 2001
10 9 8 7 6 5

Printed in Italy.

What did you think of this book? We love to hear
from our readers. Please email us at:
readerfeedback@titanemail.com or write to us at the
above address.

Paperback cover art and computer effects
by Andrew Wildman

*Botcon exclusive cover art by Geoff Senior
and Oliver Harud*

THE BEGINNING AND THE END

Back in 1991, on the letters page of *Transformers* #80 (the final issue of that run), I wrote, "for me, personally, IT NEVER ENDS". Meaning, though the comic was finally, irrevocably cancelled, I had too much invested in the characters, and worlds they inhabited, to simply shrug and move on. Oh, those words have come back to haunt me from time to time, but how true they turned out to be!

My involvement with the 'robots in disguise' began back in 1985, when I wrote my first story for the UK *Transformers* comic. Many, many more followed, and in 1989 I took over (from departing scribe Bob Budiansky) as writer on the US comic (issue #56 to be precise). At this point, the popularity of Transformers (monumental in its time) had begun to wane, and it was largely assumed that the comic would last only a few more issues at best. As it turned out, we managed twenty-six, and for me they still comprise the biggest and best body of work I ever produced.

The amount of latitude I had to steer my own course increased geometrically when Hasbro (who produced the *Transformers* toys) began to take only a peripheral interest in what we were doing. They too had moved their attention elsewhere (we tested the water with an outrageous April Fool's gag, in the form of a draft story outline in which every Transformer died and mechanical sheep vied with giant nuns!), and I was free to go 'epic' on *Transformers*. I was further blessed with an editor (Rob Tokar) who was happy for me to do so, and an artist (Andrew Wildman, with whom I'd worked on the UK comic) who ate 'epic' for lunch. We were set, we were rolling...

The issues collected herein form the first part of what, for want of a better catchall title, I call 'the Unicron Saga', and ran from issue #69 to #80 (though it actually began, as a sub-plot, back in issue #61). Unicron was one of many characters I had freely usurped from *Transformers: The Movie* (a superb animated feature that utilised lofty voice talents such as Leonard Nimoy, Eric Idle, Robert Stack and, incredibly, Orson Welles as Unicron). I gleefully stirred the movie elements into the ongoing comic-based war between the heroic Autobots and the evil Decepticons, and the resultant no-holds-barred, all-guns-blazing, this-issue-everyone-dies brew is here (or at least here and in the next book, *End of the Road*) to enjoy again.

Transformers has kept coming back for me, it really did never end. I wrote the entire 12-issue run of *Transformers: Generation 2*, a couple of *Beast Wars: Transformers* comics (and a bunch of text stories) for various US and UK Transformers conventions and the final episode of the first *Vanimated serie* a two-part sto ous *Transformers*-based projects, the idea I cherished above all was getting those original comics back in print, collected and wrapped in a brand-spanking new cover.

Thanks to Titan Books, and the faith they had in my cavalier assertions that there really was still a market out there, I'm now in a position to sit back smugly and display these volumes on my shelf for all to see. Satisfied doesn't even begin to cover it.

Simon Furman, London, 2001

BITS AND PIECES

Some things never go away. Some things come back to haunt you. And now and then some things return solely to remind you how much fun life can be.

Even though it's now over a decade ago, I can still remember how pleased I was to be given the chance to draw *Transformers* for Marvel US. I'd previously worked on various Marvel UK titles, but this was to be my first foray into the world of American comics. The real stuff (well, kind of). *Transformers* was seen by many, including myself, as a potential springboard onto more mainstream Marvel books. It was, after all, a toy book; a licensed product with all the red tape and limitations that inevitably seems to entail. The strange thing is, we had more freedom on this book than on any I have worked on since.

The challenge of taking a bunch of tin boxes and breathing life into them was accepted with relish, and I remember feeling very clearly that there was a real chance here to put my personal stamp on the book. Simon fleshed out the characters, gave them depth and personality, and in turn I began to add in all those bits and pieces that make up a true individual. Each character had subtly different physical attributes; eyes full of expression (often because that's all you had to work with), teeth (that occasionally fell out) and countless numbers of screws, rivets and bits of wire. There's a whole lot of other stuff in there too, things that can still pop out of backgrounds, previously unnoticed. Spectacles, screwdrivers, plugs, vacuum cleaners, toasters... the list is endless. It was a whole world we were creating and I felt it was my duty to add in all the ephemera.

Looking back through these pages inevitably brings a smile to my face and reminds me that comics are, above all else, meant to be fun.

Fond memories indeed.

Andrew Wildman, Oxford, 2001

WAR WITHOUT END!

Cybertron: a distant metal planet populated by robots able to transform their bodies into vehicles, beast forms and cutting edge technological hardware. A world of harmony dedicated to universal peace.

Until civil war tore it apart!

The evil Decepticons, a renegade splinter faction dedicated only to conquest and evil. Their agenda was straightforward: enslave Cybertron and transform it into a colossal war-world, with which to devastate the galaxy. Led by the malevolent Megatron, they struck without warning, tearing apart the intellectual idyll.

But under the command of the noble and dauntless Optimus Prime the other Transformers rallied and fought back. They dubbed themselves Autobots, and strove to uphold the ideals of their god-like progenitor Primus, whose dream of universal peace had been passed down the generations like a torch.

The conflict raged for countless millennia, Cybertron shook under the devastating Decepticon assault and the universe held its breath. Then, in an audacious attempt to tip the balance of power, the Ark — a giant spacecraft — was launched. On board were Optimus Prime and a hand-picked crew of Autobots, their mission to secure a supply of energon. Rich in power, the fuel of choice for Transformers, energon was the key to winning the war.

But Megatron was ready, waiting. The Ark was ambushed in deep space, and boarded by Decepticon warriors. To prevent the Ark falling into Megatron's clutches, Prime locked the giant ship on a collision course with a nearby planet, where it crashed with devastating force. All aboard suffered a complete systems shutdown.

The Autobots and Decepticons awoke millions of years later, restored and recreated by the Ark's computer. Their secondary modes had been adapted to blend in with what the computer assumed — logically — were the local lifeforms. The war began anew…

… on Earth.

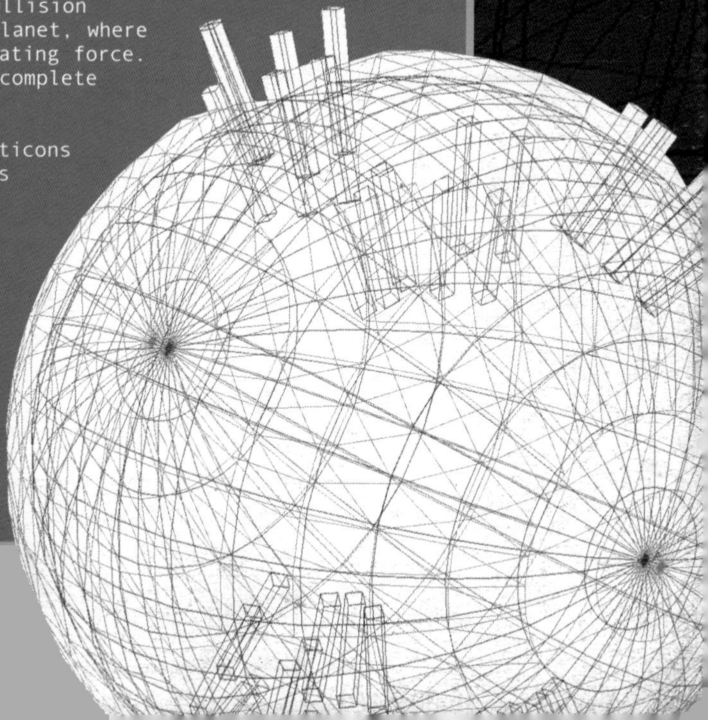

WHO'S WHO IN THE

OPTIMUS PRIME (AUTOBOT) — The most noble and dedicated of all the Autobots, holder of the Creation Matrix, the sacred life-force of the Transformers. Transforms into a truck/trailer, with mobile command base.

MEGATRON (DECEPTICON) — Megatron is the ultimate enemy of all free-thinking lifeforms. Cold, calculating and utterly remorseless, he cares only about his quest for ultimate power. Transforms into a gun of vast destructive force.

GRIMLOCK (DINOBOT) — Leader of the Dinobots (Swoop, Snarl, Slag and Sludge), allied, more or less, to the Autobots. Brash, stubborn and headstrong, Grimlock is nevertheless fiercely protective of those under his command. Transforms into a Tyrannosaurus Rex.

SCORPONOK (DECEPTICON) — Part Transformer, part alien humanoid, Scorponok is a binary-bonded being known as a Headmaster. As leaders fell by the wayside, he seized control of the Decepticons. But his dual nature may be his undoing. Transforms into a giant scorpion.

RATCHET (AUTOBOT) — Dedicated to the preservation of life, Ratchet is a healer first and foremost, a warrior only by necessity. His skill in the surgery is matched only by his courage and capacity for self-sacrifice. Transforms into an ambulance.

G.B. BLACKROCK (HUMAN) — The billionaire head of Blackrock Industries has lost much to the Transformers. His oil rigs were targeted by the Decepticons, his employees attacked. Now he strikes back, using his resources to recruit and train super-powered humans.

TRANSFORMERS UNIVERSE

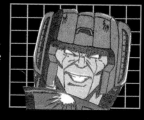

STARSCREAM (DECEPTICON) – Megatron's second-in-command… when he isn't conniving and stabbing him in the back. Treacherous, self-serving and, ultimately, cowardly, Starscream is always looking after #1. Transforms into a hypersonic jet.

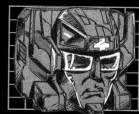

FORTRESS MAXIMUS (AUTOBOT) – Valiant, courageous, powerful beyond measure… and disillusioned. Once Autobot leader on Cybertron, Fortress Maximus is now a Headmaster, binary-bonded to human Spike Witwicky. Transforms into a battle station.

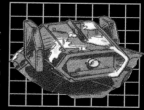

SHOCKWAVE (DECEPTICON) – The world is a coldly logical place for Shockwave, and it is only logical that he rules it. When Megatron was incapacitated he was quick to seize power, and doesn't intend to relinquish it without a fight. Transforms into a Cybertronian flying gun.

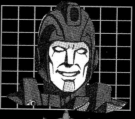

HOT ROD (AUTOBOT) – Young (relatively speaking), wild and with a need for speed, Hot Rod wants to take the world by the scruff of the neck and shake it. Prone to ignore any and all advice, he often finds himself in over his head. Transforms into a turbo-charged racecar.

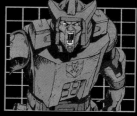

GALVATRON (DECEPTICON) – Plucked from an alternate future, Galvatron is Megatron re-born. Crafted by the planet-devouring Unicron from Megatron's remains, Galvatron is awesomely powerful and utterly insane. Transforms into a cannon.

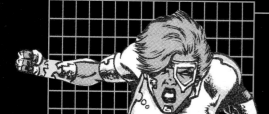

CIRCUIT BREAKER (HUMAN) – Josie Beller was paralysed when electrical feedback from a Decepticon plasma burst struck her. The accident left her with the ability to manipulate and disrupt robot circuitry, and now she wages a one-woman war against

PRELUDE TO DISASTER:
── THE STORY SO FAR ──

A As the battle rages on Earth, across the galaxy on Cybertron the balance of power shifts. With Megatron absent, other Decepticon leaders seize command, and the remaining Autobots are forced into hiding, fighting a guerrilla war against their oppressors.

At the forefront of the Autobot resistance stands Emirate Xaaron, an advocate of peace forced into the ways of war. His campaign is given a much-needed boost with the arrival of reinforcements from Earth, including Dinobot commander Grimlock, Jazz and Bumblebee.

Their appearance on Cybertron is timely, but also tragic. Autobot surgeon Ratchet, who had restored and recreated Grimlock and the others as enhanced 'Pretenders' (complete with a secondary outer shell), perished in his efforts to thwart another of Megatron's insane schemes. Both were destroyed when explosives Megatron had intended for the Ark were detonated within his own base.

THIS TIME -- *YOU STAY DEAD!*

The renewed Autobot offensive draws the attention of Thunderwing, the Decepticons' current overlord on Cybertron. His Mayhem Attack Squad — Bludgeon, Stranglehold and Octopunch — is summarily despatched to deal with the new arrivals. During the battle that follows, Grimlock, Jazz, Bumblebee and the Micromaster Rescue Patrol are accidentally transported into the very heart of Cybertron. There,

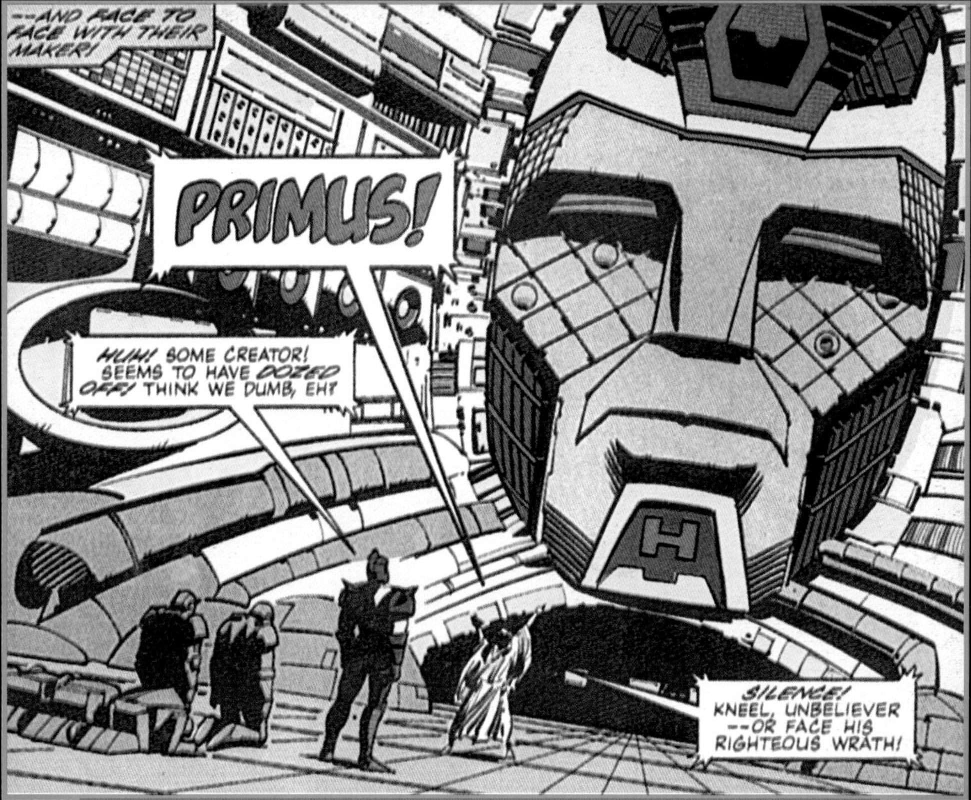
--AND FACE TO FACE WITH THEIR MAKER!
PRIMUS!
HUH! SOME CREATOR! SEEMS TO HAVE DOZED OFF! THINK WE DUMB, EH?
SILENCE! KNEEL, UNBELIEVER --OR FACE HIS RIGHTEOUS WRATH!

they discover that the entire core of the planet is Primus, their god-like creator.

In order to hide Cybertron from the planet-devouring creature known as Unicron, Primus has instigated a total systems shutdown. To all intents and purposes, he is asleep. Unicron and Primus are ancient enemies, and the chaos-bringer yearns for the destruction of Cybertron above all else.

But unknown to the Autobots, Bludgeon, Octopunch and Stranglehold have also been transported to Cybertron's core. The battle continues there, and a stray blast strikes Primus – immediately shocking him into full consciousness. His waking scream is heard on the far fringes of known space… by Unicron.

Apprised of the dire situation, Optimus Prime formulates a desperate plan to thwart the approaching chaos-bringer. They need the Creation Matrix, the lifeforce of

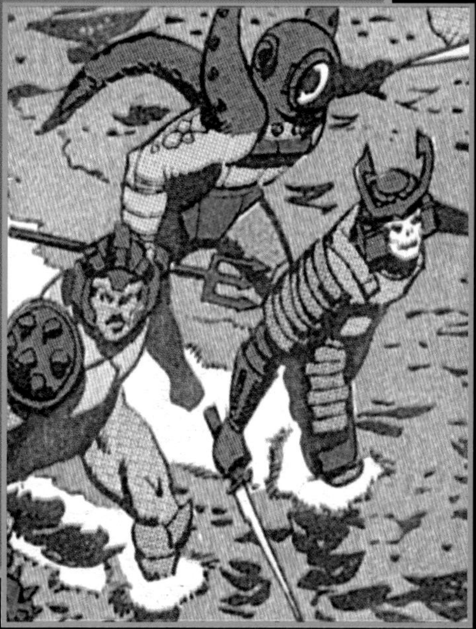

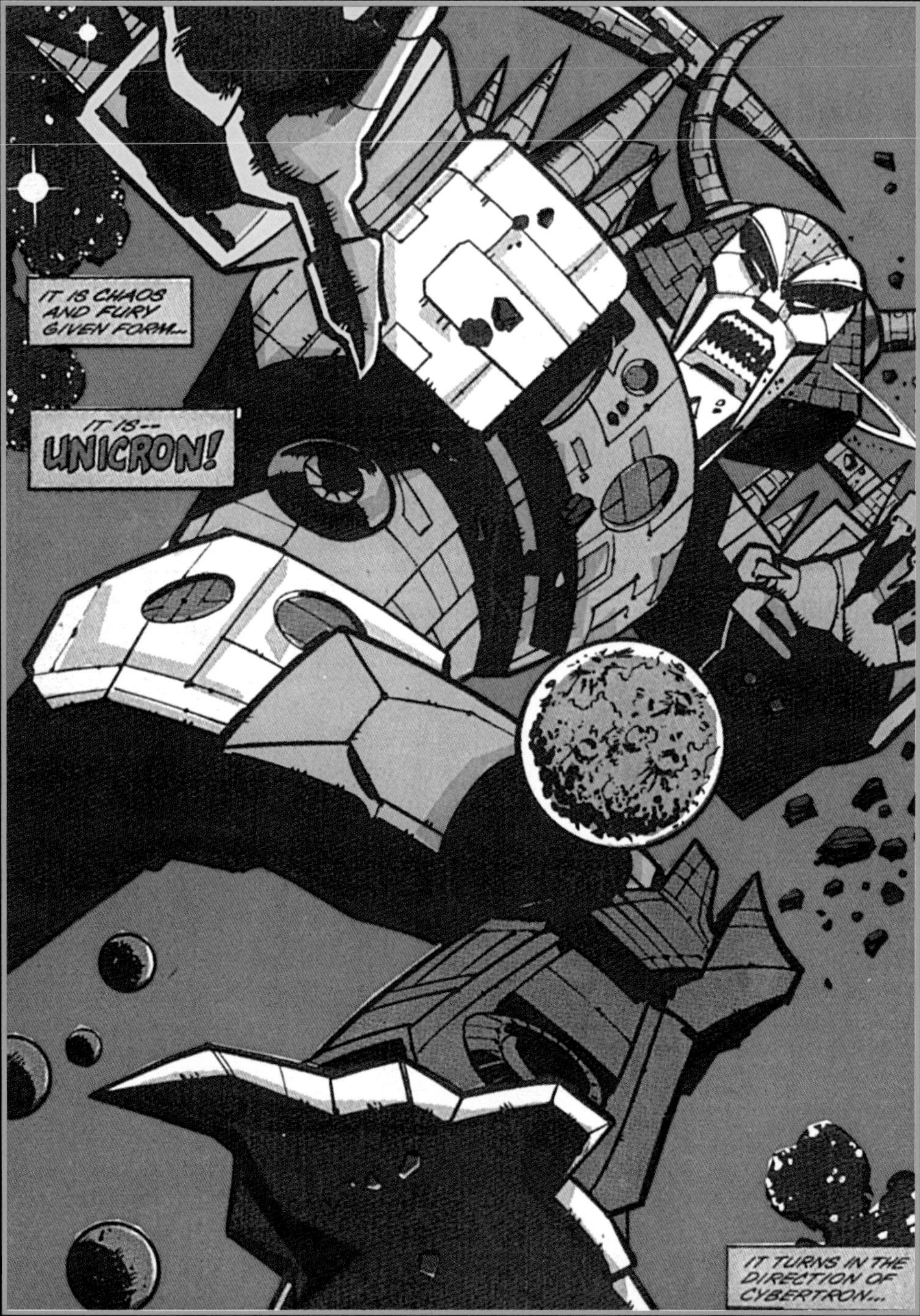
IT IS CHAOS AND FURY GIVEN FORM...
IT IS--
UNICRON!
IT TURNS IN THE DIRECTION OF CYBERTRON...

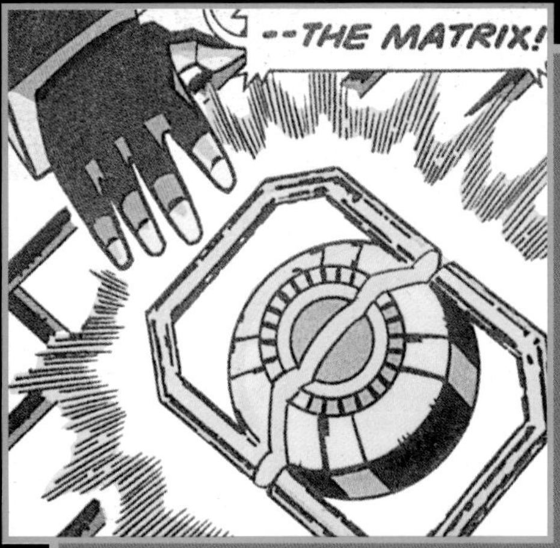
--THE MATRIX!

Primus, the one thing that can destroy Unicron. But the Matrix is gone, lost, and a desperate quest to locate it begins.

Meanwhile, on Earth, local Decepticon leader Scorponok is having problems of his own. Many of those under his command have noisily voiced their misgivings about his leadership. His decision to allow the traitorous Starscream to rejoin their ranks has not found favour. Starscream himself is only too happy to exploit the situation.

His first scheme involves a meta-powered human named Hector Dialonzo. Dialonzo has already demonstrated a knack for totalling Transformers, and Starscream wants him as a weapon he can point at Scorponok. But his plans are thwarted by the arrival of G.B. Blackrock and his human anti-robot strike team.

Away from Earth, the Matrix quest goes badly. Several of the searching teams of Autobots are captured by Thunderwing, who wants the Matrix for himself. Thunderwing's task is made easier when it is discovered that the Matrix, previously pure, has been tainted by evil. Thunderwing possesses the sacred lifeforce and turns it against the Autobots. To save the lives of all aboard the Ark, Optimus Prime is forced to blast Thunderwing — and the Matrix — out into space.

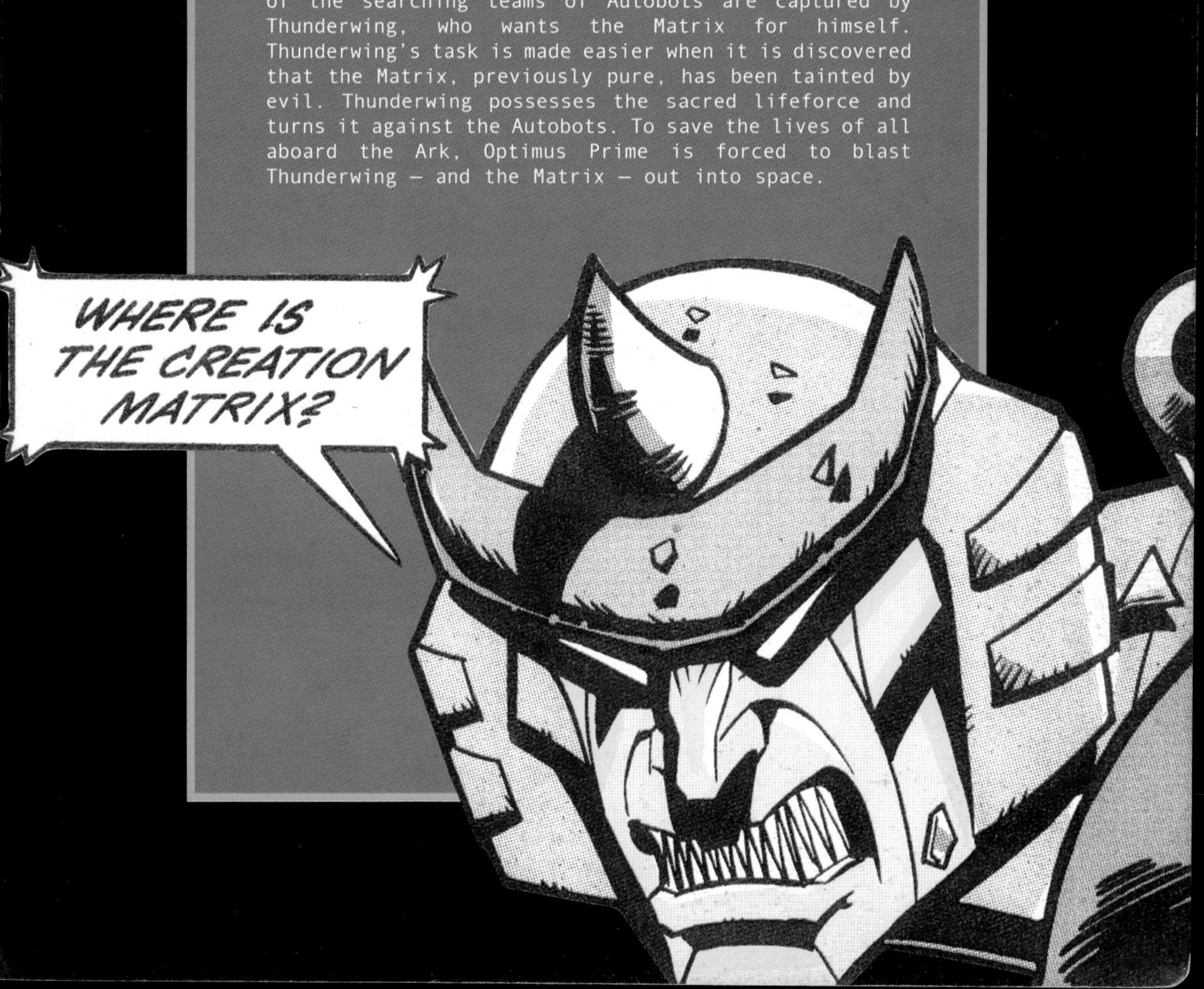
WHERE IS THE CREATION MATRIX?

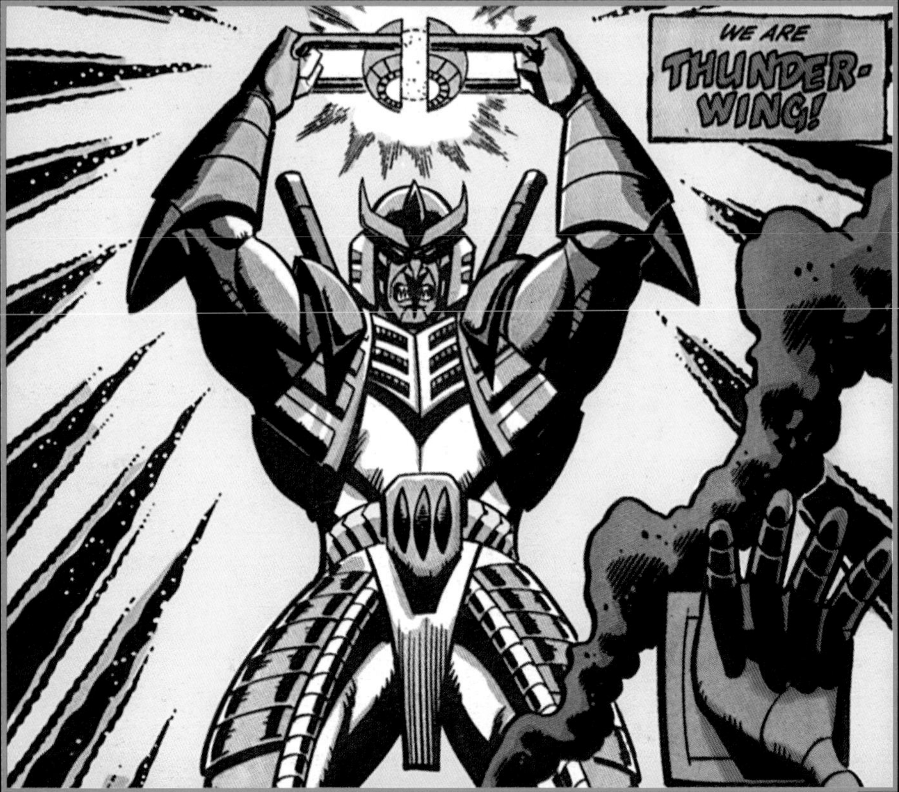
WE ARE THUNDER-WING!

Unicron is also making preparations. He sends his mindless robotic agents, Hook, Line and Sinker, to the future of an alternate Earth. Here, the planet is completely under Decepticon rule, and only a few Autobots remain alive. Hook, Line and Sinker target Decepticon leader Galvatron (a recreated future version of Megatron) and capture him. All four return to the present day… where Unicron waits.

Now read on…

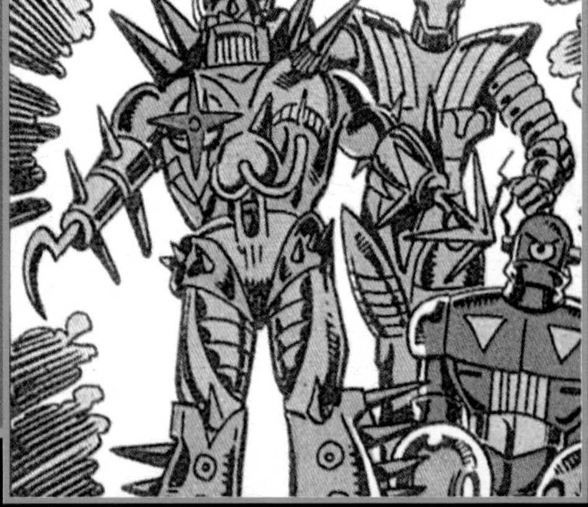
BUT...
GALVATRON-- WE HAVE COME FOR YOU!

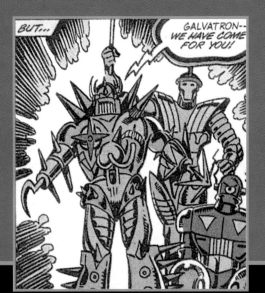

They **were** the dream--mechanical beings able to transform their bodies into vehicles, machinery and weapons; a last line of defense against the chaos-bringer, **Unicron**! They **are** at war, heroic **Autobot** pitted against evil **Decepticon**, both on their homeworld, the metal planet called **Cybertron**, and here on our **Earth**. They **are** the galaxy's last hope, **they are**-- TRANSFORMERS

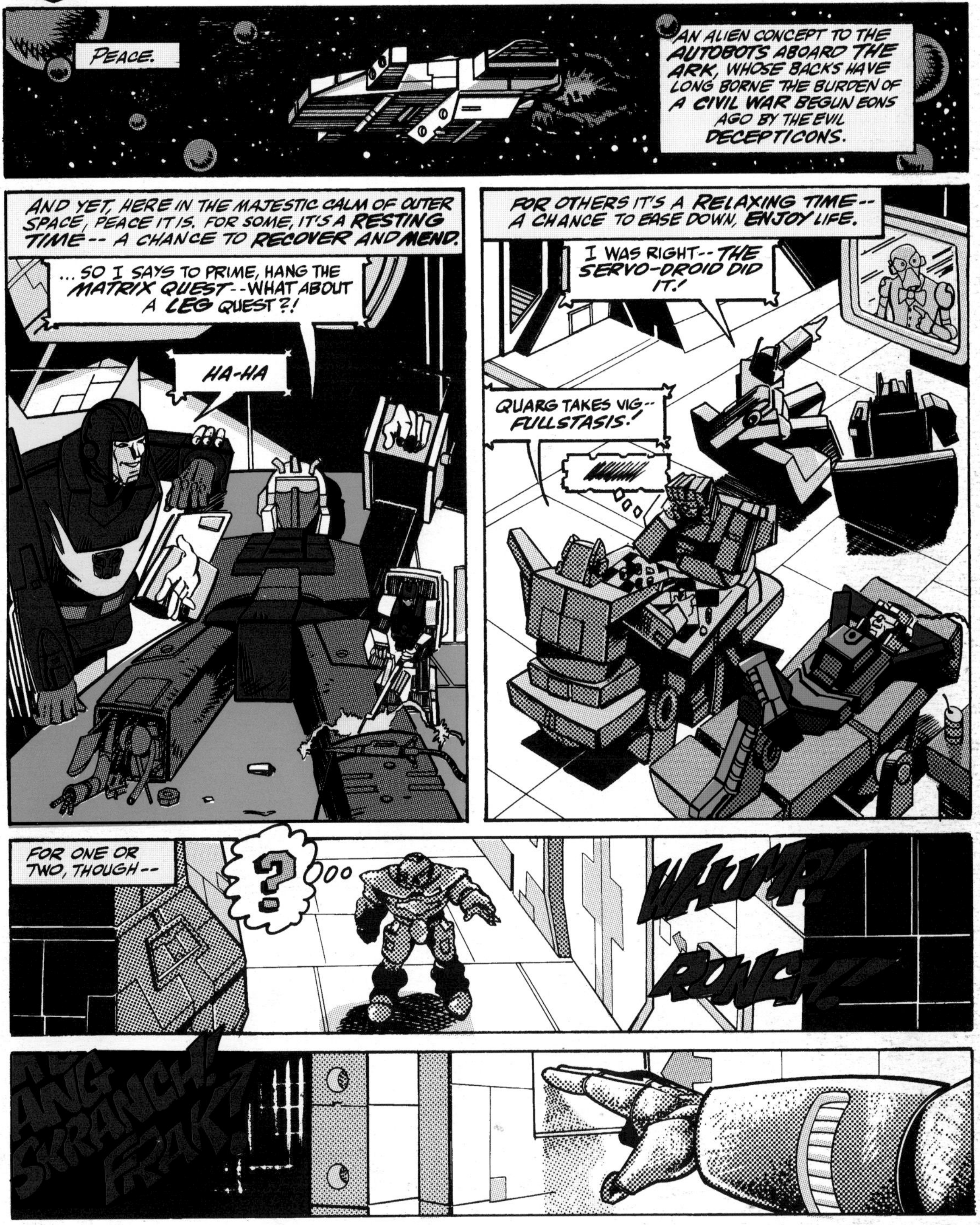
PEACE.
AN ALIEN CONCEPT TO THE AUTOBOTS ABOARD THE ARK, WHOSE BACKS HAVE LONG BORNE THE BURDEN OF A CIVIL WAR BEGUN EONS AGO BY THE EVIL DECEPTICONS.
AND YET, HERE IN THE MAJESTIC CALM OF OUTER SPACE, PEACE IT IS. FOR SOME, IT'S A RESTING TIME -- A CHANCE TO RECOVER AND MEND.
...SO I SAYS TO PRIME, HANG THE MATRIX QUEST--WHAT ABOUT A LEG QUEST?!
HA-HA
FOR OTHERS IT'S A RELAXING TIME -- A CHANCE TO EASE DOWN, ENJOY LIFE.
I WAS RIGHT-- THE SERVO-DROID DID IT!
QUARG TAKES VIG-- FULLSTASIS!
FOR ONE OR TWO, THOUGH --
?
WHUMP
RUNCH
ANG SKRANCH! FRAK!

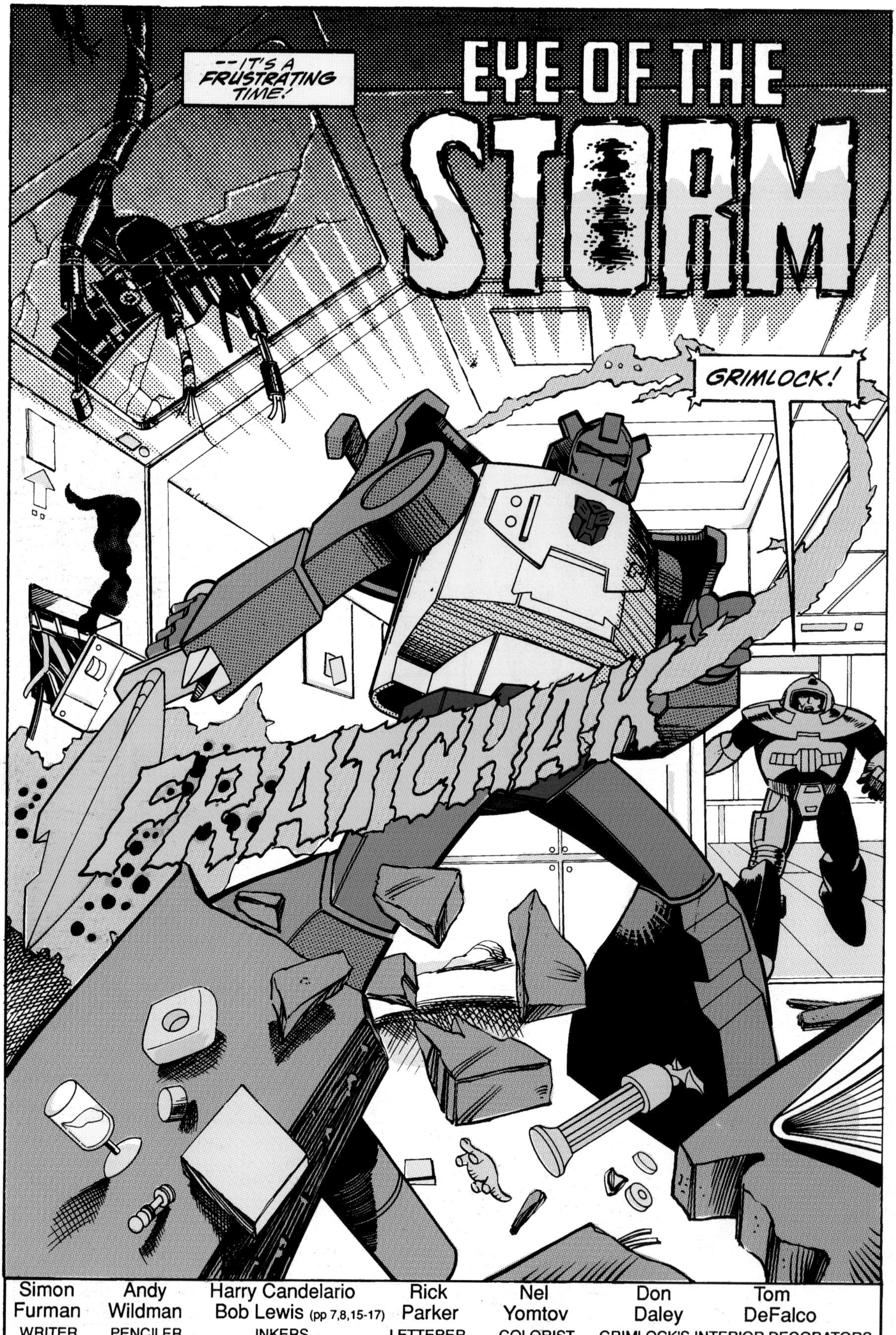
--IT'S A FRUSTRATING TIME!
EYE OF THE STORM
GRIMLOCK!
KRATCHAK

Simon Furman	Andy Wildman	Harry Candelario Bob Lewis (pp 7,8,15-17)	Rick Parker	Nel Yomtov	Don Daley	Tom DeFalco
WRITER	PENCILER	INKERS	LETTERER	COLORIST	GRIMLOCK'S INTERIOR DECORATORS	

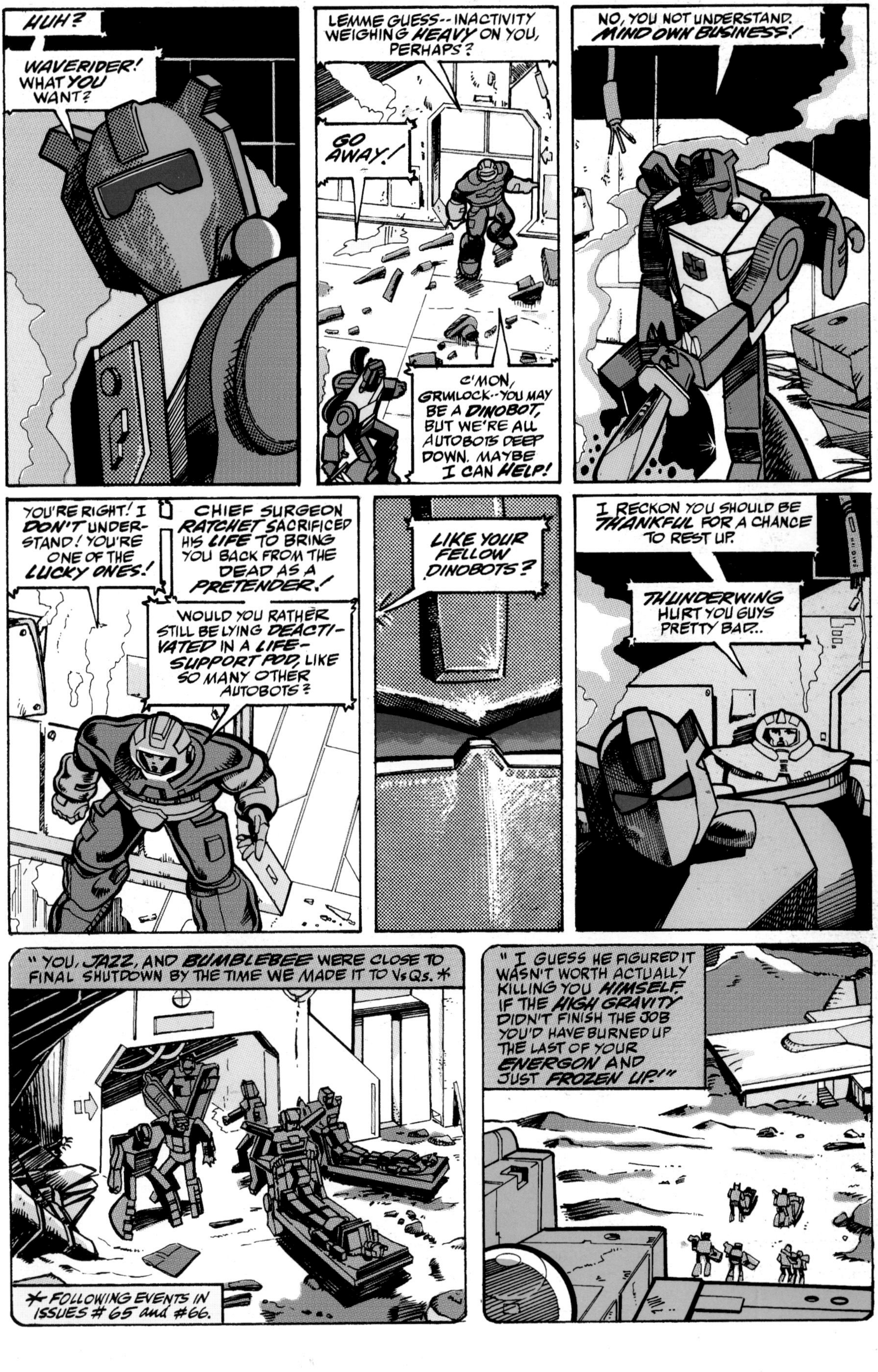

HUH?
WAVERIDER! WHAT YOU WANT?
LEMME GUESS-- INACTIVITY WEIGHING HEAVY ON YOU, PERHAPS?
GO AWAY!
C'MON, GRIMLOCK--YOU MAY BE A DINOBOT, BUT WE'RE ALL AUTOBOTS DEEP DOWN. MAYBE I CAN HELP!
NO, YOU NOT UNDERSTAND. MIND OWN BUSINESS!
YOU'RE RIGHT! I DON'T UNDERSTAND! YOU'RE ONE OF THE LUCKY ONES!
CHIEF SURGEON RATCHET SACRIFICED HIS LIFE TO BRING YOU BACK FROM THE DEAD AS A PRETENDER!
WOULD YOU RATHER STILL BE LYING DEACTIVATED IN A LIFE-SUPPORT POD, LIKE SO MANY OTHER AUTOBOTS?
LIKE YOUR FELLOW DINOBOTS?
I RECKON YOU SHOULD BE THANKFUL FOR A CHANCE TO REST UP.
THUNDERWING HURT YOU GUYS PRETTY BAD...
"YOU, JAZZ, AND BUMBLEBEE WERE CLOSE TO FINAL SHUTDOWN BY THE TIME WE MADE IT TO VsQs. *
* FOLLOWING EVENTS IN ISSUES #65 and #66.
"I GUESS HE FIGURED IT WASN'T WORTH ACTUALLY KILLING YOU HIMSELF. IF THE HIGH GRAVITY DIDN'T FINISH THE JOB YOU'D HAVE BURNED UP THE LAST OF YOUR ENERGON AND JUST FROZEN UP!"

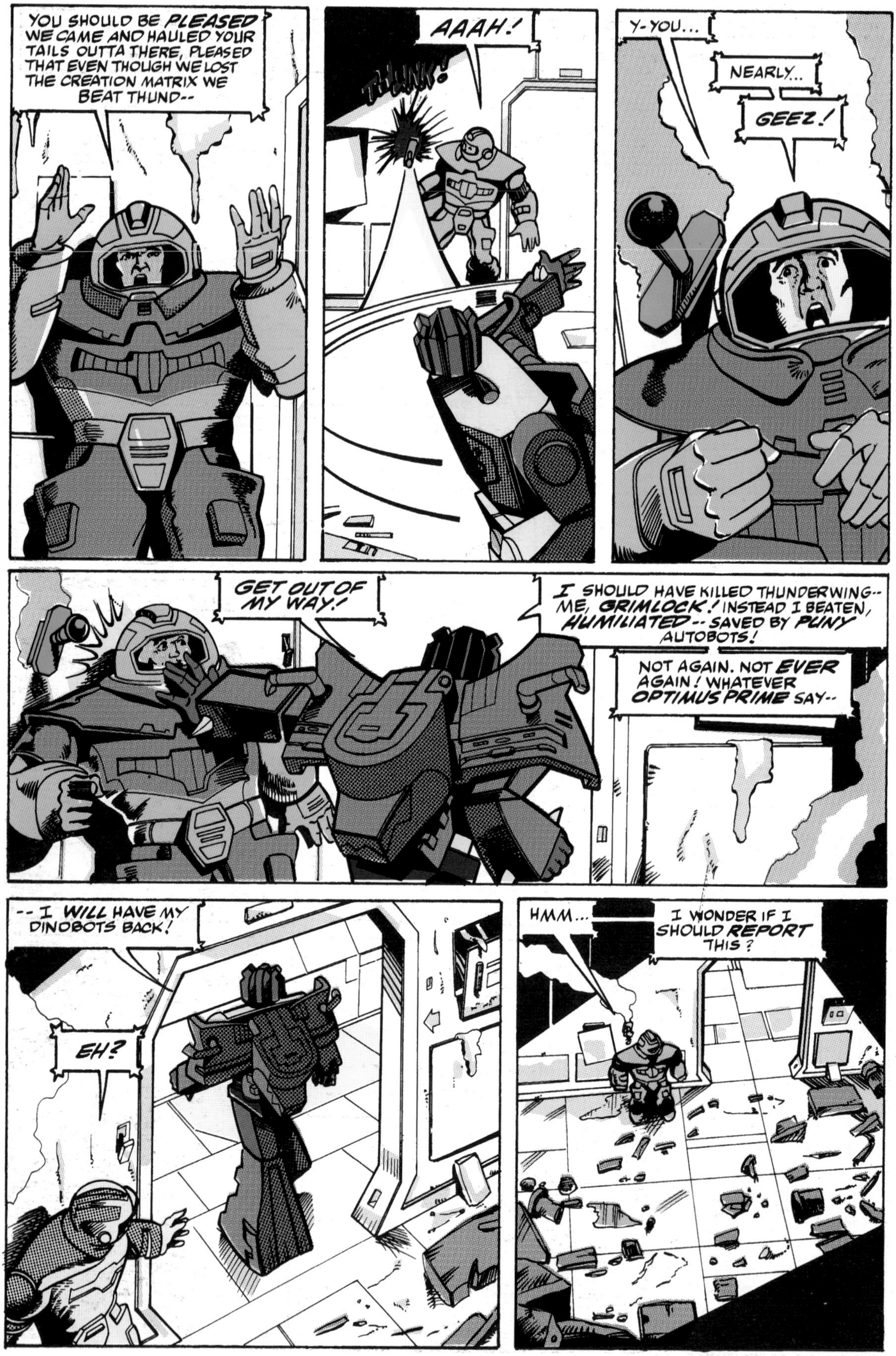
YOU SHOULD BE PLEASED WE CAME AND HAULED YOUR TAILS OUTTA THERE, PLEASED THAT EVEN THOUGH WE LOST THE CREATION MATRIX WE BEAT THUND--
AAAH!
THUNK!
Y-YOU...
NEARLY...
GEEZ!
GET OUT OF MY WAY!
I SHOULD HAVE KILLED THUNDERWING-- ME, GRIMLOCK! INSTEAD I BEATEN, HUMILIATED-- SAVED BY PUNY AUTOBOTS!
NOT AGAIN. NOT EVER AGAIN! WHATEVER OPTIMUS PRIME SAY--
--I WILL HAVE MY DINOBOTS BACK!
EH?
HMM...
I WONDER IF I SHOULD REPORT THIS?

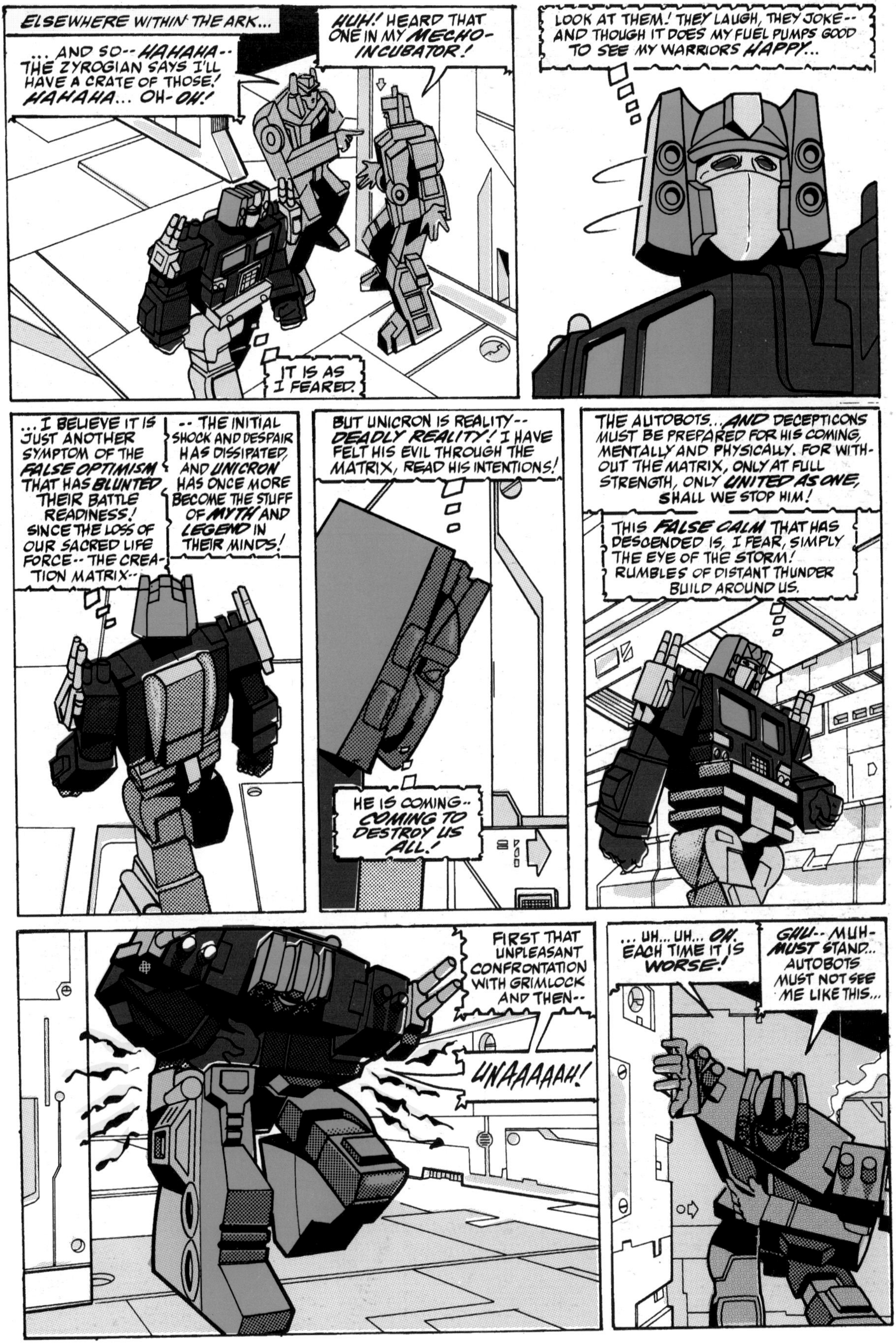

ELSEWHERE WITHIN THE ARK...
... AND SO-- HAHAHA-- THE ZYROGIAN SAYS I'LL HAVE A CRATE OF THOSE! HAHAHA... OH-OH!
HUH! HEARD THAT ONE IN MY MECHO-INCUBATOR!
IT IS AS I FEARED.
LOOK AT THEM! THEY LAUGH, THEY JOKE-- AND THOUGH IT DOES MY FUEL PUMPS GOOD TO SEE MY WARRIORS HAPPY...
... I BELIEVE IT IS JUST ANOTHER SYMPTOM OF THE FALSE OPTIMISM THAT HAS BLUNTED THEIR BATTLE READINESS! SINCE THE LOSS OF OUR SACRED LIFE FORCE-- THE CREATION MATRIX--
-- THE INITIAL SHOCK AND DESPAIR HAS DISSIPATED, AND UNICRON HAS ONCE MORE BECOME THE STUFF OF MYTH AND LEGEND IN THEIR MINDS!
BUT UNICRON IS REALITY-- DEADLY REALITY! I HAVE FELT HIS EVIL THROUGH THE MATRIX, READ HIS INTENTIONS!
HE IS COMING-- COMING TO DESTROY US ALL!
THE AUTOBOTS... AND DECEPTICONS MUST BE PREPARED FOR HIS COMING, MENTALLY AND PHYSICALLY. FOR WITHOUT THE MATRIX, ONLY AT FULL STRENGTH, ONLY UNITED AS ONE, SHALL WE STOP HIM!
THIS FALSE CALM THAT HAS DESCENDED IS, I FEAR, SIMPLY THE EYE OF THE STORM! RUMBLES OF DISTANT THUNDER BUILD AROUND US.
FIRST THAT UNPLEASANT CONFRONTATION WITH GRIMLOCK AND THEN--
UNAAAAAH!
... UH... UH... OH. EACH TIME IT IS WORSE!
GHU-- MUH- MUST STAND... AUTOBOTS MUST NOT SEE ME LIKE THIS...

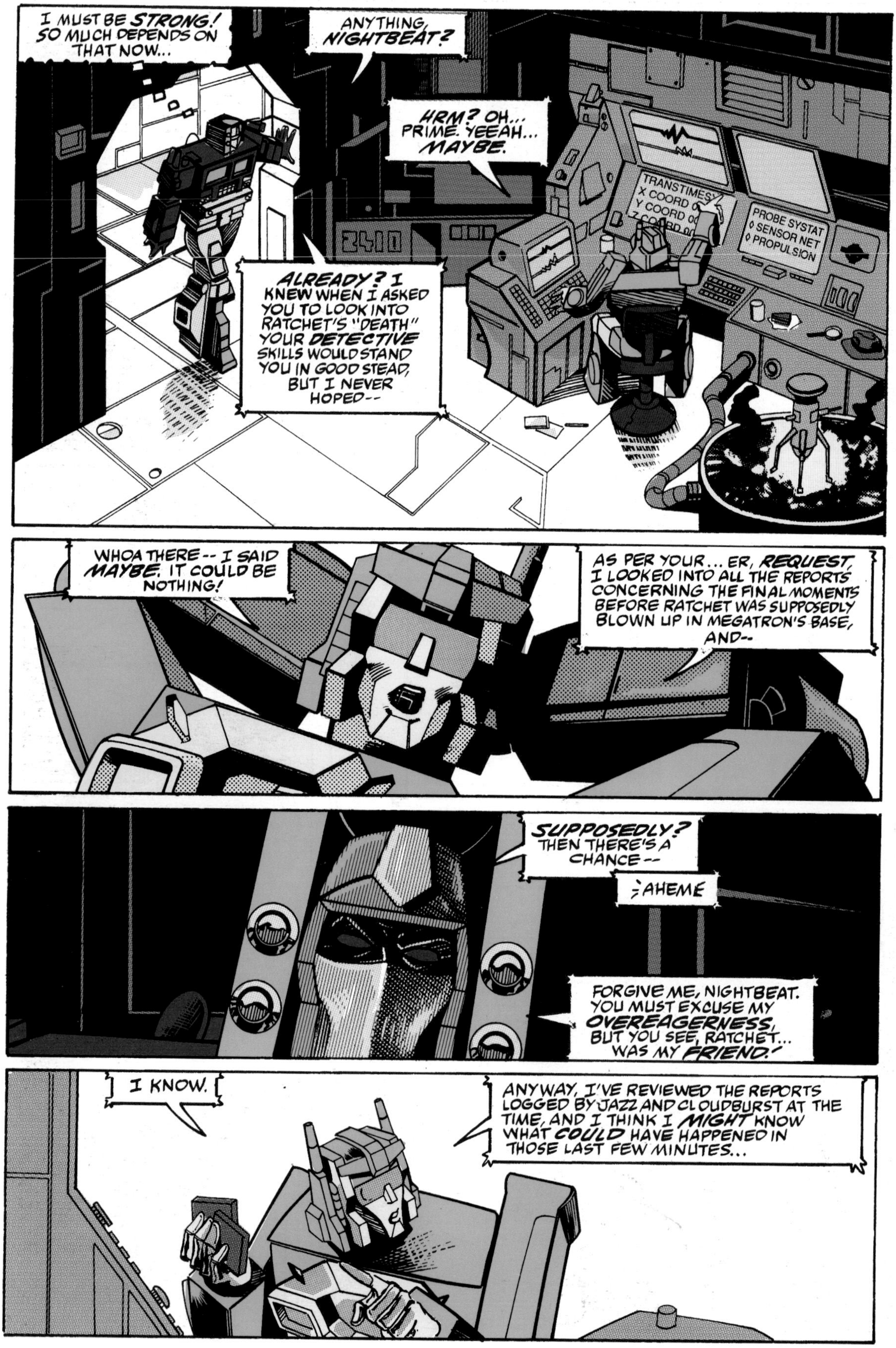
I MUST BE STRONG! SO MUCH DEPENDS ON THAT NOW...
ANYTHING, NIGHTBEAT?
HRM? OH... PRIME. YEEAH... MAYBE.
TRANSTIMES
X COORD
Y COORD
PROBE SYSTAT
◊ SENSOR NET
◊ PROPULSION
ALREADY? I KNEW WHEN I ASKED YOU TO LOOK INTO RATCHET'S "DEATH" YOUR DETECTIVE SKILLS WOULD STAND YOU IN GOOD STEAD, BUT I NEVER HOPED--
WHOA THERE -- I SAID MAYBE. IT COULD BE NOTHING!
AS PER YOUR... ER, REQUEST, I LOOKED INTO ALL THE REPORTS CONCERNING THE FINAL MOMENTS BEFORE RATCHET WAS SUPPOSEDLY BLOWN UP IN MEGATRON'S BASE, AND--
SUPPOSEDLY? THEN THERE'S A CHANCE--
AHEM
FORGIVE ME, NIGHTBEAT. YOU MUST EXCUSE MY OVEREAGERNESS, BUT YOU SEE, RATCHET... WAS MY FRIEND.
I KNOW.
ANYWAY, I'VE REVIEWED THE REPORTS LOGGED BY JAZZ AND CLOUDBURST AT THE TIME, AND I THINK I MIGHT KNOW WHAT COULD HAVE HAPPENED IN THOSE LAST FEW MINUTES...

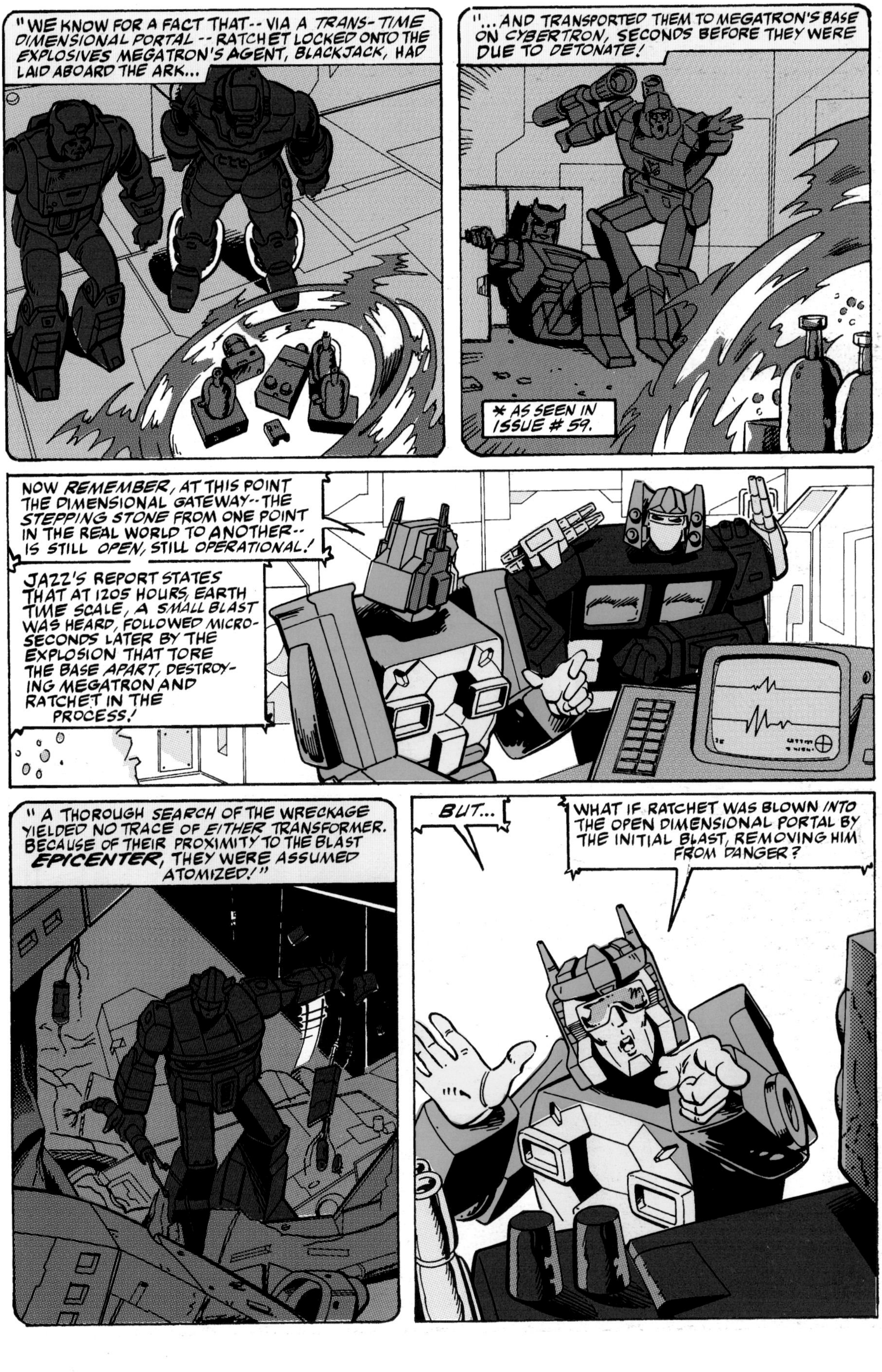
"WE KNOW FOR A FACT THAT-- VIA A TRANS-TIME DIMENSIONAL PORTAL -- RATCHET LOCKED ONTO THE EXPLOSIVES MEGATRON'S AGENT, BLACKJACK, HAD LAID ABOARD THE ARK...
"...AND TRANSPORTED THEM TO MEGATRON'S BASE ON CYBERTRON, SECONDS BEFORE THEY WERE DUE TO DETONATE!
* AS SEEN IN ISSUE # 59.
NOW REMEMBER, AT THIS POINT THE DIMENSIONAL GATEWAY-- THE STEPPING STONE FROM ONE POINT IN THE REAL WORLD TO ANOTHER-- IS STILL OPEN, STILL OPERATIONAL!
JAZZ'S REPORT STATES THAT AT 1205 HOURS, EARTH TIME SCALE, A SMALL BLAST WAS HEARD, FOLLOWED MICRO-SECONDS LATER BY THE EXPLOSION THAT TORE THE BASE APART, DESTROY-ING MEGATRON AND RATCHET IN THE PROCESS!
"A THOROUGH SEARCH OF THE WRECKAGE YIELDED NO TRACE OF EITHER TRANSFORMER. BECAUSE OF THEIR PROXIMITY TO THE BLAST EPICENTER, THEY WERE ASSUMED ATOMIZED!"
BUT...
WHAT IF RATCHET WAS BLOWN INTO THE OPEN DIMENSIONAL PORTAL BY THE INITIAL BLAST, REMOVING HIM FROM DANGER?

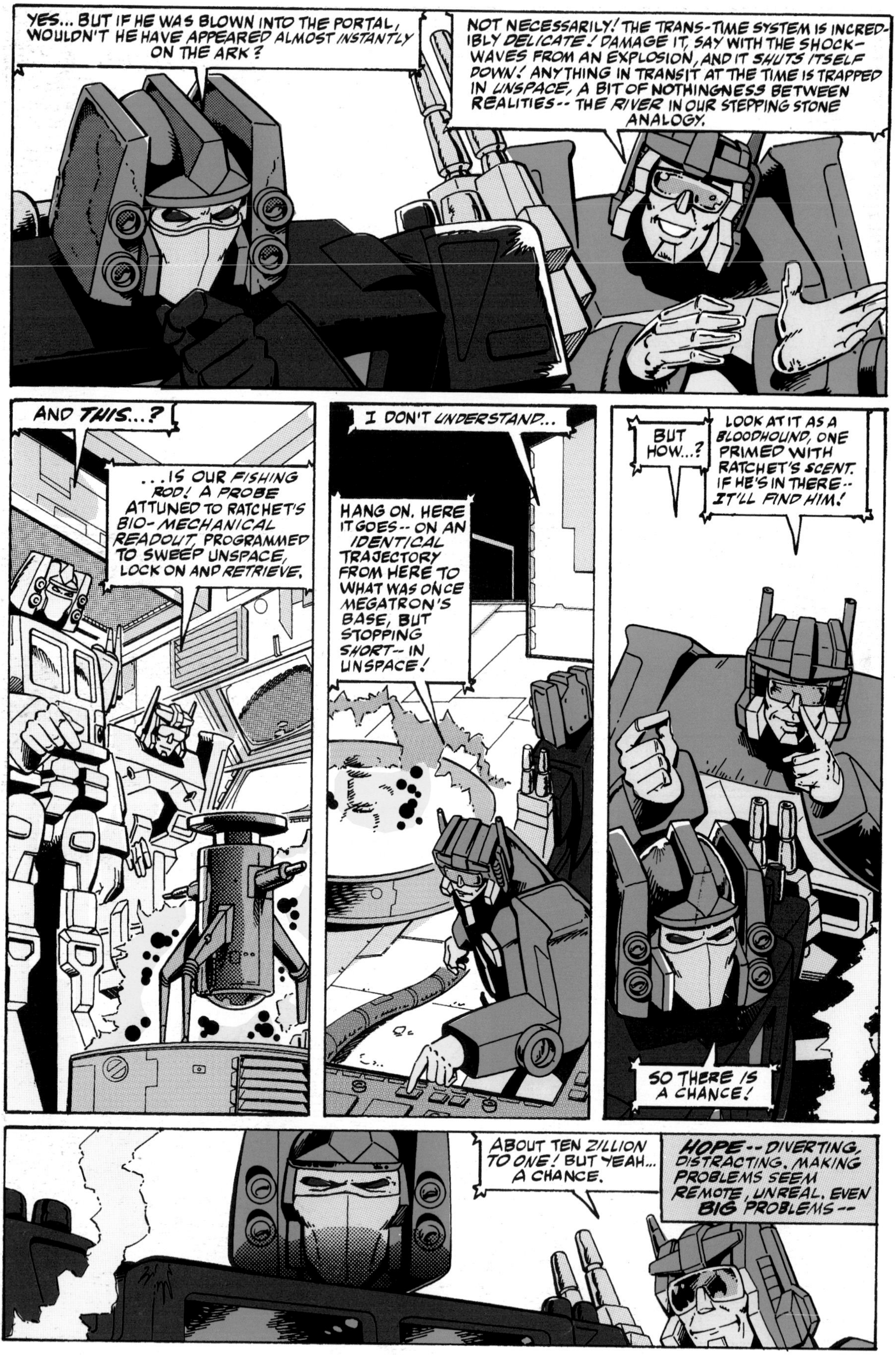
YES... BUT IF HE WAS BLOWN INTO THE PORTAL, WOULDN'T HE HAVE APPEARED ALMOST INSTANTLY ON THE ARK?
NOT NECESSARILY! THE TRANS-TIME SYSTEM IS INCREDIBLY DELICATE! DAMAGE IT, SAY WITH THE SHOCKWAVES FROM AN EXPLOSION, AND IT SHUTS ITSELF DOWN! ANYTHING IN TRANSIT AT THE TIME IS TRAPPED IN UNSPACE, A BIT OF NOTHINGNESS BETWEEN REALITIES-- THE RIVER IN OUR STEPPING STONE ANALOGY.
AND THIS...?
...IS OUR FISHING ROD! A PROBE ATTUNED TO RATCHET'S BIO-MECHANICAL READOUT, PROGRAMMED TO SWEEP UNSPACE, LOCK ON AND RETRIEVE.
I DON'T UNDERSTAND...
HANG ON. HERE IT GOES-- ON AN IDENTICAL TRAJECTORY FROM HERE TO WHAT WAS ONCE MEGATRON'S BASE, BUT STOPPING SHORT-- IN UNSPACE!
BUT HOW...?
LOOK AT IT AS A BLOODHOUND, ONE PRIMED WITH RATCHET'S SCENT. IF HE'S IN THERE-- IT'LL FIND HIM!
SO THERE IS A CHANCE!
ABOUT TEN ZILLION TO ONE! BUT YEAH... A CHANCE.
HOPE-- DIVERTING, DISTRACTING, MAKING PROBLEMS SEEM REMOTE, UNREAL. EVEN BIG PROBLEMS--

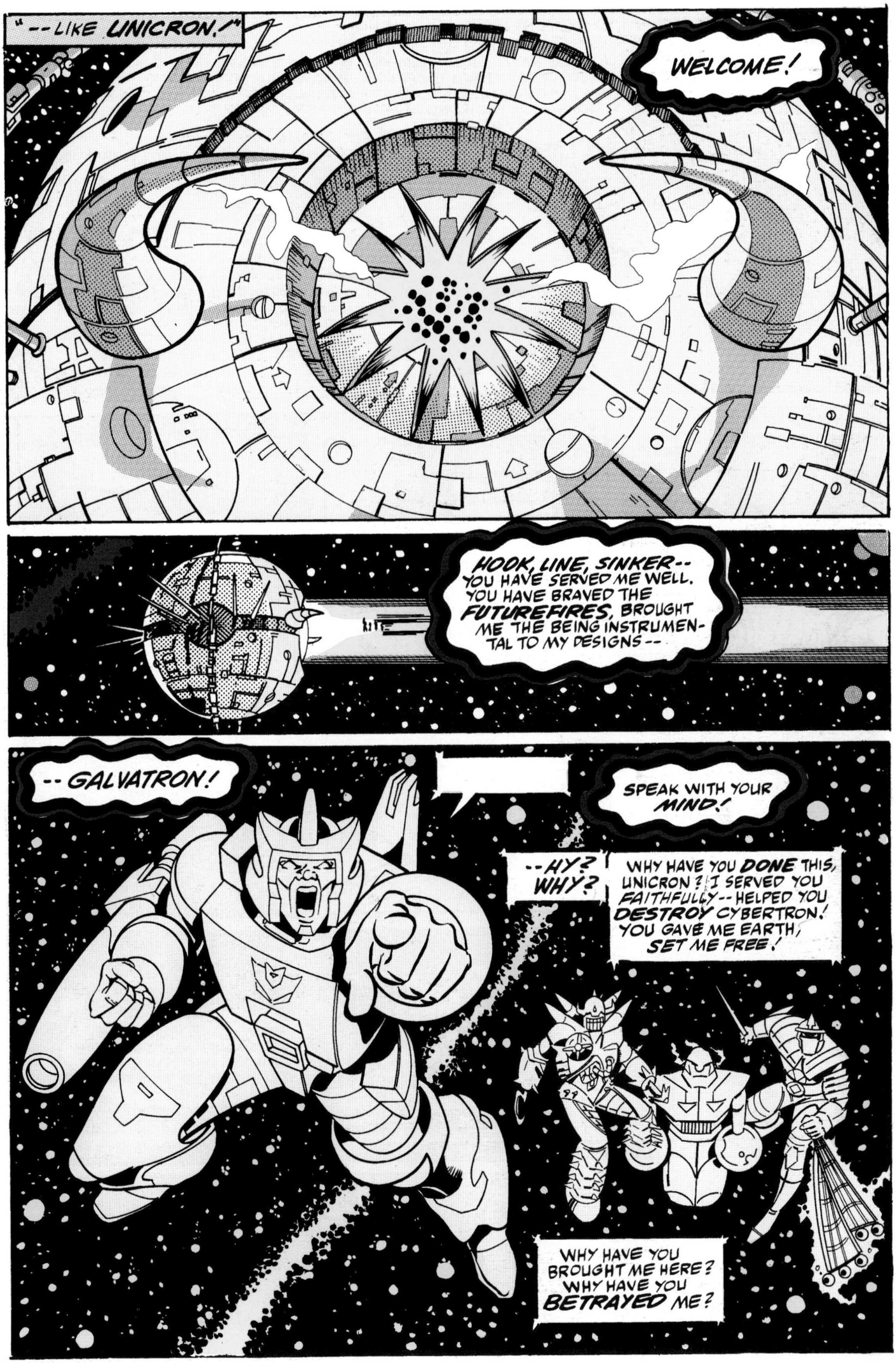
"--LIKE UNICRON!"
WELCOME!
HOOK, LINE, SINKER-- YOU HAVE SERVED ME WELL. YOU HAVE BRAVED THE FUTUREFIRES, BROUGHT ME THE BEING INSTRUMENTAL TO MY DESIGNS--
--GALVATRON!
SPEAK WITH YOUR MIND!
--HY? WHY?
WHY HAVE YOU DONE THIS, UNICRON? I SERVED YOU FAITHFULLY-- HELPED YOU DESTROY CYBERTRON! YOU GAVE ME EARTH, SET ME FREE!
WHY HAVE YOU BROUGHT ME HERE? WHY HAVE YOU BETRAYED ME?

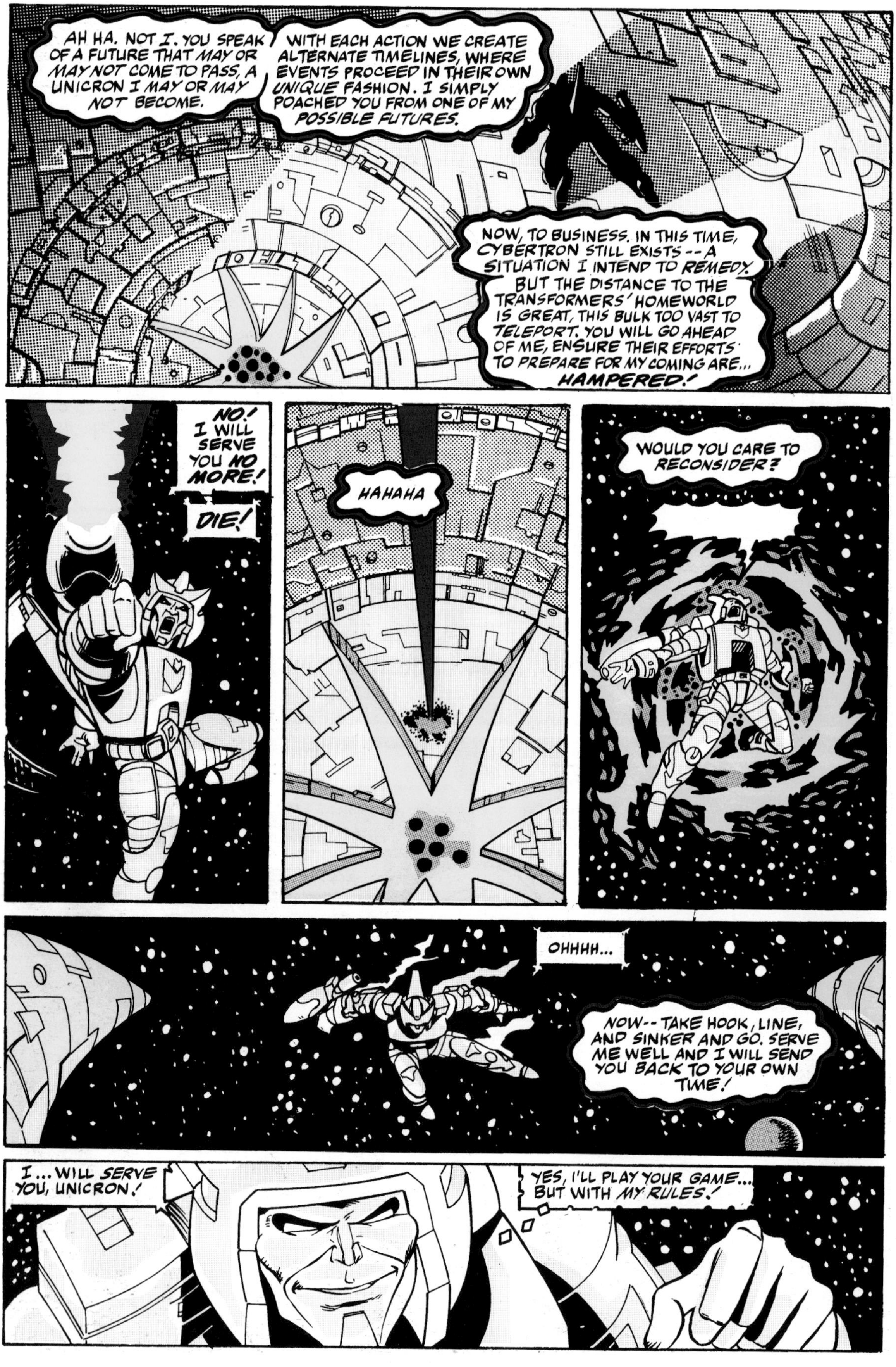
AH HA. NOT I. YOU SPEAK OF A FUTURE THAT MAY OR MAY NOT COME TO PASS, A UNICRON I MAY OR MAY NOT BECOME.
WITH EACH ACTION WE CREATE ALTERNATE TIMELINES, WHERE EVENTS PROCEED IN THEIR OWN UNIQUE FASHION. I SIMPLY POACHED YOU FROM ONE OF MY POSSIBLE FUTURES.
NOW, TO BUSINESS. IN THIS TIME, CYBERTRON STILL EXISTS -- A SITUATION I INTEND TO REMEDY. BUT THE DISTANCE TO THE TRANSFORMERS' HOMEWORLD IS GREAT, THIS BULK TOO VAST TO TELEPORT. YOU WILL GO AHEAD OF ME, ENSURE THEIR EFFORTS TO PREPARE FOR MY COMING ARE... HAMPERED!
NO! I WILL SERVE YOU NO MORE!
DIE!
HAHAHA
WOULD YOU CARE TO RECONSIDER?
OHHHH...
NOW-- TAKE HOOK, LINE, AND SINKER AND GO. SERVE ME WELL AND I WILL SEND YOU BACK TO YOUR OWN TIME!
I... WILL SERVE YOU, UNICRON!
YES, I'LL PLAY YOUR GAME... BUT WITH MY RULES!

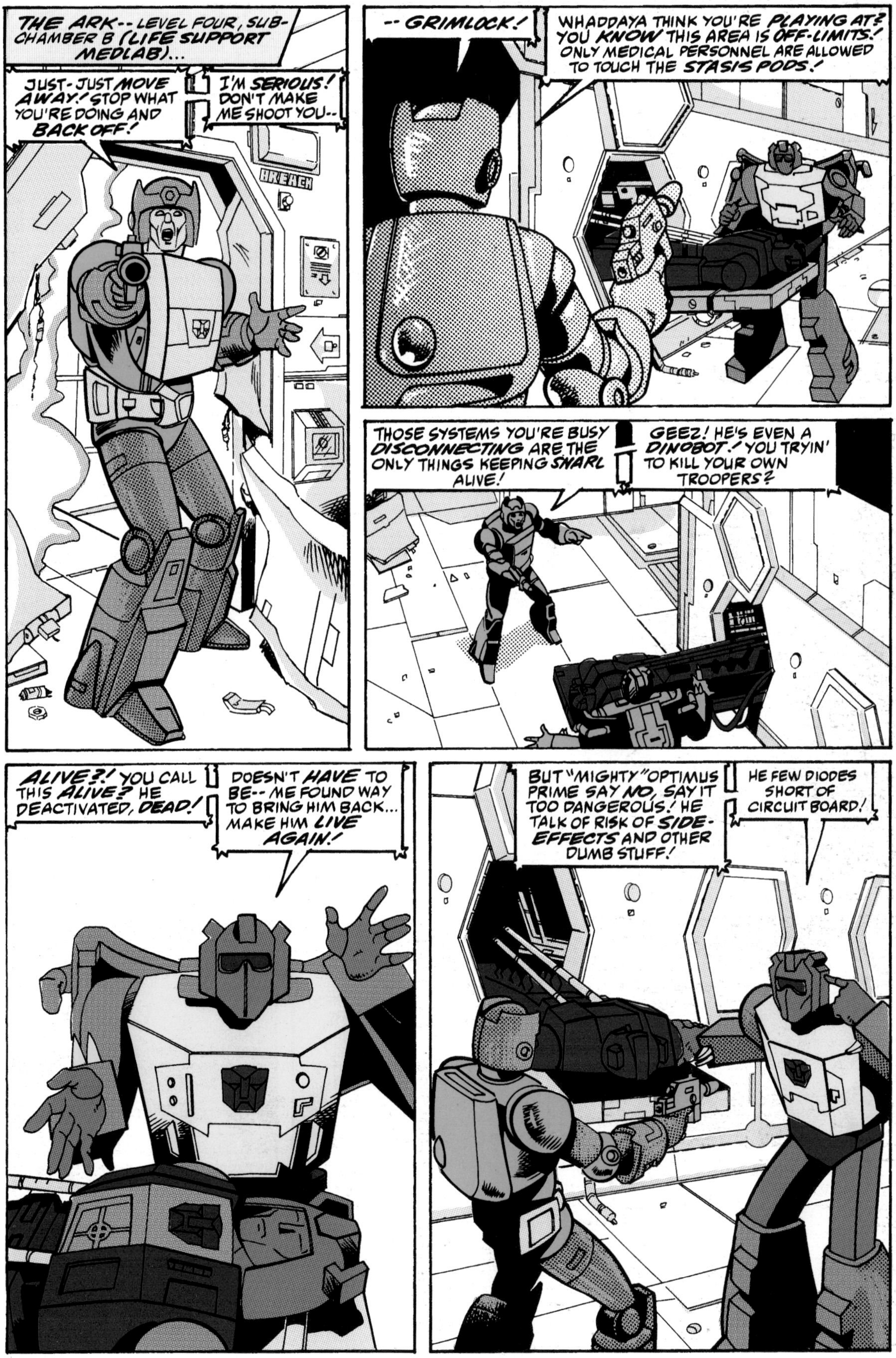
THE ARK-- LEVEL FOUR, SUB-CHAMBER B (LIFE SUPPORT MEDLAB)...
JUST- JUST MOVE AWAY! STOP WHAT YOU'RE DOING AND BACK OFF!
I'M SERIOUS! DON'T MAKE ME SHOOT YOU--
BREACH
-- GRIMLOCK!
WHADDAYA THINK YOU'RE PLAYING AT? YOU KNOW THIS AREA IS OFF-LIMITS! ONLY MEDICAL PERSONNEL ARE ALLOWED TO TOUCH THE STASIS PODS!
THOSE SYSTEMS YOU'RE BUSY DISCONNECTING ARE THE ONLY THINGS KEEPING SNARL ALIVE!
GEEZ! HE'S EVEN A DINOBOT! YOU TRYIN' TO KILL YOUR OWN TROOPERS?
ALIVE?! YOU CALL THIS ALIVE? HE DEACTIVATED, DEAD!
DOESN'T HAVE TO BE-- ME FOUND WAY TO BRING HIM BACK... MAKE HIM LIVE AGAIN!
BUT "MIGHTY" OPTIMUS PRIME SAY NO, SAY IT TOO DANGEROUS! HE TALK OF RISK OF SIDE-EFFECTS AND OTHER DUMB STUFF!
HE FEW DIODES SHORT OF CIRCUIT BOARD!

BUT *ME* WILLING TO TAKE RISK!

MY DINOBOTS-- I KNOW *THEY* BE WILLING TO TAKE RISK, TOO! BETTER TO TRY AND FAIL-- BETTER *DEATH* THAN THIS MOCKERY OF LIFE!

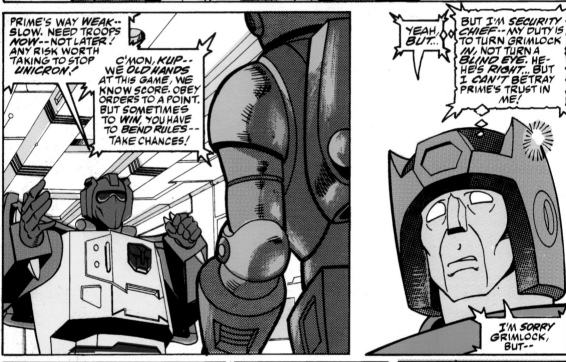

PRIME'S WAY WEAK-- SLOW. NEED TROOPS *NOW*-- NOT LATER! ANY RISK WORTH TAKING TO STOP *UNICRON!*

C'MON, *KUP*-- WE OLD HANDS AT THIS GAME, WE KNOW SCORE. OBEY ORDERS TO A POINT. BUT SOMETIMES TO *WIN*, YOU HAVE TO BEND RULES-- TAKE CHANCES!

YEAH, BUT...

BUT I'M SECURITY *CHIEF*-- MY DUTY IS TO TURN GRIMLOCK *IN*, NOT TURN A *BLIND EYE*. HE-- HE'S *RIGHT*... BUT I *CAN'T* BETRAY PRIME'S TRUST IN ME!

I'M *SORRY* GRIMLOCK, BUT--

PRIME!

YEAH?

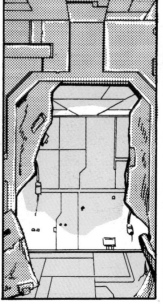

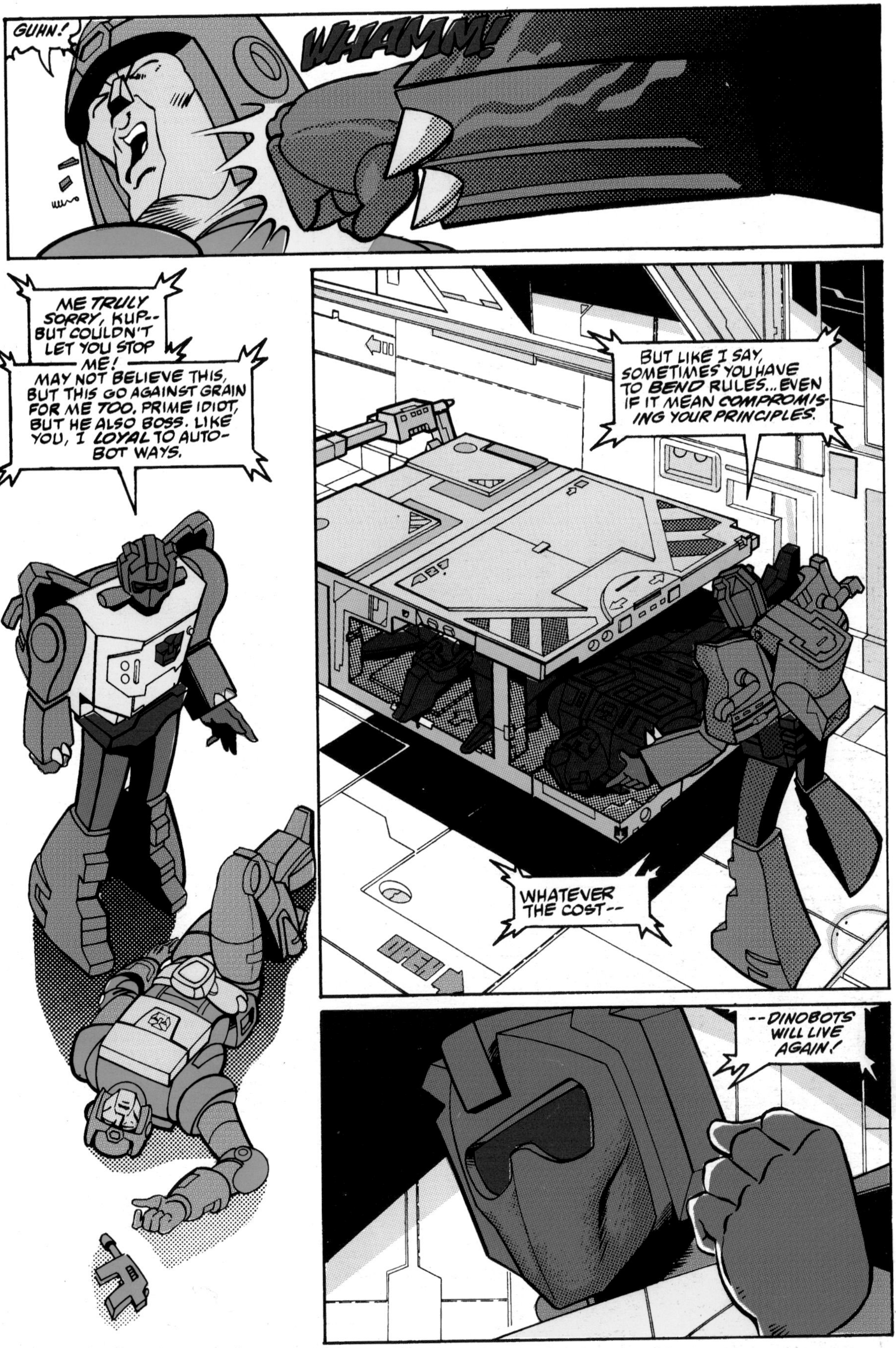
GUHN!
WHAMM!
ME TRULY SORRY, KUP-- BUT COULDN'T LET YOU STOP ME!
MAY NOT BELIEVE THIS, BUT THIS GO AGAINST GRAIN FOR ME TOO. PRIME IDIOT, BUT HE ALSO BOSS. LIKE YOU, I LOYAL TO AUTO-BOT WAYS.
BUT LIKE I SAY, SOMETIMES YOU HAVE TO BEND RULES...EVEN IF IT MEAN COMPROMIS-ING YOUR PRINCIPLES.
WHATEVER THE COST--
--DINOBOTS WILL LIVE AGAIN!

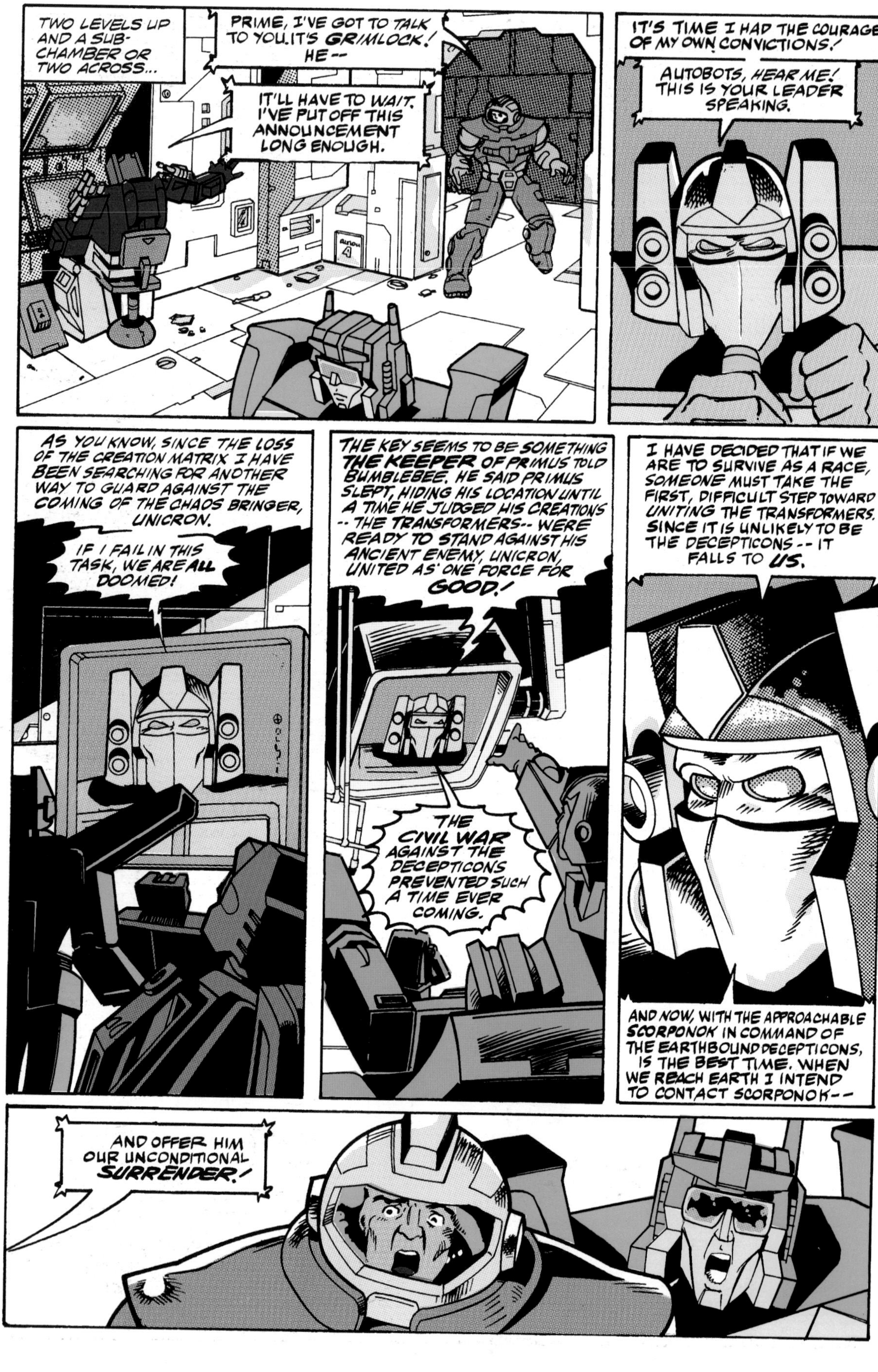
TWO LEVELS UP AND A SUB-CHAMBER OR TWO ACROSS...
PRIME, I'VE GOT TO TALK TO YOU. IT'S GRIMLOCK! HE--
IT'LL HAVE TO WAIT. I'VE PUT OFF THIS ANNOUNCEMENT LONG ENOUGH.
IT'S TIME I HAD THE COURAGE OF MY OWN CONVICTIONS!
AUTOBOTS, HEAR ME! THIS IS YOUR LEADER SPEAKING.
AS YOU KNOW, SINCE THE LOSS OF THE CREATION MATRIX I HAVE BEEN SEARCHING FOR ANOTHER WAY TO GUARD AGAINST THE COMING OF THE CHAOS BRINGER, UNICRON.
IF I FAIL IN THIS TASK, WE ARE ALL DOOMED!
THE KEY SEEMS TO BE SOMETHING THE KEEPER OF PRIMUS TOLD BUMBLEBEE. HE SAID PRIMUS SLEPT, HIDING HIS LOCATION UNTIL A TIME HE JUDGED HIS CREATIONS -- THE TRANSFORMERS-- WERE READY TO STAND AGAINST HIS ANCIENT ENEMY, UNICRON, UNITED AS ONE FORCE FOR GOOD!
THE CIVIL WAR AGAINST THE DECEPTICONS PREVENTED SUCH A TIME EVER COMING.
I HAVE DECIDED THAT IF WE ARE TO SURVIVE AS A RACE, SOMEONE MUST TAKE THE FIRST, DIFFICULT STEP TOWARD UNITING THE TRANSFORMERS. SINCE IT IS UNLIKELY TO BE THE DECEPTICONS -- IT FALLS TO US.
AND NOW, WITH THE APPROACHABLE SCORPONOK IN COMMAND OF THE EARTHBOUND DECEPTICONS, IS THE BEST TIME. WHEN WE REACH EARTH I INTEND TO CONTACT SCORPONOK--
AND OFFER HIM OUR UNCONDITIONAL SURRENDER!

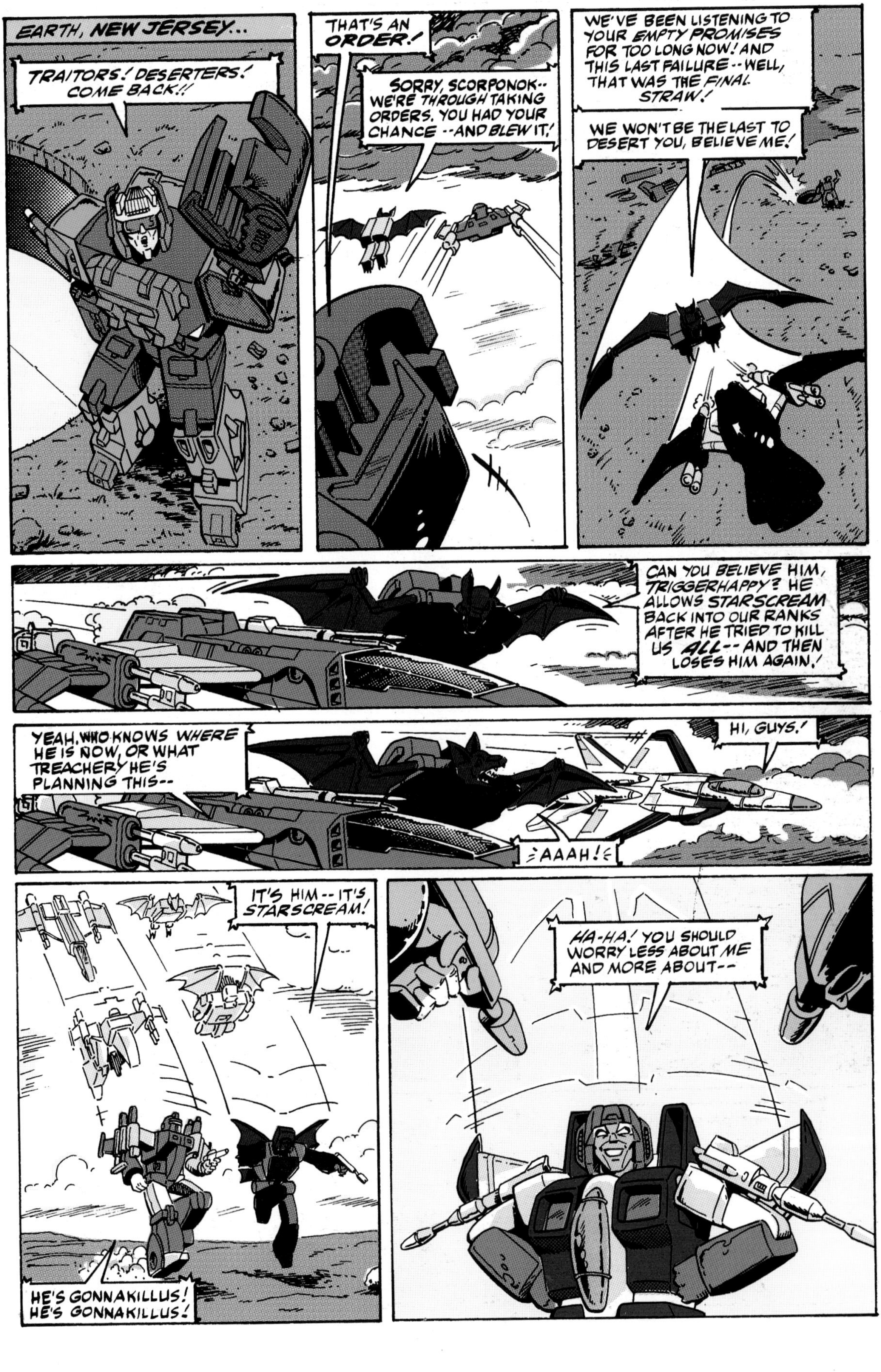
EARTH, NEW JERSEY...
TRAITORS! DESERTERS! COME BACK!!
THAT'S AN ORDER!
SORRY, SCORPONOK-- WE'RE THROUGH TAKING ORDERS. YOU HAD YOUR CHANCE --AND BLEW IT!
WE'VE BEEN LISTENING TO YOUR EMPTY PROMISES FOR TOO LONG NOW! AND THIS LAST FAILURE -- WELL, THAT WAS THE FINAL STRAW!
WE WON'T BE THE LAST TO DESERT YOU, BELIEVE ME!
CAN YOU BELIEVE HIM, TRIGGERHAPPY? HE ALLOWS STARSCREAM BACK INTO OUR RANKS AFTER HE TRIED TO KILL US ALL-- AND THEN LOSES HIM AGAIN!
YEAH, WHO KNOWS WHERE HE IS NOW, OR WHAT TREACHERY HE'S PLANNING THIS--
HI, GUYS!
AAAH!
IT'S HIM -- IT'S STARSCREAM!
HE'S GONNAKILLUS! HE'S GONNAKILLUS!
HA-HA! YOU SHOULD WORRY LESS ABOUT ME AND MORE ABOUT--

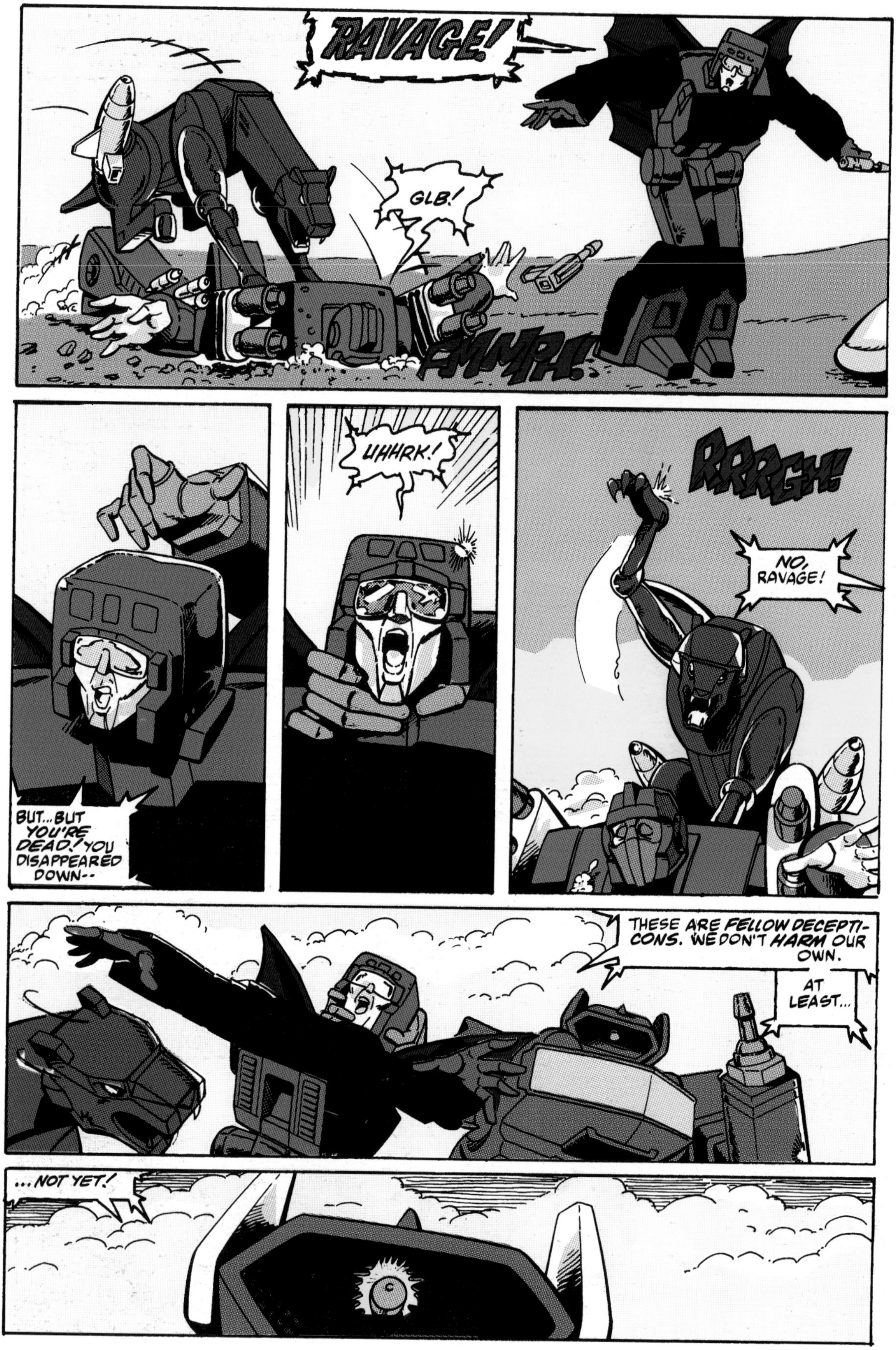
RAVAGE!
GLB!
FMMPH!
UHHRK!
RRRGH!
NO, RAVAGE!
BUT... BUT YOU'RE DEAD! YOU DISAPPEARED DOWN--
THESE ARE FELLOW DECEPTICONS. WE DON'T HARM OUR OWN.
AT LEAST...
... NOT YET!

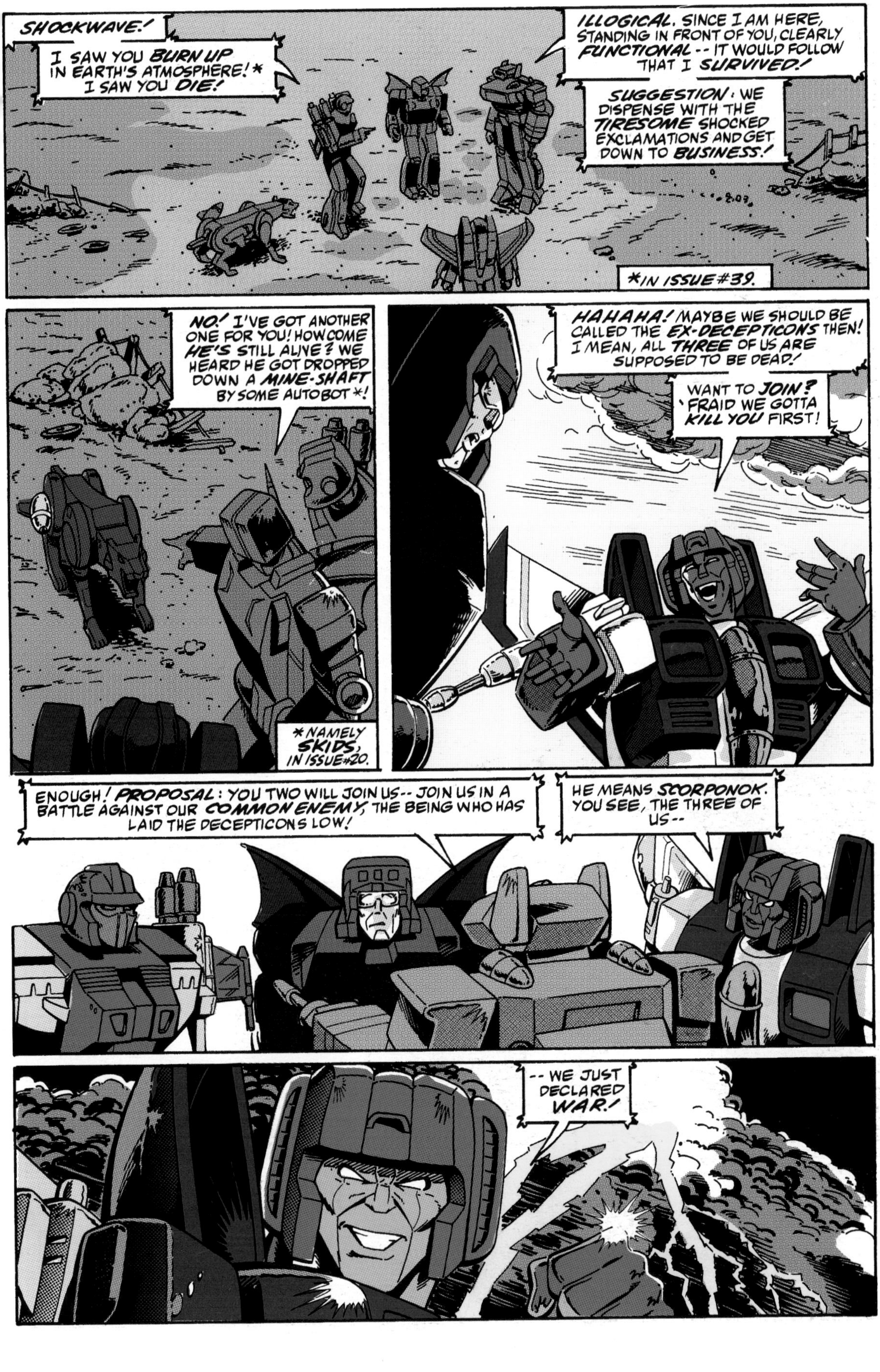
SHOCKWAVE!
I SAW YOU BURN UP IN EARTH'S ATMOSPHERE!* I SAW YOU DIE!
ILLOGICAL. SINCE I AM HERE, STANDING IN FRONT OF YOU, CLEARLY FUNCTIONAL -- IT WOULD FOLLOW THAT I SURVIVED!
SUGGESTION: WE DISPENSE WITH THE TIRESOME SHOCKED EXCLAMATIONS AND GET DOWN TO BUSINESS!
*IN ISSUE #39.
NO! I'VE GOT ANOTHER ONE FOR YOU! HOW COME HE'S STILL ALIVE? WE HEARD HE GOT DROPPED DOWN A MINE-SHAFT BY SOME AUTOBOT*!
*NAMELY SKIDS, IN ISSUE #20.
HAHAHA! MAYBE WE SHOULD BE CALLED THE EX-DECEPTICONS THEN! I MEAN, ALL THREE OF US ARE SUPPOSED TO BE DEAD!
WANT TO JOIN? 'FRAID WE GOTTA KILL YOU FIRST!
ENOUGH! PROPOSAL: YOU TWO WILL JOIN US-- JOIN US IN A BATTLE AGAINST OUR COMMON ENEMY, THE BEING WHO HAS LAID THE DECEPTICONS LOW!
HE MEANS SCORPONOK. YOU SEE, THE THREE OF US--
-- WE JUST DECLARED WAR!

THE ARK (AGAIN)...

COMPUTER--

BOOM!

-- PLOT COURSE FOR *HYDRUS FOUR* STYRAKON SYSTEM. *FULL SPEED.*

OOH. WHAT WAS *THAT?* I TOLD HOT ROD NOT TO LEAVE THE *OVEN* ON!

DID SOMETHING *HIT US?* ARE WE *UNDER ATTACK?*

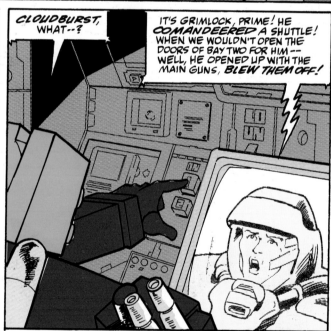

CLOUDBURST, WHAT--?

IT'S GRIMLOCK, PRIME! HE *COMANDEERED* A SHUTTLE! WHEN WE WOULDN'T OPEN THE DOORS OF BAY TWO FOR HIM -- WELL, HE OPENED UP WITH THE MAIN GUNS, *BLEW THEM OFF!*

THIS IS WHAT I WAS TRYING TO TELL YOU BEFORE, PRIME-- *SOME-THING'S UP WITH GRIMLOCK!*

I *KNOW,* WAVERIDER. I JUST DIDN'T THINK HE'D GO *THIS FAR!*

SO WHERE--?

A PLANET CALLED HYDRUS FOUR...

SCIENTISTS THERE HAD DISCOVERED A NEW SOURCE OF ENERGY THEY CALLED *NUCLEON.* NOT ONLY DID IT SEEMINGLY *CURE* THE INCURABLE, BUT IT ALSO *FUELLED* THEIR MECHANOID BIO-SYSTEMS, MAKING THEM *MORE POWERFUL* THAN BEFORE!

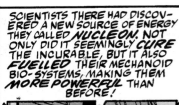

ALL WELL AND GOOD-- AND *CERTAINLY* WORTH INVESTIGATING, CONSIDERING OUR CURRENT SITUATION.

-- BUT THERE WAS A *PRICE* TO PAY FOR THIS "WONDER CURE"! THE FIRST THREE LOCALS THEY TREATED BECAME *UNHINGED,* TURNING ON THEIR SAVIORS! I DECIDED THAT THE RISK OUTWEIGHED ANY *POSSIBLE* BENEFIT AND SIMPLY *FILED* THE REPORT.

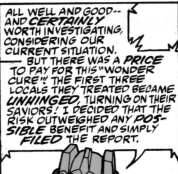

GRIMLOCK FOUND IT AND WANTED TO INVESTIGATE FURTHER. I WAS BUSY, *PREOCCUPIED...* I SAID *NO,* DIDN'T EVEN GIVE HIM A CHANCE TO STATE HIS *CASE!*

I JUST HOPE MY *MISTAKE* DOESN'T--

PRIME!

SOMETHING'S COMING THROUGH! THE PROBE'S FOUND--

FSSP!

TINK! TINK!

FOR A MOMENT THERE IS SILENCE, A FROZEN MICRO-SECOND OF UNNATURAL CALM WHILE THE WORLD SEEMS TO CATCH ITS BREATH.

THEN IT BEGINS!

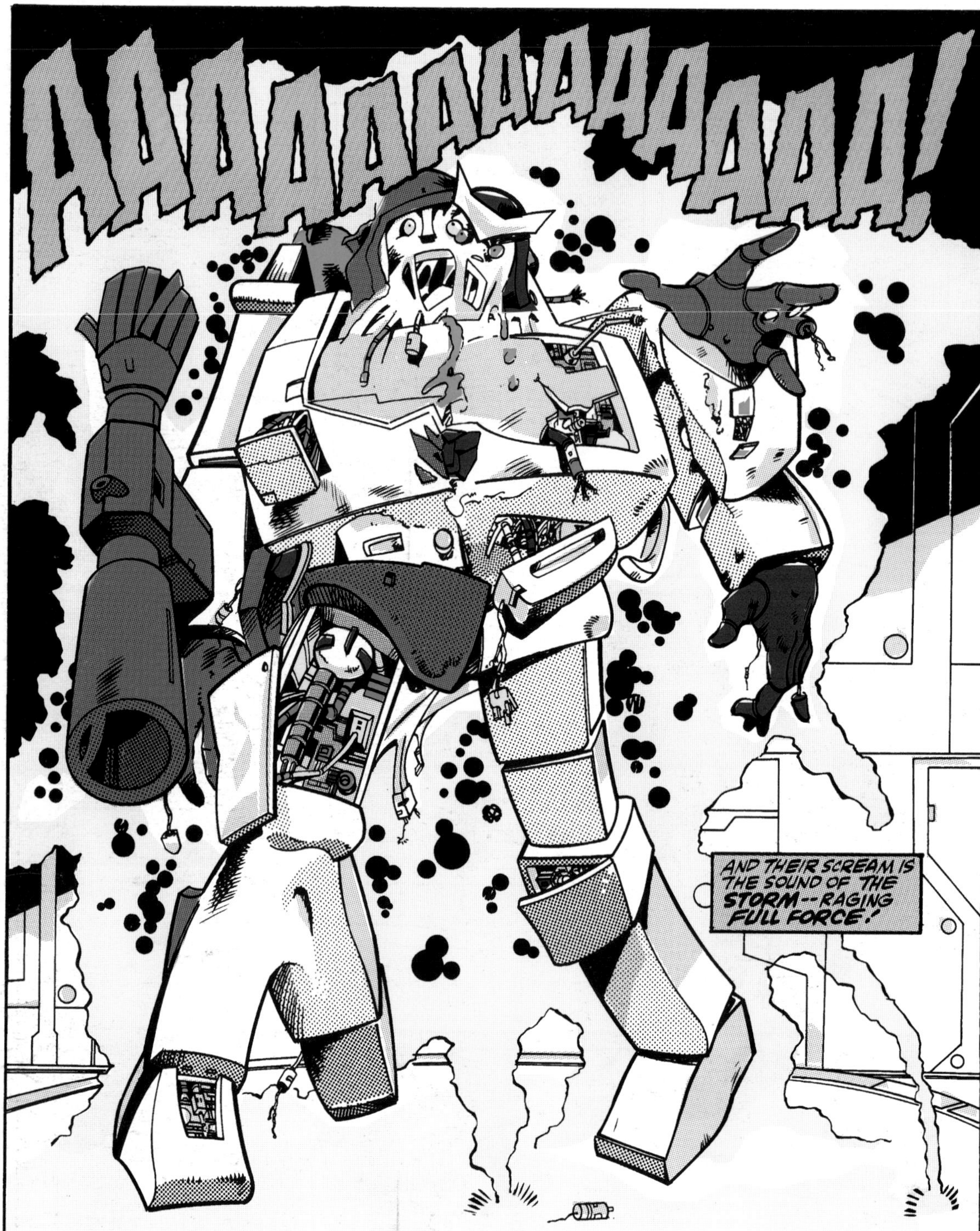
AAAAAAAAAAAAAA!
AND THEIR SCREAM IS THE SOUND OF THE STORM--RAGING FULL FORCE!

DON'T YOU DARE MISS NEXT ISSUE: **THE PRICE OF LIFE!**

They **were** the dream--mechanical beings able to transform their bodies into vehicles, machinery and weapons; a last line of defense against the chaos-bringer, **Unicron**! They **are** at war, heroic **Autobot** pitted against evil **Decepticon**, both on their homeworld, the metal planet called **Cybertron**, and here on our **Earth**. They **are** the galaxy's last hope, they **are**-- **TRANSFORMERS**

THE PRICE OF LIFE!

WHERE ONCE THERE WERE TWO, NOW THERE IS **ONE**-- A FUSED **HORROR** NO LONGER SIMPLY **DECEPTICON** OR HEROIC **AUTOBOT**!

HNNNLPAHH....

ONCE, A **LIFETIME** AGO, THEY FOUGHT -- CHIEF **SURGEON RATCHET** SEEKING TO RID THE WORLD OF THE MOST **EVIL** DECEPTICON OF ALL, **MEGATRON**, BY SACRIFICING HIS **OWN** LIFE!

HE **FAILED!**

Simon Furman	Andrew Wildman	Stephen Baskerville
WRITER	PENCILER	INKER
Rick Parker	Nel Yomtov	Rob Tokar	Tom DeFalco
LETTERER	COLORIST	SHARE ONE BRAIN

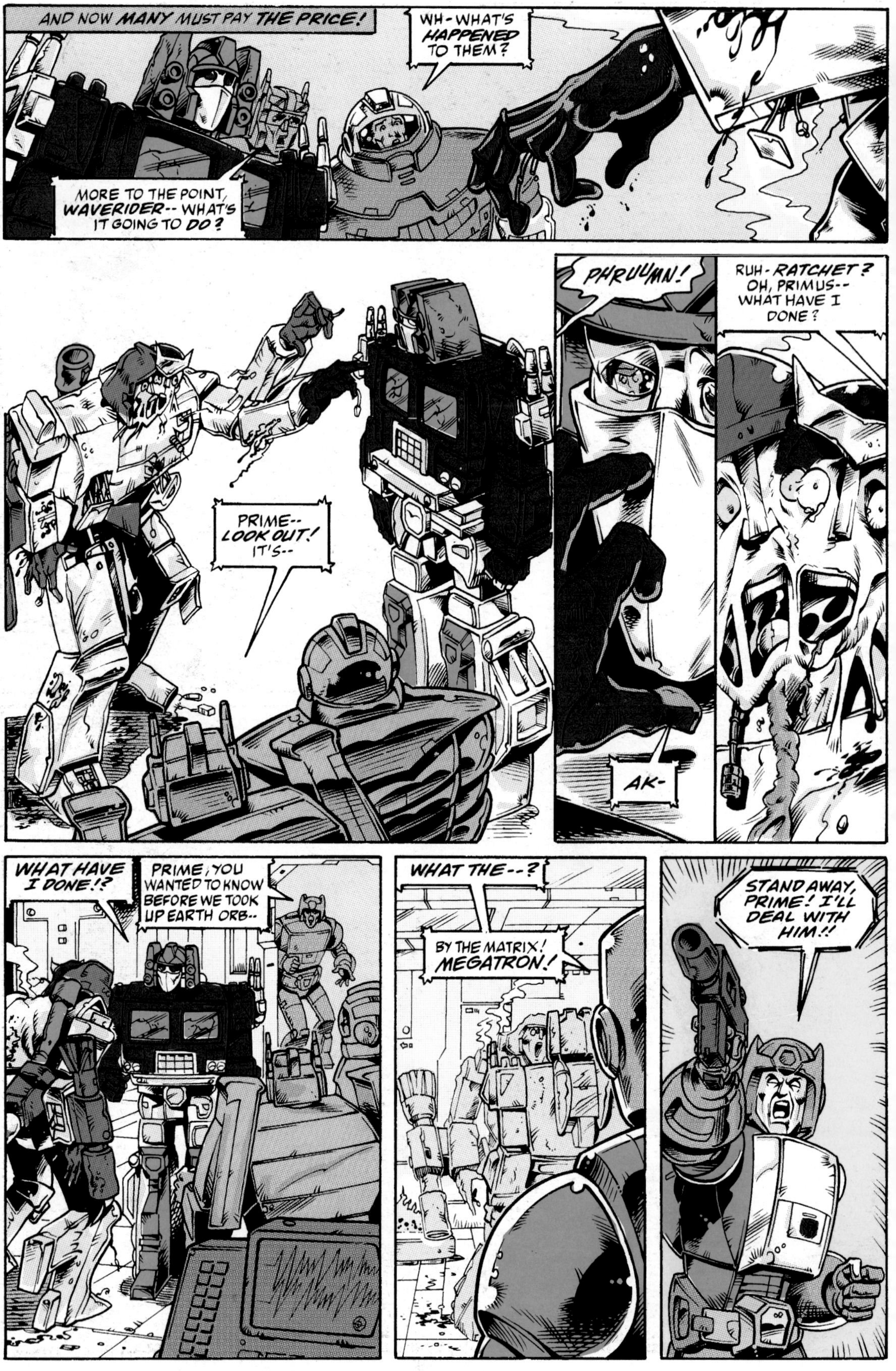
AND NOW MANY MUST PAY THE PRICE!
WH-WHAT'S HAPPENED TO THEM?
MORE TO THE POINT, WAVERIDER-- WHAT'S IT GOING TO DO?
PRIME-- LOOK OUT! IT'S--
PHRUUMN!
AK-
RUH-RATCHET? OH, PRIMUS-- WHAT HAVE I DONE?
WHAT HAVE I DONE!?
PRIME, YOU WANTED TO KNOW BEFORE WE TOOK UP EARTH ORB--
WHAT THE--?
BY THE MATRIX! MEGATRON!
STAND AWAY, PRIME! I'LL DEAL WITH HIM!!

WHAT? KUP-- DON'T.!! IT'S--

PRUM!

PRUUUM!

UUNAAH!

YOU'RE HISTORY, SCUMBALL!

RUUUAAH!

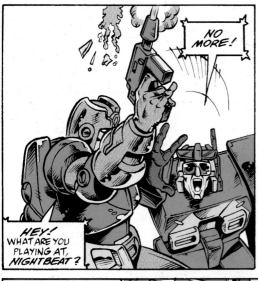

NO MORE!

HEY! WHAT ARE YOU PLAYING AT, NIGHTBEAT?

TAKE A CLOSE LOOK, KUP! THAT'S NOT JUST MEGATRON-- THAT'S MEGATRON AND RATCHET! OUR RATCHET!

RATCHET? I THOUGHT HE DIED WHEN MEGATRON'S BASE ON CYBERTRON BLEW UP! *

*IN ISSUE # 59.

SO DID WE ALL! BUT I'VE FOUND OUT SINCE THAT THERE WERE ACTUALLY TWO EXPLOSIONS. IT'S MY THEORY THAT SOMEHOW THE FIRST FUSED THEM TOGETHER--

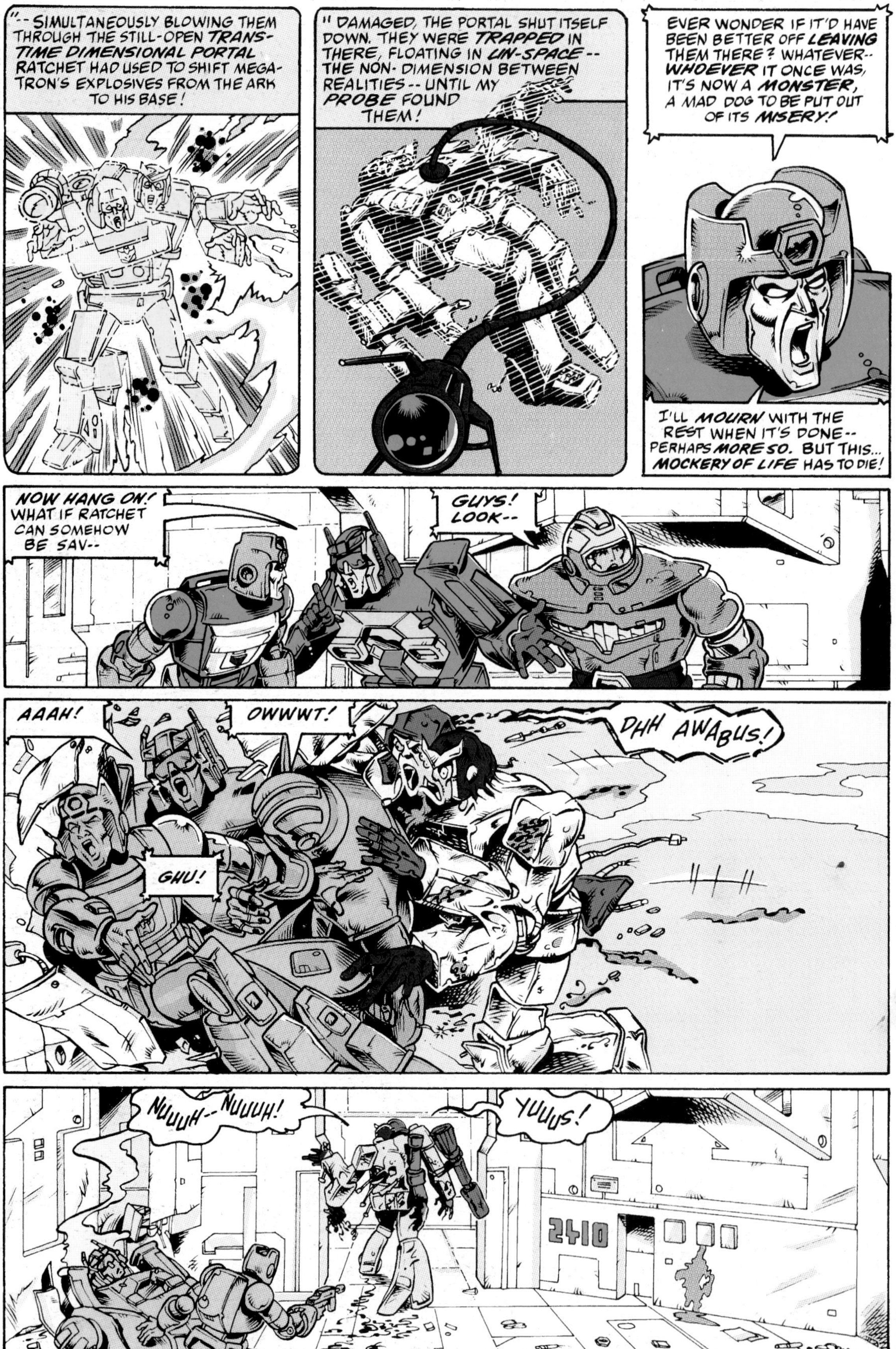
"-- SIMULTANEOUSLY BLOWING THEM THROUGH THE STILL-OPEN TRANS-TIME DIMENSIONAL PORTAL RATCHET HAD USED TO SHIFT MEGATRON'S EXPLOSIVES FROM THE ARK TO HIS BASE!
"DAMAGED, THE PORTAL SHUT ITSELF DOWN. THEY WERE TRAPPED IN THERE, FLOATING IN UN-SPACE -- THE NON-DIMENSION BETWEEN REALITIES -- UNTIL MY PROBE FOUND THEM!
EVER WONDER IF IT'D HAVE BEEN BETTER OFF LEAVING THEM THERE? WHATEVER -- WHOEVER IT ONCE WAS, IT'S NOW A MONSTER, A MAD DOG TO BE PUT OUT OF ITS MISERY!
I'LL MOURN WITH THE REST WHEN IT'S DONE -- PERHAPS MORE SO. BUT THIS... MOCKERY OF LIFE HAS TO DIE!
NOW HANG ON! WHAT IF RATCHET CAN SOMEHOW BE SAV--
GUYS! LOOK--
AAAH!
OWWWT!
DHH AWABUS!
GHU!
NUUUH -- NUUUH!
YUUUS!
2410

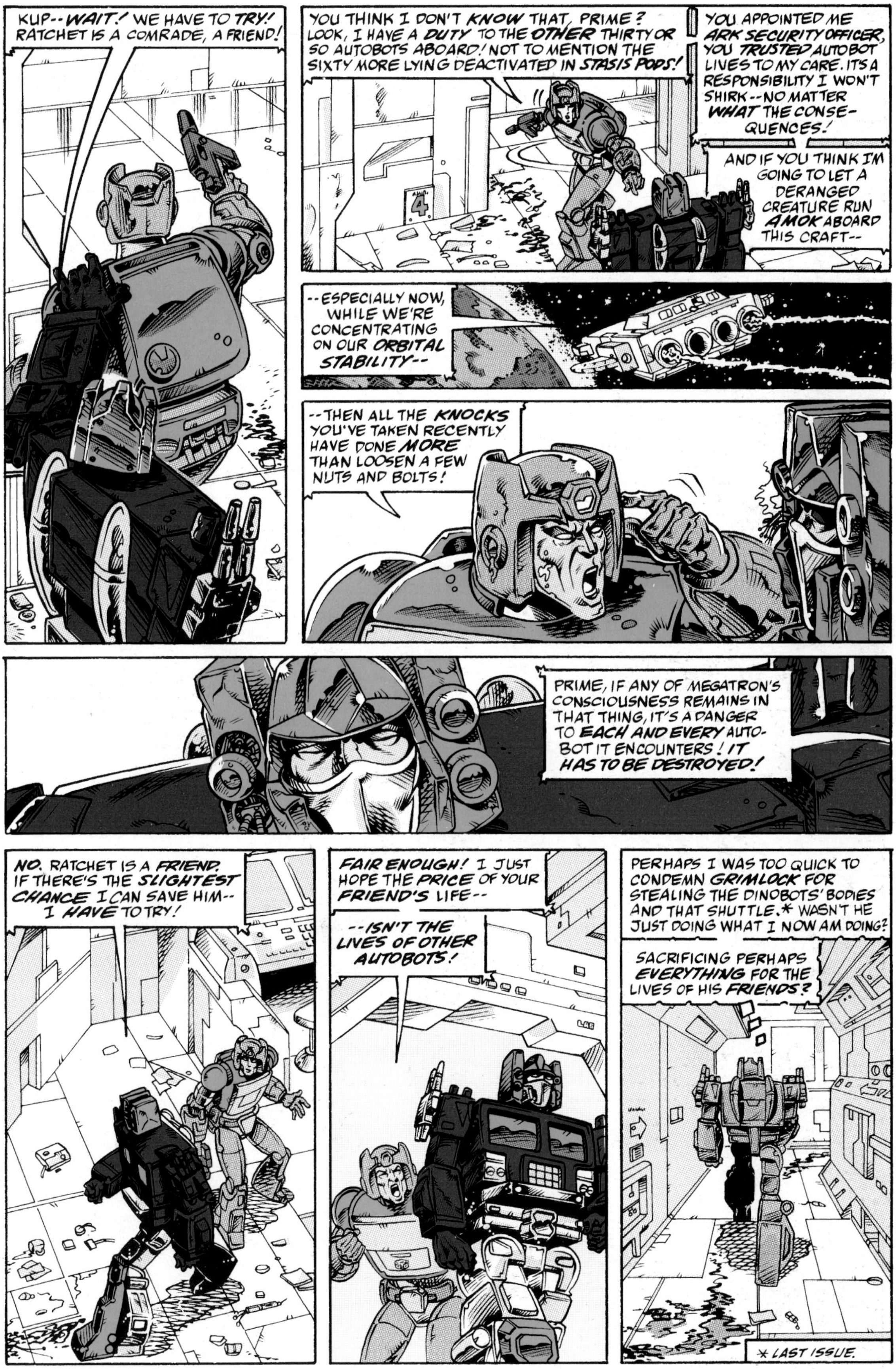
KUP--WAIT! WE HAVE TO TRY! RATCHET IS A COMRADE, A FRIEND!
YOU THINK I DON'T KNOW THAT, PRIME? LOOK, I HAVE A DUTY TO THE OTHER THIRTY OR SO AUTOBOTS ABOARD! NOT TO MENTION THE SIXTY MORE LYING DEACTIVATED IN STASIS PODS!
YOU APPOINTED ME ARK SECURITY OFFICER, YOU TRUSTED AUTOBOT LIVES TO MY CARE. IT'S A RESPONSIBILITY I WON'T SHIRK--NO MATTER WHAT THE CONSE-QUENCES!
AND IF YOU THINK I'M GOING TO LET A DERANGED CREATURE RUN AMOK ABOARD THIS CRAFT--
--ESPECIALLY NOW, WHILE WE'RE CONCENTRATING ON OUR ORBITAL STABILITY--
--THEN ALL THE KNOCKS YOU'VE TAKEN RECENTLY HAVE DONE MORE THAN LOOSEN A FEW NUTS AND BOLTS!
PRIME, IF ANY OF MEGATRON'S CONSCIOUSNESS REMAINS IN THAT THING, IT'S A DANGER TO EACH AND EVERY AUTO-BOT IT ENCOUNTERS! IT HAS TO BE DESTROYED!
NO. RATCHET IS A FRIEND. IF THERE'S THE SLIGHTEST CHANCE I CAN SAVE HIM-- I HAVE TO TRY!
FAIR ENOUGH! I JUST HOPE THE PRICE OF YOUR FRIEND'S LIFE--
--ISN'T THE LIVES OF OTHER AUTOBOTS!
PERHAPS I WAS TOO QUICK TO CONDEMN GRIMLOCK FOR STEALING THE DINOBOTS' BODIES AND THAT SHUTTLE.* WASN'T HE JUST DOING WHAT I NOW AM DOING?
SACRIFICING PERHAPS EVERYTHING FOR THE LIVES OF HIS FRIENDS?
* LAST ISSUE.

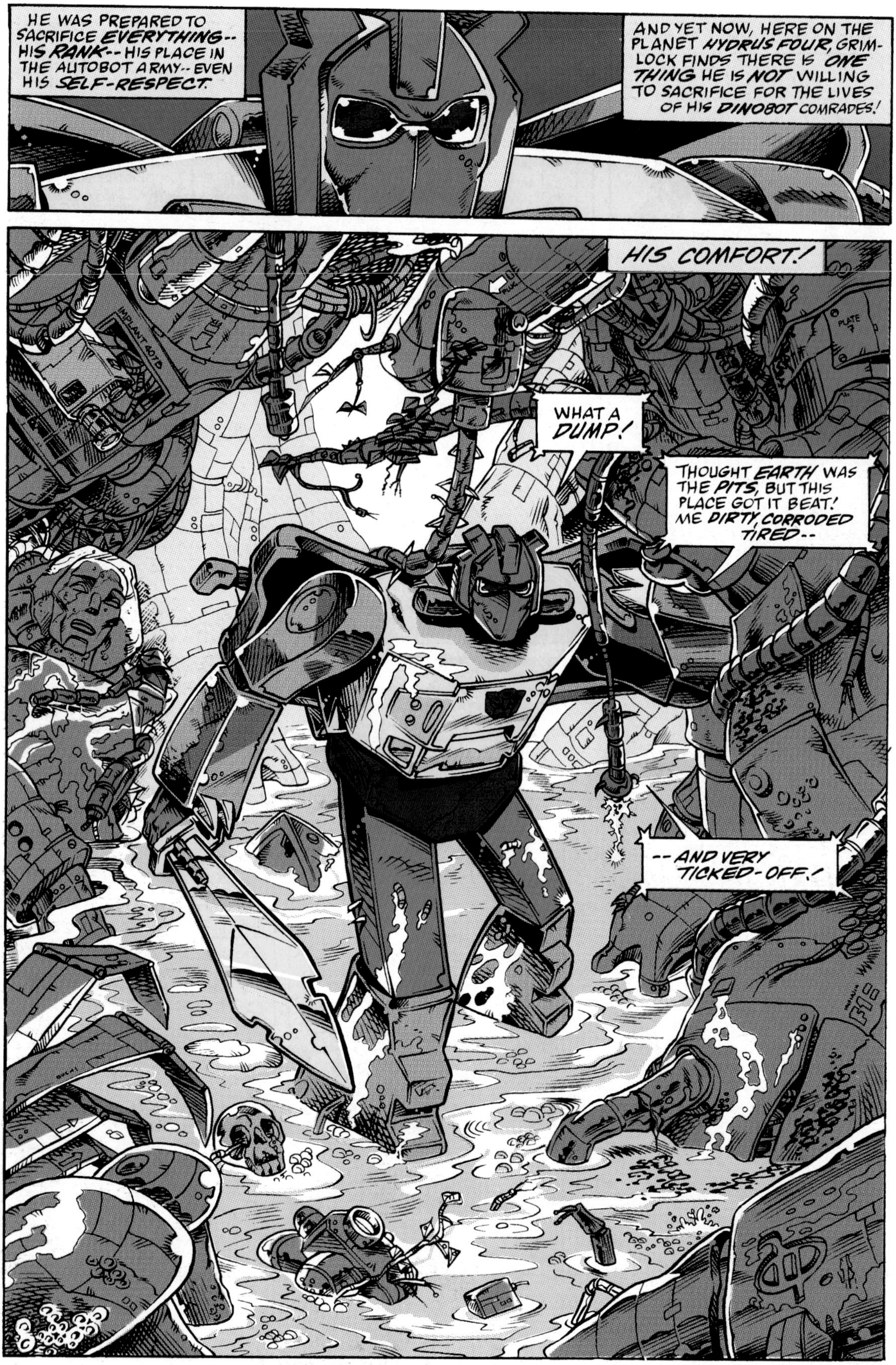
HE WAS PREPARED TO SACRIFICE EVERYTHING-- HIS RANK-- HIS PLACE IN THE AUTOBOT ARMY-- EVEN HIS SELF-RESPECT.
AND YET NOW, HERE ON THE PLANET HYDRUS FOUR, GRIMLOCK FINDS THERE IS ONE THING HE IS NOT WILLING TO SACRIFICE FOR THE LIVES OF HIS DINOBOT COMRADES!
HIS COMFORT!
WHAT A DUMP!
THOUGHT EARTH WAS THE PITS, BUT THIS PLACE GOT IT BEAT! ME DIRTY, CORRODED TIRED--
--AND VERY TICKED-OFF!

@$※#£!!

WHERE DUMB GUIDE GO *NOW*? PAID ENOUGH FOR HIM -- EXPECT *GOOD SERVICE!*

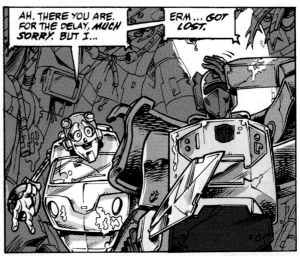

AH. THERE YOU ARE. FOR THE DELAY, *MUCH SORRY.* BUT I...

ERM ... *GOT LOST.*

MUST BE *MAD!* REMIND ME SOMEONE, PLEASE --

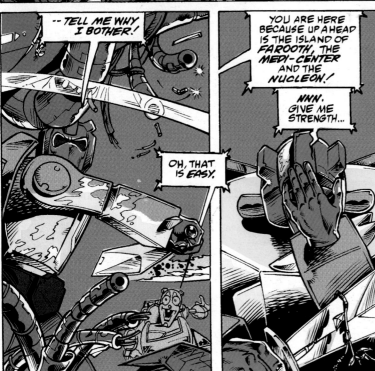

-- TELL ME WHY I BOTHER!

OH, THAT IS *EASY.*

YOU ARE HERE BECAUSE UP AHEAD IS THE ISLAND OF *FAROOTH,* THE *MEDI-CENTER* AND THE *NUCLEON!*

NNN. GIVE ME STRENGTH...

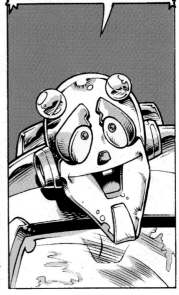

AND THE NUCLEON, OF COURSE, IS WHAT YOU ARE *SEEKING.* THIS WONDERFUL NEW *ENERGY* IS THE GIVER OF *LIFE* WHERE THERE IS NONE. THE SOURCE IS THE *WELL,* AND THE MEDI-CENTER IS THE *TAP.*

BUT IT IS AS I AM *WARNING* YOU, THIS NUCLEON HAS BAD *SIDE-EFFECTS*. THE FIRST THREE HYDRUSIANS TO BE TREATED WENT BERSERK--

--*CUCKOO, GAGA BARKING MAD.* YOU UNDERSTAND?

THEN MUCH *BADNESS.* THEY SLAUGHTER THEIR DOCTORS, *SEAL OFF* ISLAND. ANYONE GET *TOO CLOSE* --

-- THEY ARE BEING *KILLED*...

UH?

OHDEAROH DEAROHDEAR! MASTER GRIMLOCK?

MASTER GRIMLO--

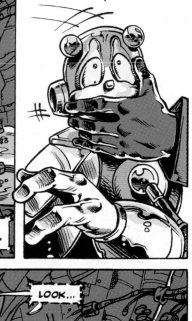

MNNGLL!

LOOK...

THERE!

AAAAAAH!

NNN!

≶ ZZSK ≶ NONE MUST PASS ≶ ZZSK ≶

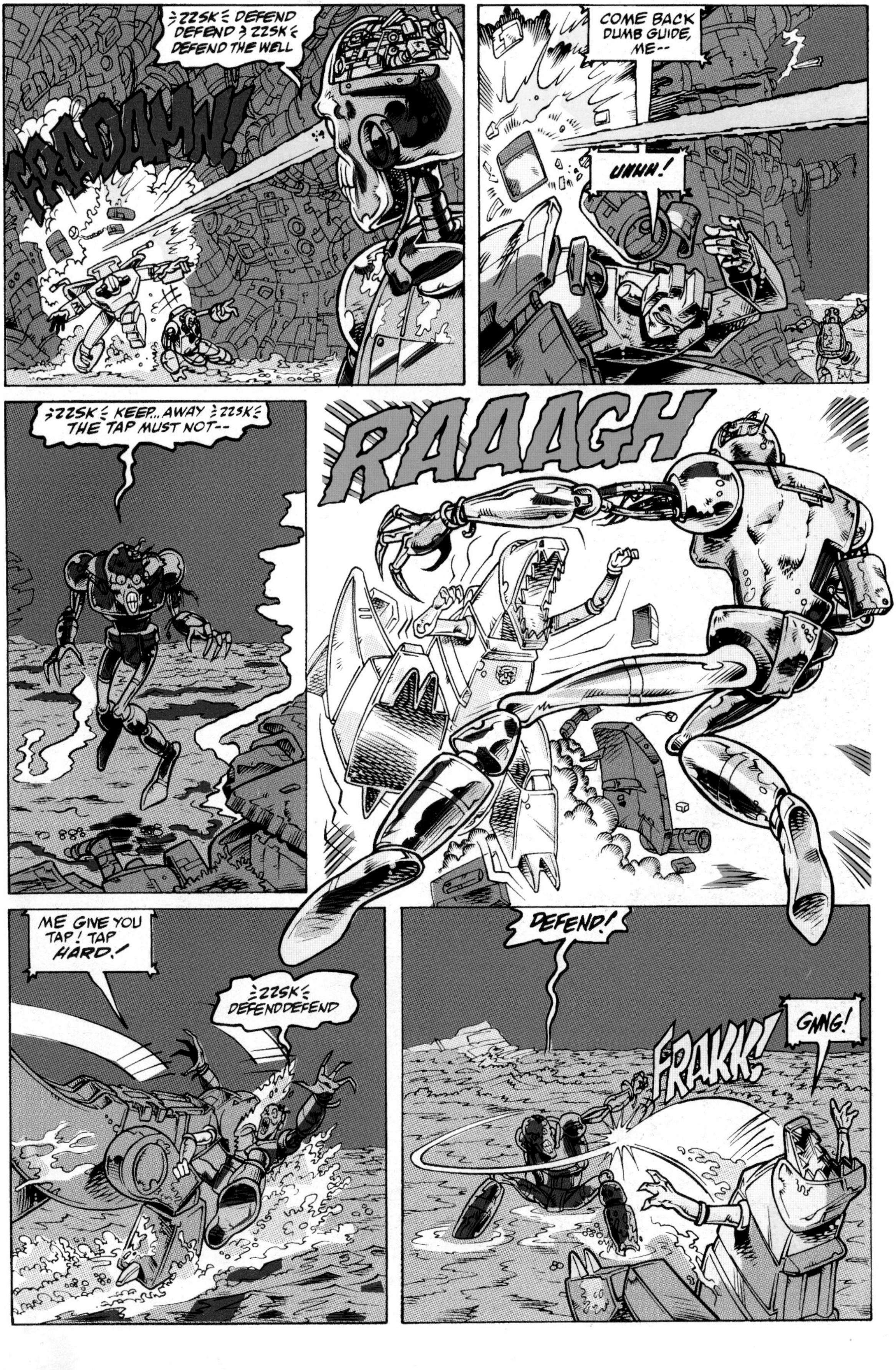
ZZSK DEFEND DEFEND ZZSK DEFEND THE WELL
FRADOOMM!
COME BACK DUMB GUIDE, ME--
UNHH!
ZZSK KEEP... AWAY ZZSK THE TAP MUST NOT--
RAAAGH
ME GIVE YOU TAP! TAP HARD!
ZZSK DEFENDDEFEND
DEFEND!
FRAKK!
GANG!

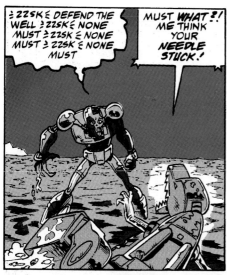

≥ZZSK≤ DEFEND THE WELL ≥ZZSK≤ NONE MUST ≥ZZSK≤ NONE MUST ≥ZZSK≤ NONE MUST

MUST *WHAT?!* ME THINK YOUR *NEEDLE STUCK!*

FEED ≥ZZSK≤ NONE MUST FEED ≥ZZSK≤

DEFEND!

UUH! ENOUGH!!

FRRSSH!

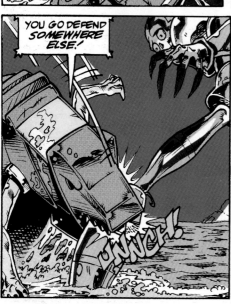

YOU GO DEFEND *SOMEWHERE ELSE!*

UNNGH!

ME THROW YOU SO FAR YOU --

UHK?

SKT!

PWHH! PWHH! EUUU... THIS THING MORE *DEAD* THAN *ALIVE!* AND YET --

≥CRK≤ DEFEND ≥ZZSK≤ WELL ≥1XZ≤

-- SOME FORCE KEEP IT *STRUGGLING,* KEEP IT *FIGHTING!*

IS NO WAY TO *LIVE!* BETTER *DEAD.*

GHHU! ME *NO TASTE* FOR THIS! THIS NOT *WARRIOR'S WORK* --

-- ME *SURGEON,* CUTTING AWAY *DISEASED TISSUE!*

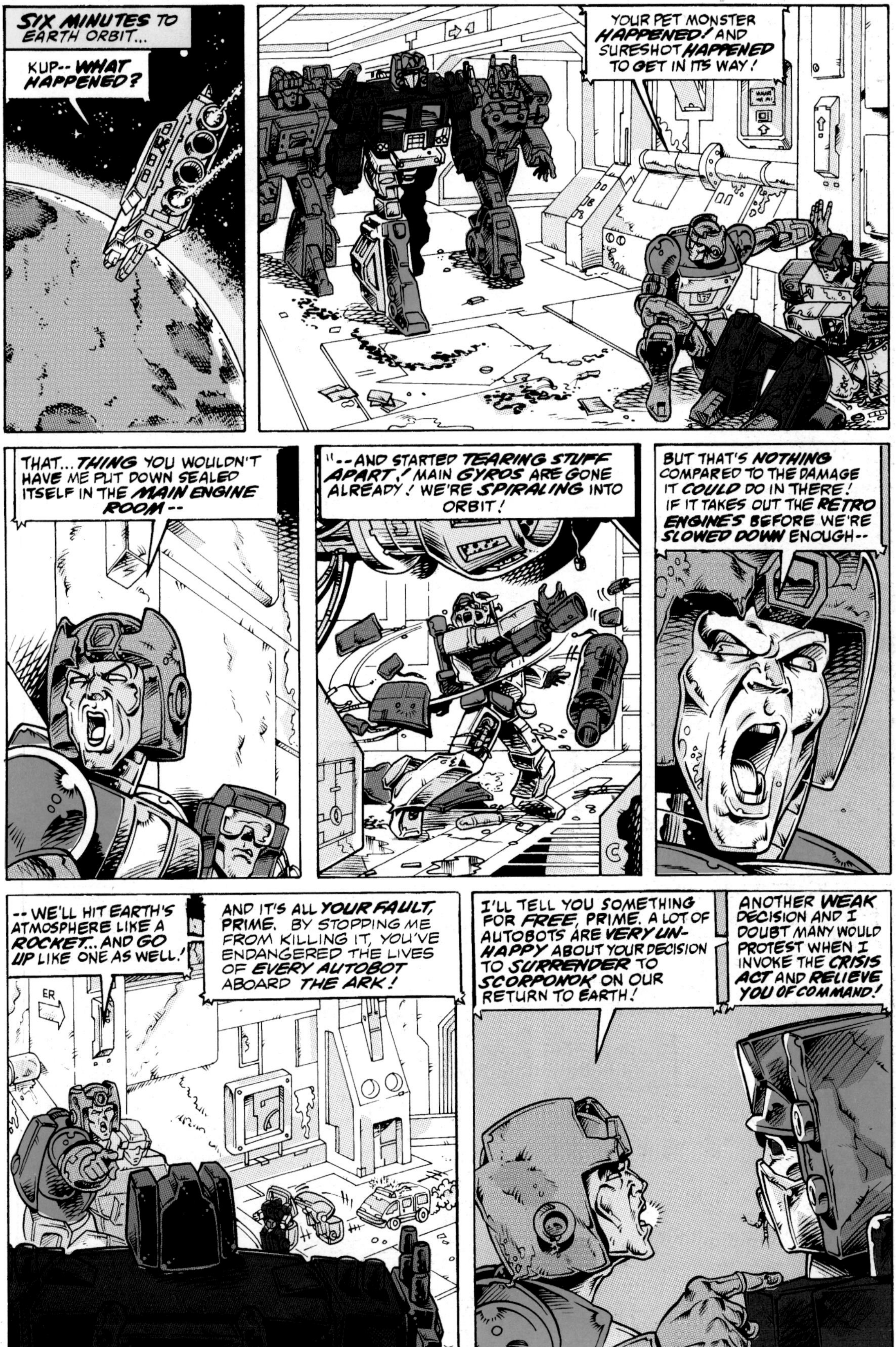
SIX MINUTES TO EARTH ORBIT...
KUP-- WHAT HAPPENED?
YOUR PET MONSTER HAPPENED! AND SURESHOT HAPPENED TO GET IN ITS WAY!
THAT... THING YOU WOULDN'T HAVE ME PUT DOWN SEALED ITSELF IN THE MAIN ENGINE ROOM--
"--AND STARTED TEARING STUFF APART! MAIN GYROS ARE GONE ALREADY! WE'RE SPIRALING INTO ORBIT!
BUT THAT'S NOTHING COMPARED TO THE DAMAGE IT COULD DO IN THERE! IF IT TAKES OUT THE RETRO ENGINES BEFORE WE'RE SLOWED DOWN ENOUGH--
--WE'LL HIT EARTH'S ATMOSPHERE LIKE A ROCKET... AND GO UP LIKE ONE AS WELL!
AND IT'S ALL YOUR FAULT, PRIME. BY STOPPING ME FROM KILLING IT, YOU'VE ENDANGERED THE LIVES OF EVERY AUTOBOT ABOARD THE ARK!
ER
I'LL TELL YOU SOMETHING FOR FREE, PRIME. A LOT OF AUTOBOTS ARE VERY UN-HAPPY ABOUT YOUR DECISION TO SURRENDER TO SCORPONOK ON OUR RETURN TO EARTH!
ANOTHER WEAK DECISION AND I DOUBT MANY WOULD PROTEST WHEN I INVOKE THE CRISIS ACT AND RELIEVE YOU OF COMMAND!

WE'RE OUT OF TIME.

DESTROY THE CREATURE!

KRAAAANG!

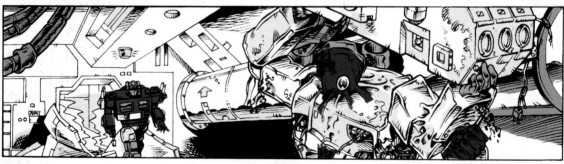

KUP, THERE'S GOT TO BE *ANOTHER WAY!* RATCHET SACRIFICED *EVERYTHING* TO SAVE US--CAN WE DO *LESS?*

I...

I LIKE IT *NO BETTER* THAN YOU, *SURESHOT!* BUT I'M SURE *RATCHET HIMSELF* WOULD *AGREE* WITH ME. IF THE CREATURE DESTROYS US, HIS SACRIFICE BECOMES *POINTLESS!*

BESIDES...

WOULD *YOU* WANT TO LIVE IF YOU WERE LIKE *THAT?*

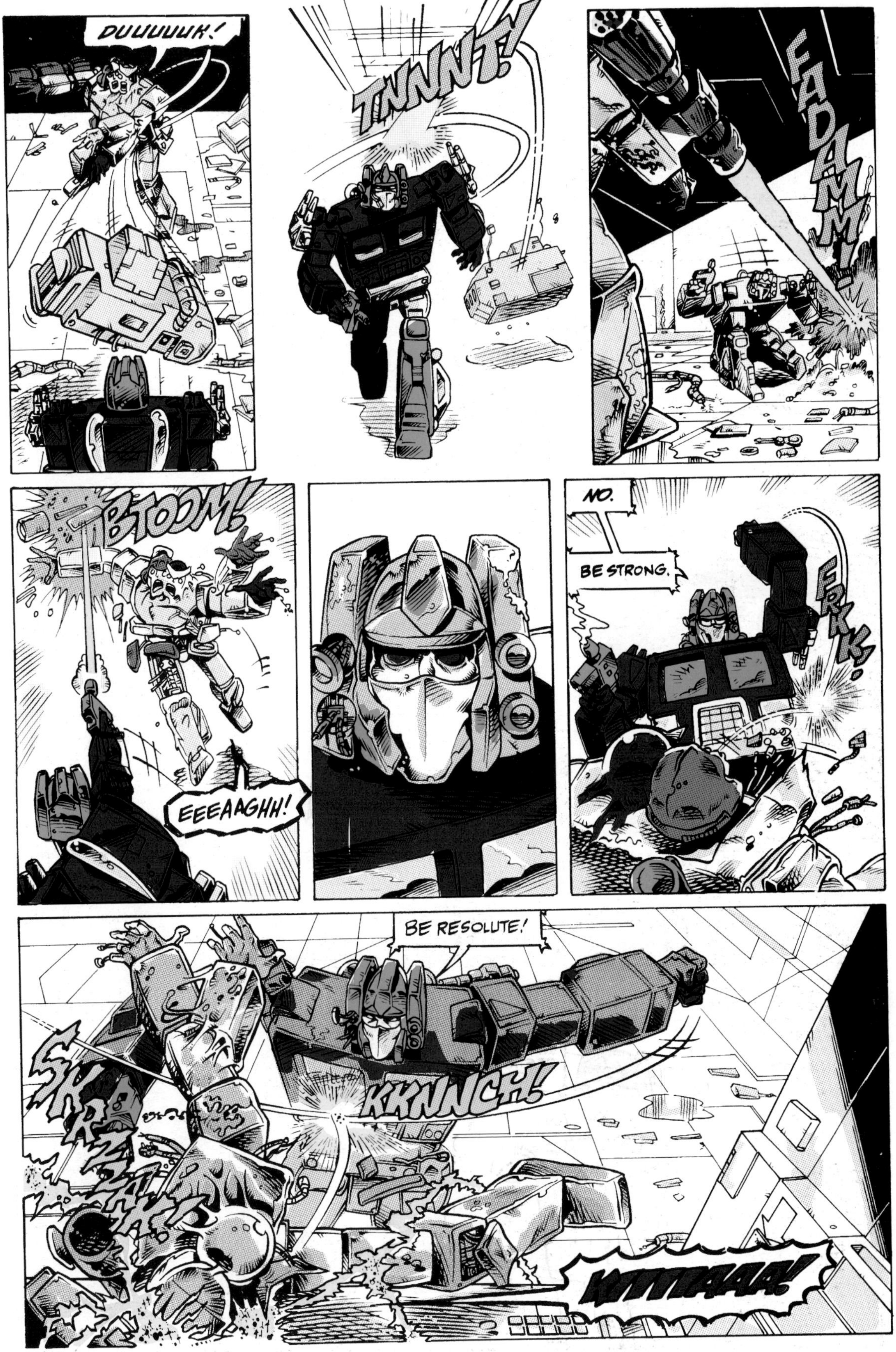

DUUUUUK!
TNNNT!
FADAMM!
BTOOM!
EEEAAGHH!
NO.
BE STRONG.
FRKK!
BE RESOLUTE!
SKRAKKK!
KKNNCH!
KWMAAA!

BE MERCILESS!

I-- --CANNOT! IT IS NOT MY WAY, NOT THE AUTOBOT WAY! MATRIX FORGIVE ME, BUT I CA--

WHA--?

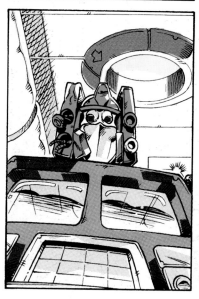

PLUUUUS!

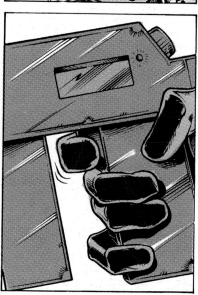

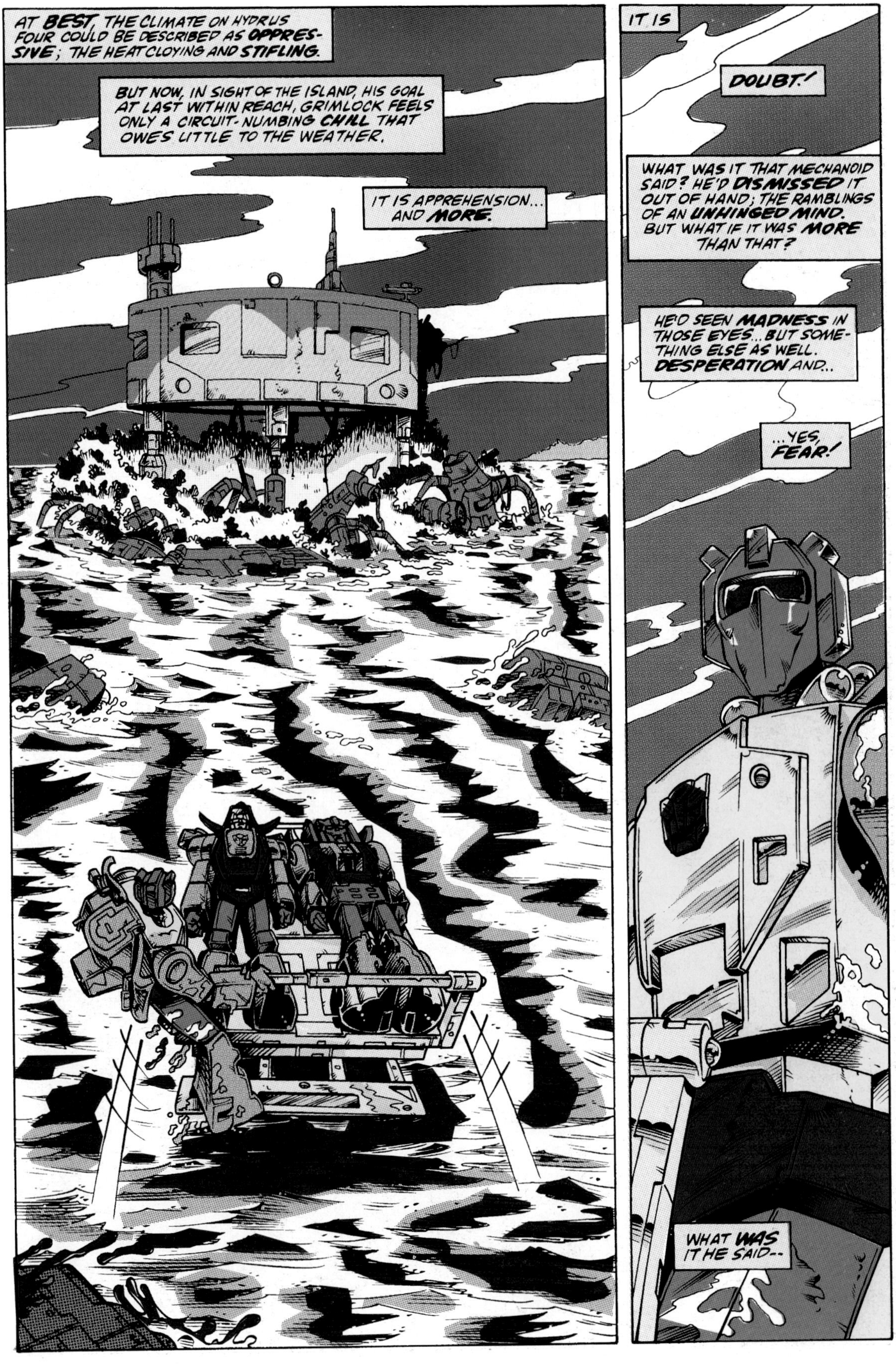
AT BEST, THE CLIMATE ON HYDRUS FOUR COULD BE DESCRIBED AS OPPRESSIVE; THE HEAT CLOYING AND STIFLING.
BUT NOW, IN SIGHT OF THE ISLAND, HIS GOAL AT LAST WITHIN REACH, GRIMLOCK FEELS ONLY A CIRCUIT-NUMBING CHILL THAT OWES LITTLE TO THE WEATHER.
IT IS APPREHENSION... AND MORE.
IT IS
DOUBT!
WHAT WAS IT THAT MECHANOID SAID? HE'D DISMISSED IT OUT OF HAND; THE RAMBLINGS OF AN UNHINGED MIND. BUT WHAT IF IT WAS MORE THAN THAT?
HE'D SEEN MADNESS IN THOSE EYES... BUT SOMETHING ELSE AS WELL. DESPERATION AND...
...YES, FEAR!
WHAT WAS IT HE SAID--

NONE MUST FEED!

UUH!

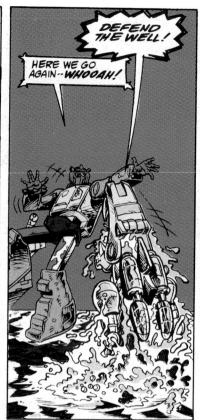

DEFEND THE WELL!

HERE WE GO AGAIN-- WHOOAH!

GLLB!

SPSSSSH!

SKTCH!

THIS MAD! WHAT I TRYING TO PROVE? I REALLY DO ALL THIS TO GET DINOBOTS BACK? OR DO I JUST WANT TO UP-STAGE PRIME, SHOW AUTO-BOTS ME KNOW BETTER THAN HIM?

DON'T KNOW! DON'T WANT TO KNOW--

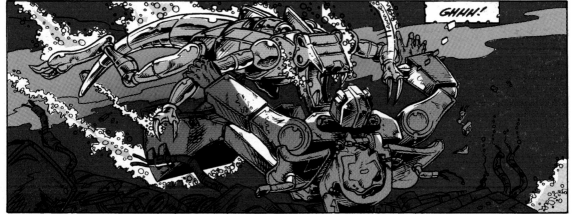

GHHH!

DUMB! HE GOT ME!

TEAR ME TO PIECES--

UNLESS...

KKKITCH!

UUH! WHAT A WASTE! WHAT A TERRIBLE WASTE OF LIFE!

ME JUST WANT THIS OVER WITH-- FINISHED!

WELCOME.

UHH!

WELCOME TO THE ISLAND OF *SPILLED TEARS* -- THE LAND ≋*UUH*≋ OF *CRUSHED ILLUSIONS* AND BROKEN ≋*GHU*≋ PROMISES.

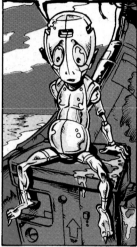

HUNN! YOU SURE *LOUSY* TOURIST GUIDE!

LET ME GUESS -- *NOME MUST FEED*, RIGHT? ME GETTING THE HANG OF THIS NOW. ME SUPPOSE IT BE TOO MUCH TO ASK WE DON'T FIGHT.

≋*UHK*≋ FIGHT ME? OH, NO, I MERELY WISH TO *WARN* YOU--

-- ABOUT NUCLEON!

YOU WILL DOUBTLESS SEEK LIFE FOR YOUR COMRADES, BUT ≋*AK*≋ WILL THEY WANT LIFE IF -- IF IT COMES LIKE THIS? NUCLEON AFFECTS NO TYPE OF MECHANOID IN THE SAME WAY. WHAT I ASK--

-- WILL IT DO TO *TRANSFORMERS?*

ER... MAKE US *STRONG*, MAKE US *POWERFUL!*

HA-HA ≋*GGN*≋ YES, YES. IT WILL DO *THAT* ALL RIGHT. BUT *WHAT ELSE?* WILL IT EAT YOU FROM THE IN-SIDE OUT? WILL IT DISTORT YOUR BODIES?

-- OR WILL IT MAKE YOU *CRAZY* LIKE MY... UH, *FRIENDS* YOU ENCOUNTERED?

WILL YOUR COMRADES *THANK* YOU FOR SAVING THEM--

-- OR *CURSE* YOU?

≋*UHH*≋ TAKE *ME* FOR EXAMPLE. I WAS SUFFERING FROM A *WASTING* DISEASE, MY CIRCUITS SLOWLY DECAYING. IT WAS *LONG*, DRAWN OUT, BUT AT LAST I'D REACHED THE *OBLIVION* I SO, ≋*URR*≋ BADLY CRAVED.

THEN THEY *CURED* ME.

ONLY THEY *DIDN'T* CURE ME! *UH-UH!* THEY BROUGHT ME BACK TO LIFE SO I COULD DIE *AGAIN* -- THIS TIME FEELING EVERY *CIRCUIT* AS IT SPUTTERS AND FADES. *ALL THANKS TO* NUCLEON!

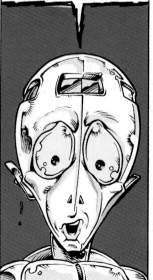

IT'S SAID ≤ UHN ≥ WE GUARD THE NUCLEON *JEALOUSLY.* NOT SO.

WE GUARD OTHERS *AGAINST* NUCLEON!

WHAT IF HE *RIGHT?* WHAT IF ME REVIVE DINOBOTS ONLY TO HAVE THEM DIE AGAIN, CURSING MY NAME? ONLY WAY TO BE SURE --

-- IS TO TEST IT *MYSELF!*

HE OPENS RECEIVING CIRCUITS IN HIS FINGERTIPS --

-- LETTING UNIMAGINABLE ENERGY FLOOD THROUGH HIM!

ME FEEL ...

...GREAT!

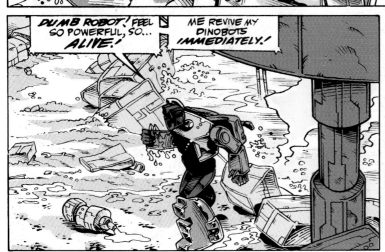

DUMB ROBOT! FEEL SO POWERFUL, SO... *ALIVE!*

ME REVIVE MY DINOBOTS *IMMEDIATELY!*

TIME WILL TELL...

THE ARK...

ARE THEY--?

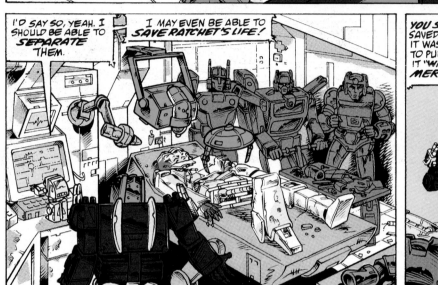

I'D SAY SO, YEAH. I SHOULD BE ABLE TO *SEPARATE* THEM.

I MAY EVEN BE ABLE TO *SAVE RATCHET'S LIFE!*

YOU SEE? HE *CAN* BE SAVED! DO YOU STILL THINK IT WAS "*WEAK*" OF ME NOT TO PULL THE TRIGGER? WAS IT "*WRONG*" TO BE MERCIFUL?

I'M AFRAID IT ISN'T QUITE AS *SIMPLE* AS THAT,

I CAN NEITHER GUARANTEE THE *STATE* OF RATCHET'S MIND OR SAVE HIM--

-- WITHOUT ALSO SAVING MEGATRON!

SOMEHOW THEIR NERVOUS SYSTEMS HAVE BEEN *BONDED* AT A *MOLECULAR LEVEL*. ONE *CANNOT* SURVIVE WITHOUT THE OTHER!

DO YOU STILL WISH ME TO PROCEED WITH THE OPERATION?

DO IT.

NEXT MONTH > THE ISSUE YOU THOUGHT YOU'D NEVER SEE (HECK, WE DIDN'T THINK WE'D SEE IT EITHER, AND WE PRODUCED IT!) **SURRENDER!**

They **were** the dream--mechanical beings able to transform their bodies into vehicles, machinery and weapons; a last line of defense against the chaos-bringer, **Unicron**! They **are** at war, heroic **Autobot** pitted against evil **Decepticon**, both on their homeworld, the metal planet called **Cybertron**, and here on our **Earth**. They **are** the galaxy's last hope; they **are**-- TRANSFORMERS

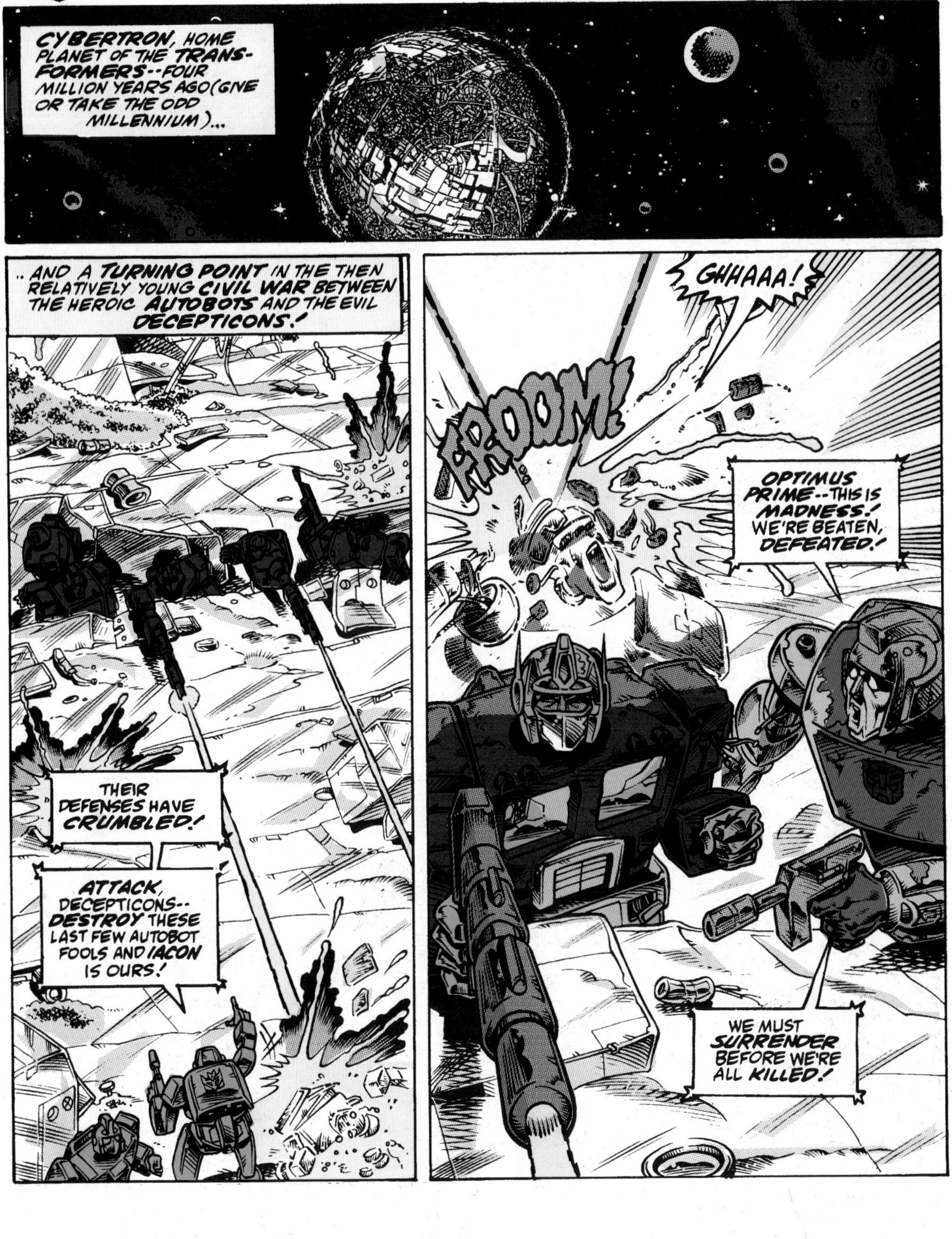
CYBERTRON, HOME PLANET OF THE TRANSFORMERS--FOUR MILLION YEARS AGO (GIVE OR TAKE THE ODD MILLENNIUM)...
..AND A TURNING POINT IN THE THEN RELATIVELY YOUNG CIVIL WAR BETWEEN THE HEROIC AUTOBOTS AND THE EVIL DECEPTICONS!
THEIR DEFENSES HAVE CRUMBLED!
ATTACK, DECEPTICONS--DESTROY THESE LAST FEW AUTOBOT FOOLS AND IACON IS OURS!
GHHAAA!
FROOM!
OPTIMUS PRIME--THIS IS MADNESS! WE'RE BEATEN, DEFEATED!
WE MUST SURRENDER BEFORE WE'RE ALL KILLED!

DO YOU HAVE THE *WHITE FLAG?*

THE FLAG..? OH, YES, *THE FLAG!*

THANK PRIMUS! I'LL TIE IT TO THE FRONT BATTLEMENTS AND--

YOU'LL *BIND MY WOUND* WITH IT, SOLDIER!

WHAT?!

YOU *HEARD ME.*

WE'RE *AUTOBOTS!* WE *NEVER* GIVE GROUND AND WE *NEVER, NEVER SURRENDER!*

NEVER SURRENDER! NEVER SURRENDER! NEVER SURRENDER!

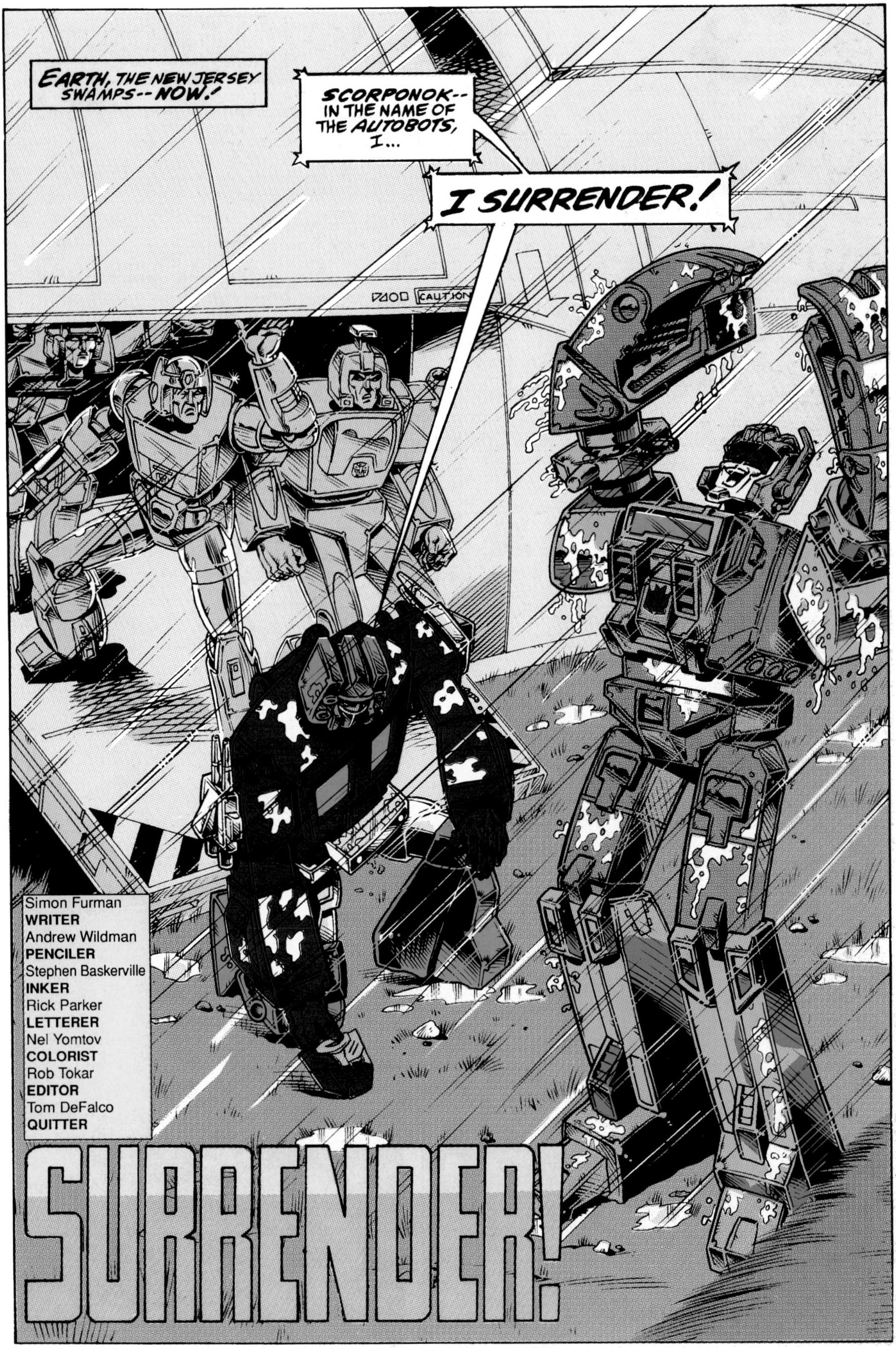
EARTH, THE NEW JERSEY SWAMPS--NOW!
SCORPONOK-- IN THE NAME OF THE AUTOBOTS, I...
I SURRENDER!
CAUTION
Simon Furman
WRITER
Andrew Wildman
PENCILER
Stephen Baskerville
INKER
Rick Parker
LETTERER
Nel Yomtov
COLORIST
Rob Tokar
EDITOR
Tom DeFalco
QUITTER
SURRENDER!

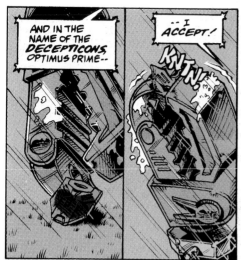

AND IN THE NAME OF THE *DECEPTICONS*, OPTIMUS PRIME--

-- I *ACCEPT!*

KNTN!

DECEPTICONS-- RELIEVE THEM OF *WEAPONS, NEBULANS* AND ANY OUTER *PRE-TENDER* SHELLS!

IT'LL BE A *PLEASURE!*

HAW-HAW! I ALWAYS KNEW YOU AUTOBOTS WERE A JOKE, BUT THIS-- THIS IS A REGULAR *COMEDY SHOW!*

AAAAAAA!

KRAKK!

UNNH!

GO ON, *APEFACE*-- LAUGH NOW!

PLEASE!

KUP--

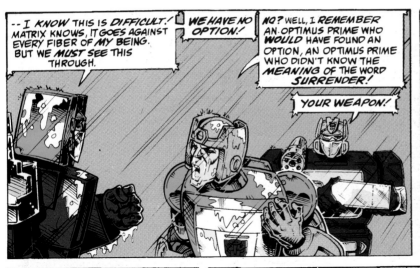

-- I KNOW THIS IS *DIFFICULT!* MATRIX KNOWS, IT GOES AGAINST EVERY FIBER OF *MY BEING.* BUT WE *MUST* SEE THIS THROUGH.

WE HAVE NO OPTION!

NO? WELL, I REMEMBER AN OPTIMUS PRIME WHO *WOULD* HAVE FOUND AN OPTION, AN OPTIMUS PRIME WHO DIDN'T KNOW THE *MEANING* OF THE WORD *SURRENDER!*

YOUR WEAPON!

AAH! HAVE IT!

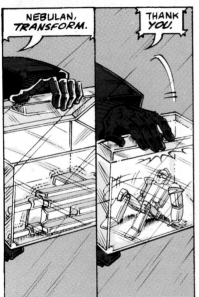

NEBULAN, TRANSFORM.

THANK *YOU.*

LET'S GO, AUTOBOT. WE'VE A NICE, COZY CEL-- I MEAN, *ROOM* FOR YOU!

IS HE RIGHT?

AM I SAVING MY RACE--

--OR DOOMING US ALL?

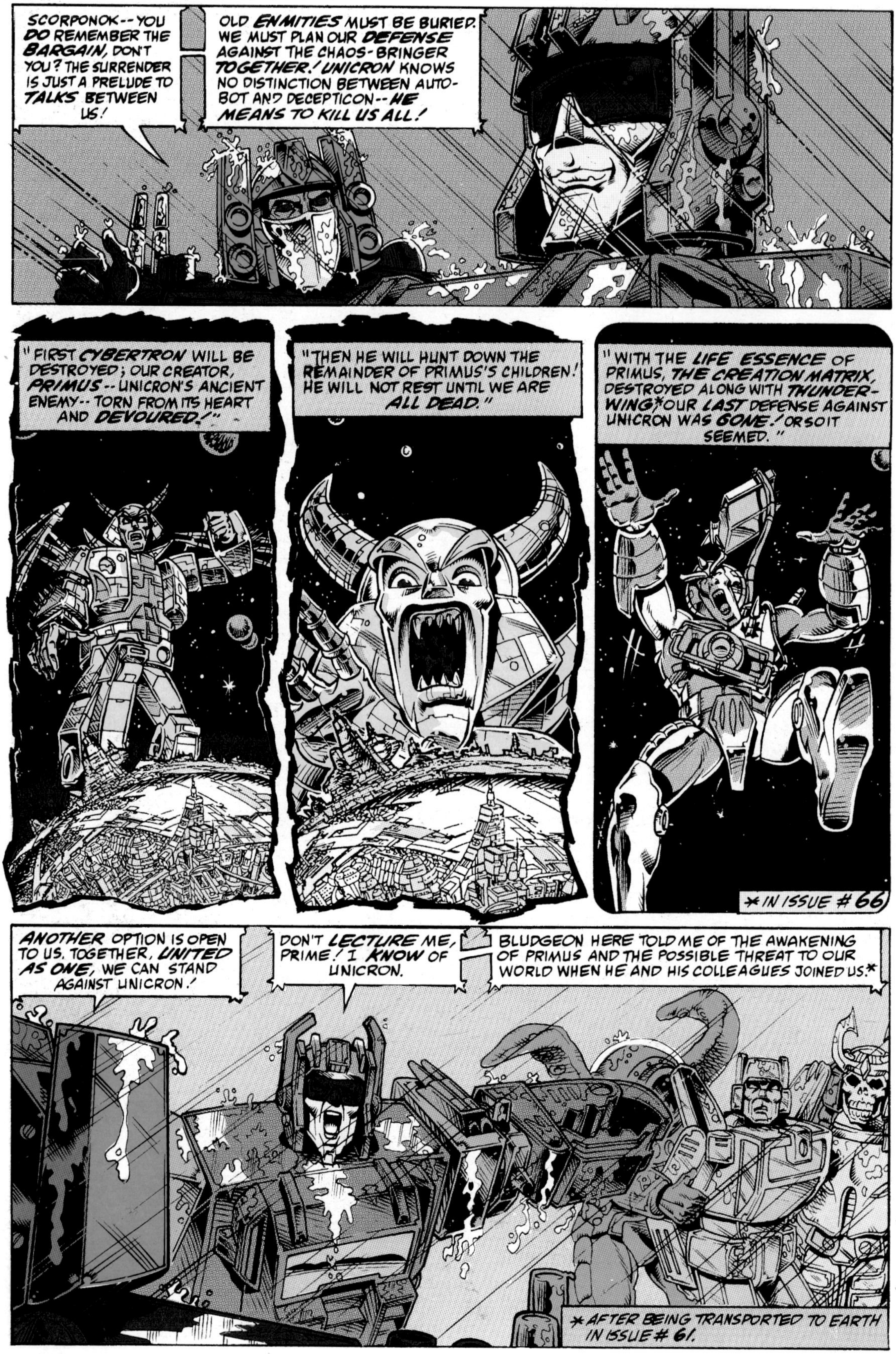
SCORPONOK -- YOU DO REMEMBER THE BARGAIN, DON'T YOU? THE SURRENDER IS JUST A PRELUDE TO TALKS BETWEEN US!
OLD ENMITIES MUST BE BURIED. WE MUST PLAN OUR DEFENSE AGAINST THE CHAOS-BRINGER TOGETHER! UNICRON KNOWS NO DISTINCTION BETWEEN AUTOBOT AND DECEPTICON -- HE MEANS TO KILL US ALL!
"FIRST CYBERTRON WILL BE DESTROYED; OUR CREATOR, PRIMUS -- UNICRON'S ANCIENT ENEMY -- TORN FROM ITS HEART AND DEVOURED!"
"THEN HE WILL HUNT DOWN THE REMAINDER OF PRIMUS'S CHILDREN! HE WILL NOT REST UNTIL WE ARE ALL DEAD."
"WITH THE LIFE ESSENCE OF PRIMUS, THE CREATION MATRIX, DESTROYED ALONG WITH THUNDERWING* OUR LAST DEFENSE AGAINST UNICRON WAS GONE! OR SO IT SEEMED."
* IN ISSUE # 66
ANOTHER OPTION IS OPEN TO US. TOGETHER, UNITED AS ONE, WE CAN STAND AGAINST UNICRON!
DON'T LECTURE ME, PRIME! I KNOW OF UNICRON.
BLUDGEON HERE TOLD ME OF THE AWAKENING OF PRIMUS AND THE POSSIBLE THREAT TO OUR WORLD WHEN HE AND HIS COLLEAGUES JOINED US.*
* AFTER BEING TRANSPORTED TO EARTH IN ISSUE # 61.

THEN HELP ME TO **DO** SOMETHING ABOUT IT! BY TRUSTING YOU, SCORPONOK, I HAVE RISKED **EVERYTHING**. BETRAY THAT TRUST--

--AND **ALL** TRANS-FORMERS WILL PAY!

YES, **YES**. WE'LL TALK SOON. **SOUNDWAVE**-- SEE THAT OUR **GUEST** IS MADE... COMFORTABLE.

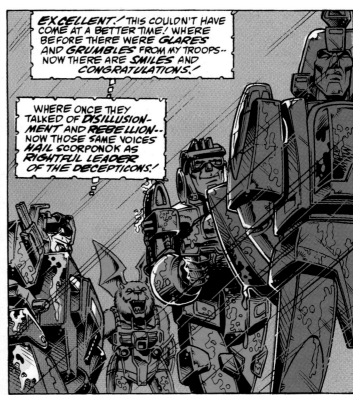

EXCELLENT! THIS COULDN'T HAVE COME AT A BETTER TIME! WHERE BEFORE THERE WERE **GLARES** AND **GRUMBLES** FROM MY TROOPS-- NOW THERE ARE **SMILES** AND CONGRATULATIONS!

WHERE ONCE THEY TALKED OF **DISILLUSION-MENT** AND **REBELLION**-- NOW THOSE SAME VOICES **HAIL** SCORPONOK AS **RIGHTFUL LEADER** OF THE DECEPTICONS!

BUT IF I STAY TRUE TO MY WORD AND **ALLY** MY FORCES WITH PRIME'S, WOULD THIS GOODWILL NOT SIMPLY BE LOST, **SWEPT AWAY** FOR THE SAKE OF A **MYTH?**

PERHAPS I SHOULD **BETRAY** PRIME. FOR THOUGH I HAVE THE **MIGHT OF SCORPONOK** BEHIND ME--

-- I AM STILL JUST **FLESH AND BLOOD**; A NEBULAN. **LORD ZARAK** IS BUT A **MAN AMONG GIANTS!**

HMM. ONE THING I **DO** KNOW, IS THAT WHEN **MINDWIPE** AND **TRIGGERHAPPY** LEARN OF MY VICTORY--

-- THOSE TWO **DESERTERS** WILL COME **CRAWLING** BACK TO ME ON THEIR HANDS AND KNEES!

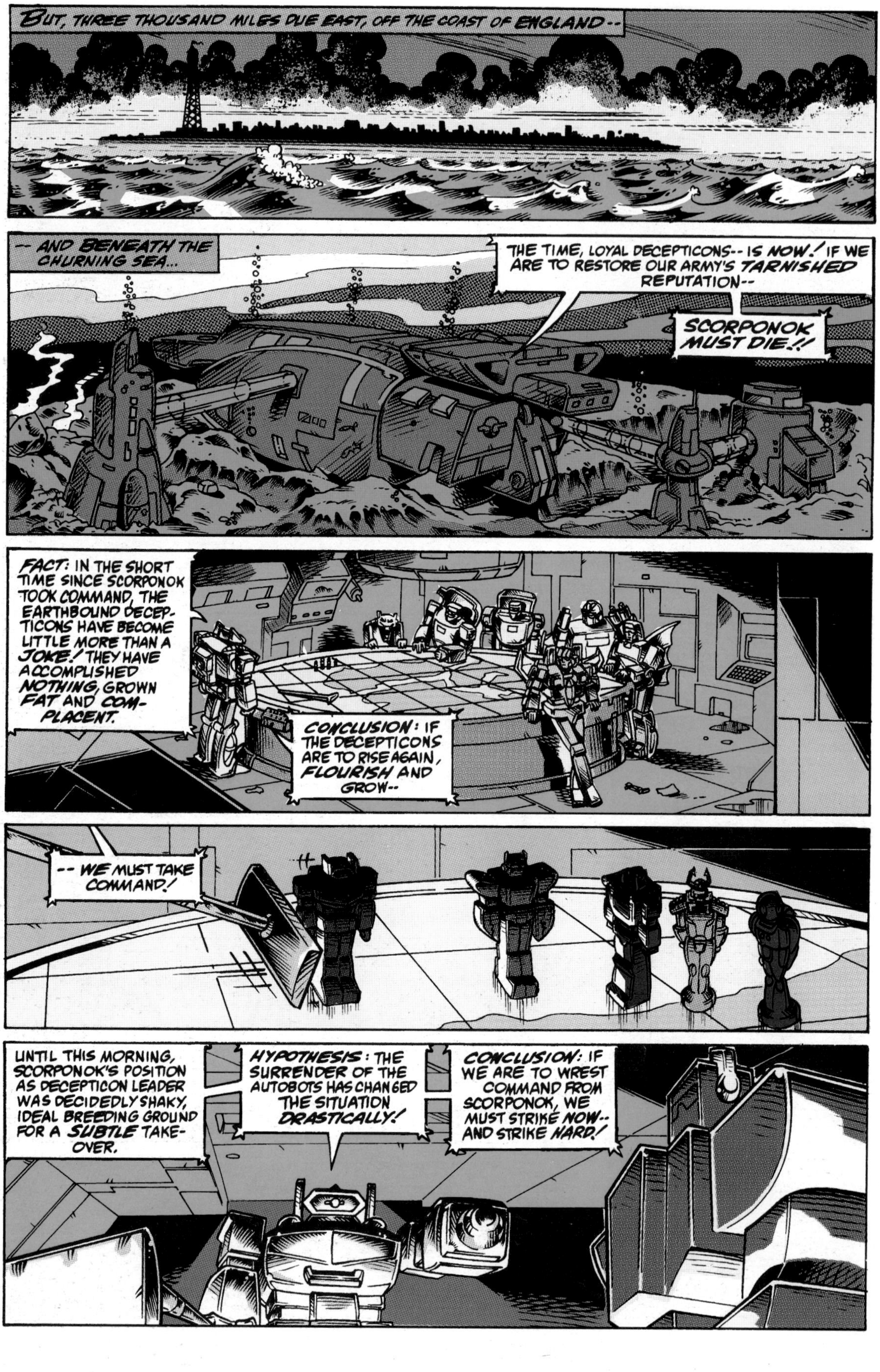
But, three thousand miles due east, off the coast of England--
-- And beneath the churning sea...
THE TIME, LOYAL DECEPTICONS-- IS NOW! IF WE ARE TO RESTORE OUR ARMY'S TARNISHED REPUTATION--
SCORPONOK MUST DIE!!
FACT: IN THE SHORT TIME SINCE SCORPONOK TOOK COMMAND, THE EARTHBOUND DECEPTICONS HAVE BECOME LITTLE MORE THAN A JOKE! THEY HAVE ACCOMPLISHED NOTHING, GROWN FAT AND COMPLACENT.
CONCLUSION: IF THE DECEPTICONS ARE TO RISE AGAIN, FLOURISH AND GROW--
-- WE MUST TAKE COMMAND!
UNTIL THIS MORNING, SCORPONOK'S POSITION AS DECEPTICON LEADER WAS DECIDEDLY SHAKY, IDEAL BREEDING GROUND FOR A SUBTLE TAKE-OVER.
HYPOTHESIS: THE SURRENDER OF THE AUTOBOTS HAS CHANGED THE SITUATION DRASTICALLY!
CONCLUSION: IF WE ARE TO WREST COMMAND FROM SCORPONOK, WE MUST STRIKE NOW-- AND STRIKE HARD!

RAVAGE, RUNAMUCK, RUNABOUT, TRIGGERHAPPY, MINDWIPE -- STARSCREAM AND I HAVE CHOSEN YOU FOR THIS GLORIOUS TASK! YOU ARE OUR WARRIORS, OUR--

HANG ON, SHOCKWAVE!

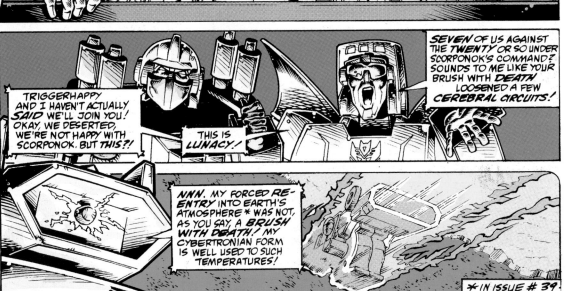

TRIGGERHAPPY AND I HAVEN'T ACTUALLY SAID WE'LL JOIN YOU! OKAY, WE DESERTED, WE'RE NOT HAPPY WITH SCORPONOK, BUT THIS?!

THIS IS LUNACY!

SEVEN OF US AGAINST THE TWENTY OR SO UNDER SCORPONOK'S COMMAND? SOUNDS TO ME LIKE YOUR BRUSH WITH DEATH LOOSENED A FEW CEREBRAL CIRCUITS!

NNN. MY FORCED RE-ENTRY INTO EARTH'S ATMOSPHERE * WAS NOT, AS YOU SAY, A BRUSH WITH DEATH! MY CYBERTRONIAN FORM IS WELL USED TO SUCH TEMPERATURES!

* IN ISSUE # 39.

OH, YEAH? THEN HOW COME YOU TOOK SO LONG TO SHOW UP AGAIN? AND WHERE DID YOU GET THIS CRAFT? AND WHY--

HUH?

I'LL MAKE IT REAL SIMPLE FOR YOU. YOU'VE SEEN AND HEARD TOO MUCH! IF YOU WANT OUT, YOU GO FEET FIRST!

≥ULP≥ IN THAT CASE-- WE'RE IN!

GOOD! THEN WE ATTACK AT ONCE!

FROOM

NEW JERSEY, AND FOR OPTIMUS PRIME THE HOURS THAT HAVE PASSED--

-- SEEM MORE LIKE WEEKS!

HOW MUCH LONGER, SOUNDWAVE? DOESN'T SCORPONOK UNDERSTAND? TIME IS RUNNING OUT!

WE HAVE TERMS TO DISCUSS, PLANS TO MAKE! WHERE IS HE?!

HE IS BUSY AT PRESENT. YOU MUST BE...PATIENT.

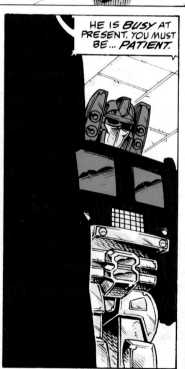

AH!

THIS IS BAD! IF SCORPONOK HAS CHANGED HIS MIND, ALL I HAVE MANAGED TO DO IS HAND HIM THE SIMPLEST OF VICTORIES!

AND YET...ONE WAY OR ANOTHER I MUST GET THAT ALLIANCE, AND GET IT SOON! FOR DIVIDED-- WE FALL!

WHAT IF IT'S ALREADY STARTED? WHAT IF UNICRON HAS ALREADY REACHED CYBERTRON?

IF I ONLY KNEW WHAT WAS HAPPENING THERE!

AND IF EVER THERE WAS A CUE FOR A LOOK IN ON THE TRANSFORMERS' HOMEWORLD--

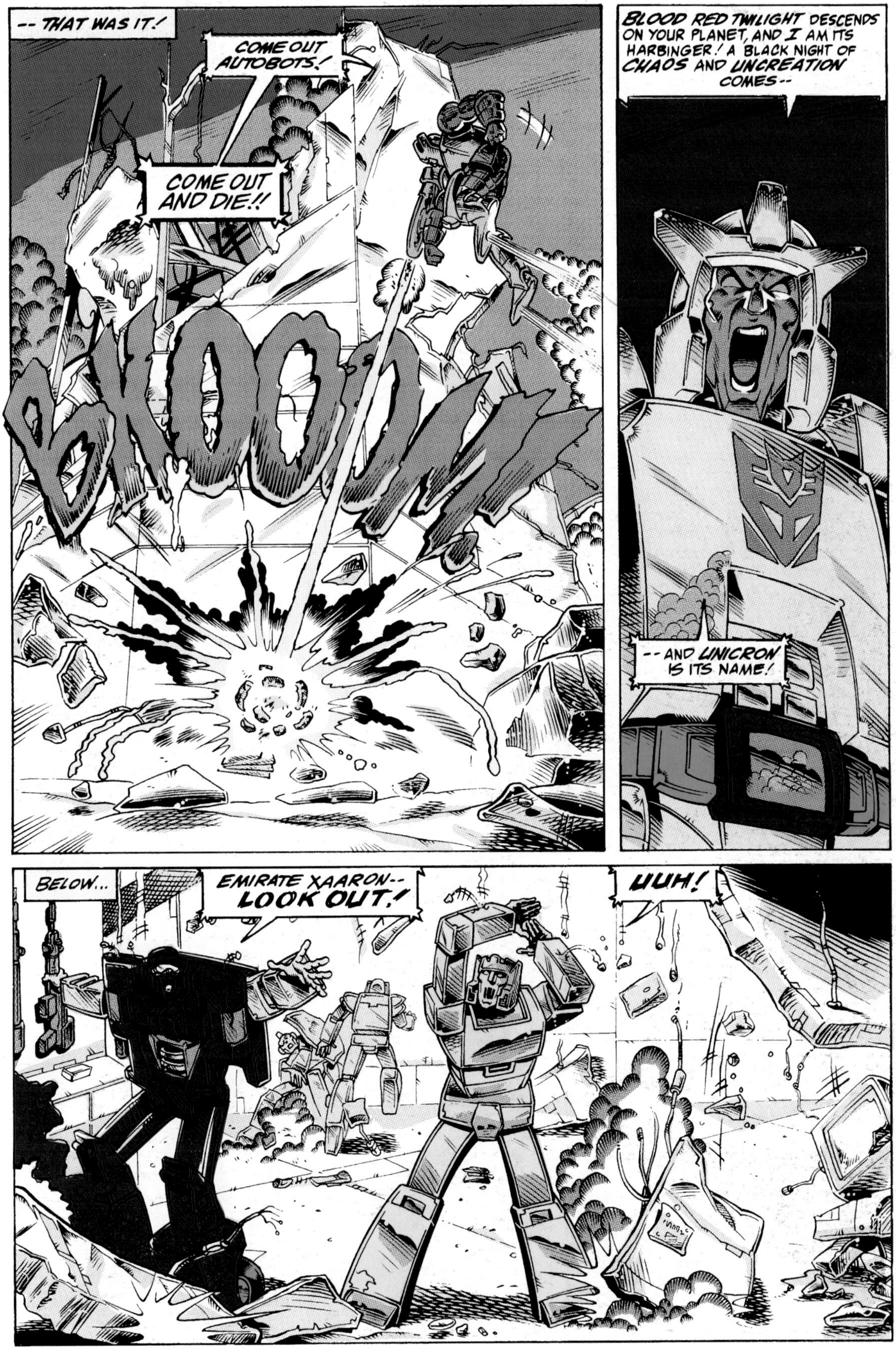
-- THAT WAS IT!
COME OUT AUTOBOTS!
COME OUT AND DIE!!
BKOOOM
BLOOD RED TWILIGHT DESCENDS ON YOUR PLANET, AND I AM ITS HARBINGER! A BLACK NIGHT OF CHAOS AND UNCREATION COMES--
--AND UNICRON IS ITS NAME!
BELOW...
EMIRATE XAARON-- LOOK OUT!
UUH!

EMIRATE XAARON, EMIRATE XAARON-- WE'RE UNDER ATTACK!

REALLY? YOUR CAPACITY FOR TACTICAL ANALYSIS IS QUITE BREATHTAKING!

AUTOBASE IS COMPROMISED, EMIRATE. YOU MUST FLEE, USE THE TUNNELS TO ESCAPE.

WE'LL HOLD OFF THE DECEPTICONS FOR AS LONG AS POSSIBLE!

MEVER! I'LL STAND AND FIGHT WITH THE REST OF YOU! EVEN IF--

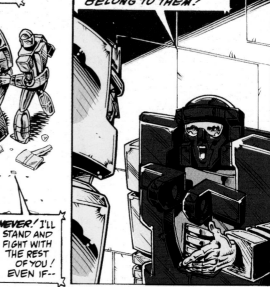

NO. WE ALWAYS KNEW DISCOVERY WAS A POSSIBILITY. WHAT'S IMPORTANT IS YOUR SURVIVAL! YOU MUST STAY ALIVE TO REBUILD AT ANOTHER AUTOBASE, REKINDLE THE FLAME!

SHOULD THE RESISTANCE MOVEMENT LOSE ITS LEADER, THE FIGHT WILL GO OUT OF OUR REMAINING WARRIORS! THE DECEPTICONS WILL HAVE WON AND CYBERTRON WILL FINALLY BELONG TO THEM!

I -- VERY WELL.

MAY PRIMUS WATCH OVER YOU!

HAH! IN MY OWN TIME I DESTROYED AN ENTIRE RACE OF AUTOBOTS, THEIR MIGHTIEST LEADER! WHAT CHANCE THEN--

--DO YOU HAVE?!

KTAMEN

ENOUGH, DECEPTICON-- ENOUGH!

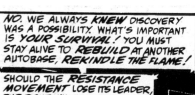

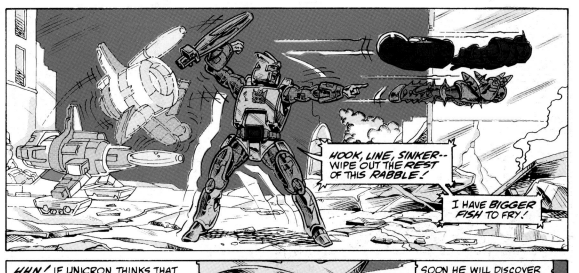

HOOK, LINE, SINKER-- WIPE OUT THE *REST* OF THIS *RABBLE!*

I HAVE *BIGGER FISH* TO FRY!

HHN! IF UNICRON THINKS THAT *I* WILL LET HIM JUST *PLUCK* ME FROM THE *FUTURE* AND TURN ME INTO SOME GLORIFIED *MESSENGER BOY*--

--HE HAS BADLY *UNDERESTIMATED* HIS OWN CREATION!

SOON HE WILL DISCOVER THAT FAR FROM BEING HIS SERVANT--*GALVATRON* IS HIS *MASTER!*

BUT FOR THE MOMENT...

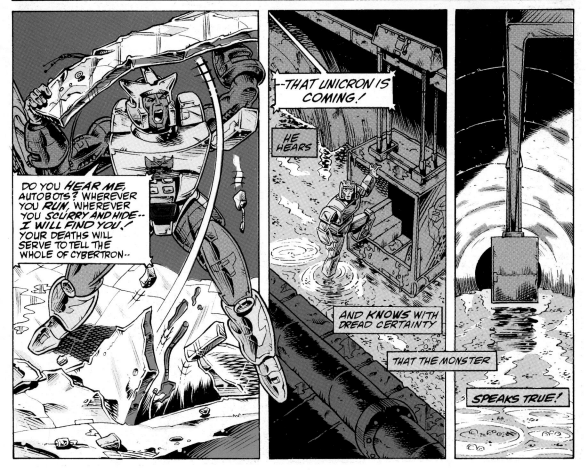

DO YOU *HEAR ME,* AUTOBOTS? WHEREVER YOU *RUN,* WHEREVER YOU *SCURRY AND HIDE*-- *I* WILL FIND YOU! YOUR DEATHS WILL SERVE TO TELL THE WHOLE OF CYBERTRON--

--THAT UNICRON IS COMING!

HE HEARS

AND *KNOWS* WITH DREAD CERTAINTY

THAT THE MONSTER

SPEAKS TRUE!

BACK TO EARTH... WITH A *BANG!*

GNNN!

THANK YOU FOR YOUR... *HOSPITALITY,* SOUNDWAVE.

BUT I'M AFRAID...

SKRRANCH!

...I MUST *BE GOING!*

SHOULD I SIT PASSIVELY, *MEEKLY,* WAITING FOR *THE END?* I THINK *NOT!*

IT IS TIME TO SALVAGE WHAT *SELF-RESPECT* I HAVE LEFT-- AND *ACT!*

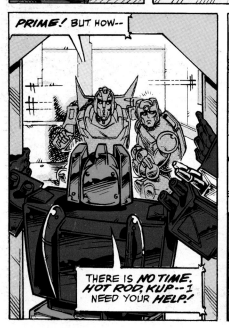

PRIME! BUT HOW--

THERE IS *NO TIME,* HOT ROD, KUP-- I NEED YOUR *HELP!*

OF COURSE! WHAT--

HOLD IT, LAD!

THIS IS *RICH,* PRIME! WHY ON CYBERTRON SHOULD WE HELP *YOU?* YOU SOLD US OUT *ONCE*-- WHAT'S TO SAY YOU WON'T DO IT *AGAIN?*

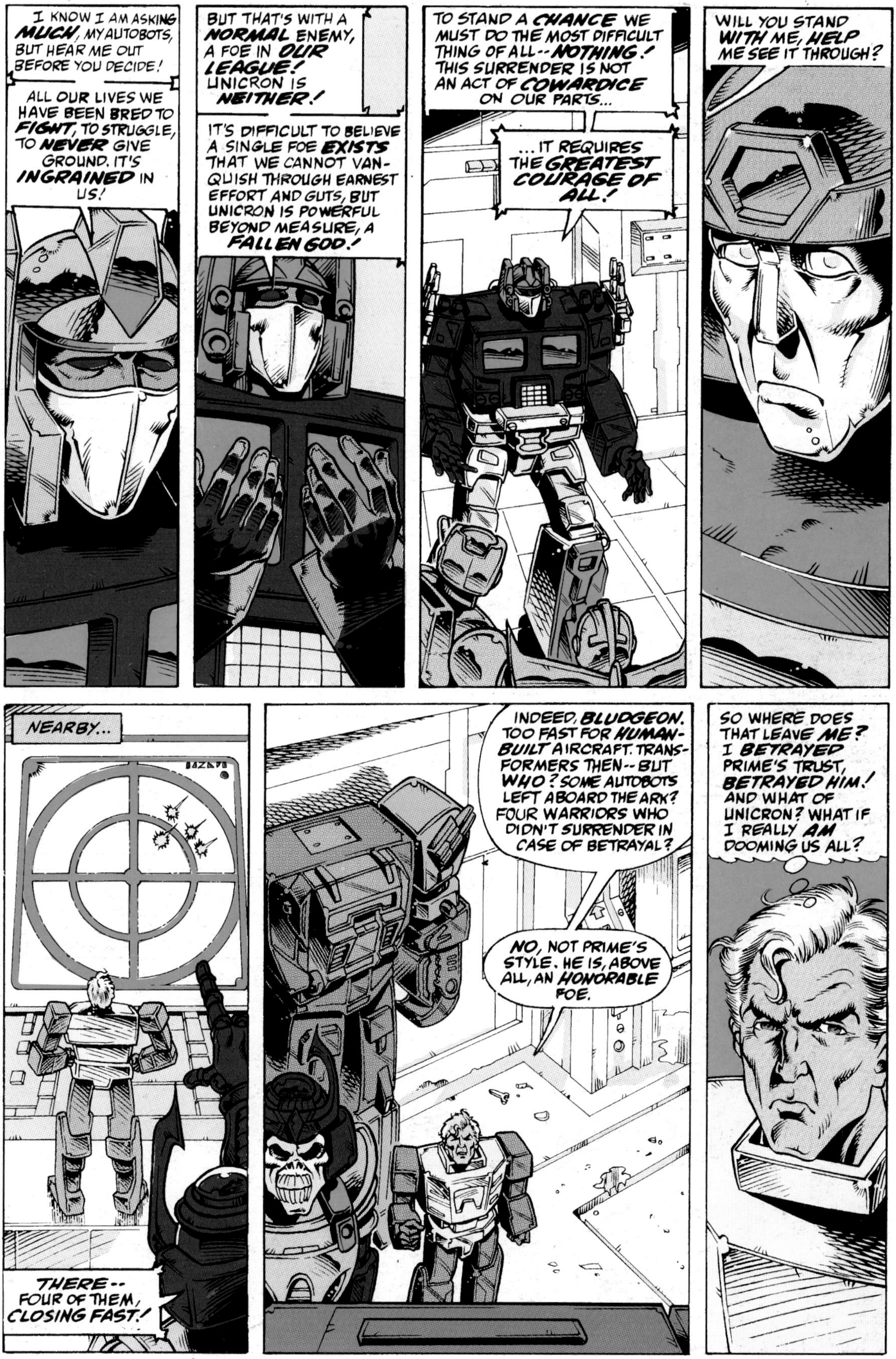
I KNOW I AM ASKING MUCH, MY AUTOBOTS, BUT HEAR ME OUT BEFORE YOU DECIDE!
ALL OUR LIVES WE HAVE BEEN BRED TO FIGHT, TO STRUGGLE, TO NEVER GIVE GROUND. IT'S INGRAINED IN US!
BUT THAT'S WITH A NORMAL ENEMY, A FOE IN OUR LEAGUE! UNICRON IS NEITHER!
IT'S DIFFICULT TO BELIEVE A SINGLE FOE EXISTS THAT WE CANNOT VANQUISH THROUGH EARNEST EFFORT AND GUTS, BUT UNICRON IS POWERFUL BEYOND MEASURE, A FALLEN GOD!
TO STAND A CHANCE WE MUST DO THE MOST DIFFICULT THING OF ALL--NOTHING! THIS SURRENDER IS NOT AN ACT OF COWARDICE ON OUR PARTS...
...IT REQUIRES THE GREATEST COURAGE OF ALL!
WILL YOU STAND WITH ME, HELP ME SEE IT THROUGH?
NEARBY...
RADAR
THERE--FOUR OF THEM, CLOSING FAST!
INDEED, BLUDGEON. TOO FAST FOR HUMAN-BUILT AIRCRAFT. TRANSFORMERS THEN--BUT WHO? SOME AUTOBOTS LEFT ABOARD THE ARK? FOUR WARRIORS WHO DIDN'T SURRENDER IN CASE OF BETRAYAL?
NO, NOT PRIME'S STYLE. HE IS, ABOVE ALL, AN HONORABLE FOE.
SO WHERE DOES THAT LEAVE ME? I BETRAYED PRIME'S TRUST, BETRAYED HIM! AND WHAT OF UNICRON? WHAT IF I REALLY AM DOOMING US ALL?

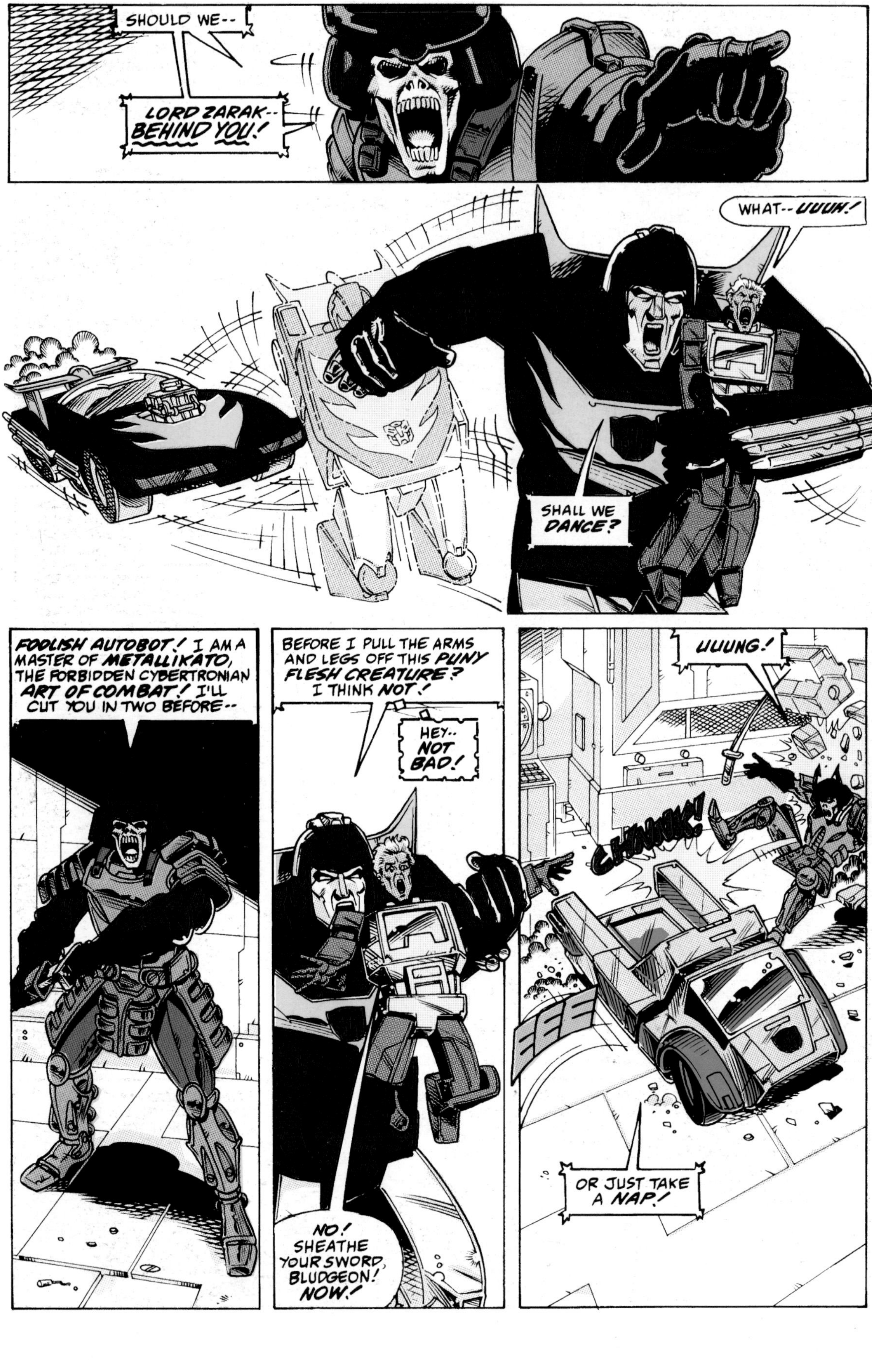
SHOULD WE--
LORD ZARAK-- BEHIND YOU!
WHAT--UUUH!
SHALL WE DANCE?
FOOLISH AUTOBOT! I AM A MASTER OF METALLIKATO, THE FORBIDDEN CYBERTRONIAN ART OF COMBAT! I'LL CUT YOU IN TWO BEFORE--
BEFORE I PULL THE ARMS AND LEGS OFF THIS PUNY FLESH CREATURE? I THINK NOT!
HEY.. NOT BAD!
NO! SHEATHE YOUR SWORD, BLUDGEON! NOW!
UUUNG!
CHUNNK!
OR JUST TAKE A NAP!

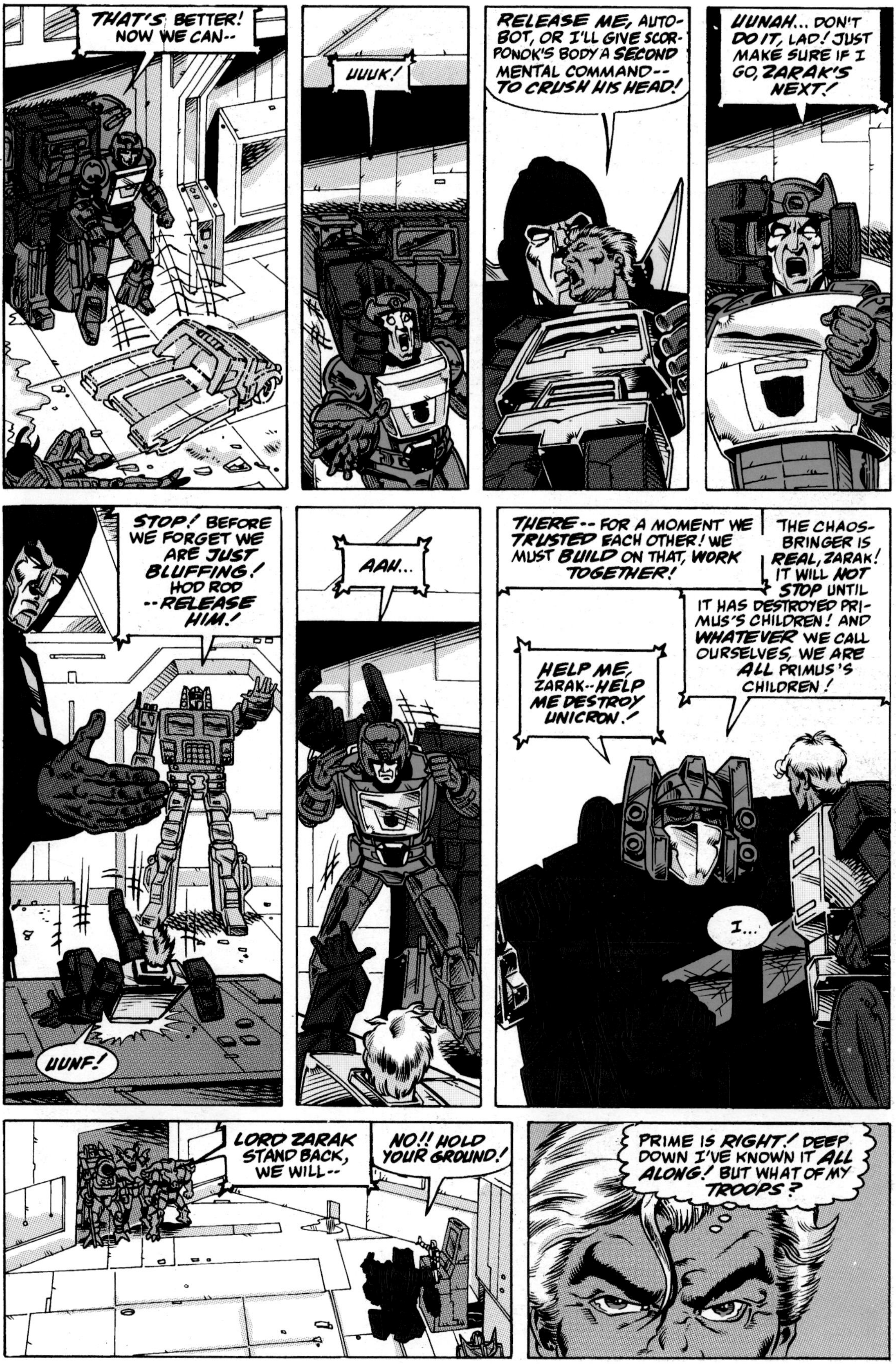
THAT'S BETTER! NOW WE CAN--
UUUK!
RELEASE ME, AUTOBOT, OR I'LL GIVE SCORPONOK'S BODY A SECOND MENTAL COMMAND-- TO CRUSH HIS HEAD!
UUNAH... DON'T DO IT, LAD! JUST MAKE SURE IF I GO, ZARAK'S NEXT!
STOP! BEFORE WE FORGET WE ARE JUST BLUFFING! HOD ROD --RELEASE HIM!
UUNF!
AAH...
THERE-- FOR A MOMENT WE TRUSTED EACH OTHER! WE MUST BUILD ON THAT, WORK TOGETHER!
THE CHAOS-BRINGER IS REAL, ZARAK! IT WILL NOT STOP UNTIL IT HAS DESTROYED PRIMUS'S CHILDREN! AND WHATEVER WE CALL OURSELVES, WE ARE ALL PRIMUS'S CHILDREN!
HELP ME, ZARAK-- HELP ME DESTROY UNICRON!
I...
LORD ZARAK STAND BACK, WE WILL--
NO!! HOLD YOUR GROUND!
PRIME IS RIGHT! DEEP DOWN I'VE KNOWN IT ALL ALONG! BUT WHAT OF MY TROOPS?

IF I SIDE WITH PRIME, THEY MAY TURN THEIR GUNS ON ME AND--

ENOUGH! I MAY BE LORD ZARAK, BUT I AM ALSO SCORPONOK-- THE MIGHTIEST DECEPTICON OF ALL!

LET OTHERS FEAR ME!

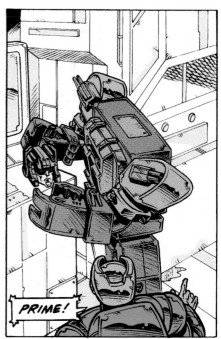

PRIME!

WE'VE GOT TO STOP--

NO! WE START TRUSTING... NOW!

SCORPONOK-- IT IS TIME FOR TALKS, FOR PLANS! WE MUST STRIKE BACK... TOGETHER!

GIVE ME YOUR HAND ON IT!

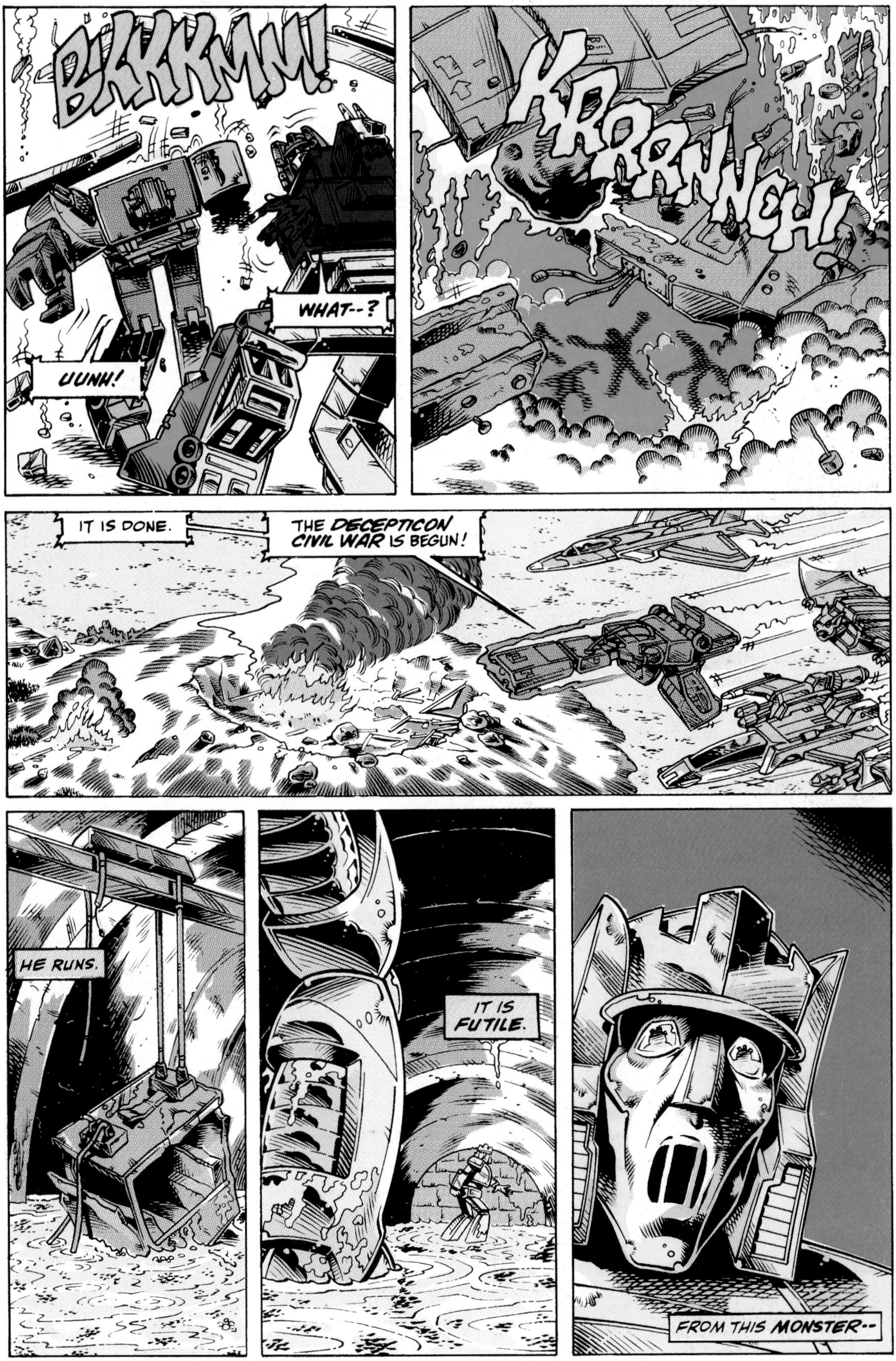

BLKKMM!
WHAT--?
UUNH!
KRRRNNCH!
IT IS DONE.
THE DECEPTICON CIVIL WAR IS BEGUN!
HE RUNS.
IT IS FUTILE.
FROM THIS MONSTER--

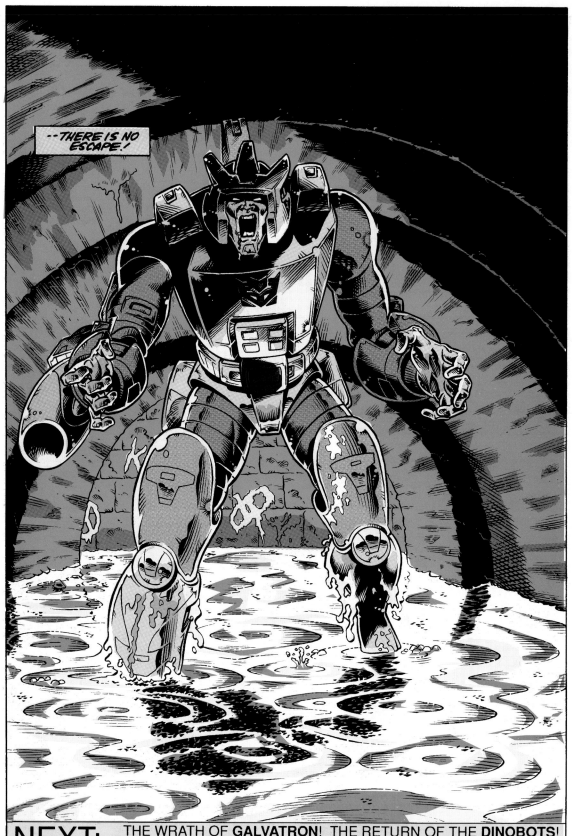

NEXT: THE WRATH OF **GALVATRON**! THE RETURN OF THE **DINOBOTS**! THE COMING OF **UNICRON**! ALL THIS. . . AND **CIVIL WAR 2!**

They **were** the dream--mechanical beings able to transform their bodies into vehicles, machinery and weapons; a last line of defense against the chaos-bringer, **Unicron**! They **are** at war, heroic **Autobot** pitted against evil **Decepticon**, both on their homeworld, the metal planet called **Cybertron**, and here on our **Earth**. They **are** the galaxy's last hope, they **are**-- **TRANSFORMERS**

...ALL THIS AND CIVIL WAR 2

WELL, THAT WAS *SHORT AND SWEET!*

MUST BE THE QUICKEST *COUP* THE DECEPTICON ARMY HAS *EVER* SEEN! AND I MEAN...

...THERE'S CERTAINLY BEEN *ENOUGH* OF THEM!

THE *NEW JERSEY* SWAMPS, *JUST FOUR MILES* FROM THE *HEART* OF *NEW YORK CITY*...

Simon Furman	Andrew Wildman	Stephen Baskerville	Rick Parker	Nel Yomtov	Rob Tokar Tom DeFalco
WRITER	PENCILER	INKER	LETTERER	COLORIST	CONSCIENTIOUS OBJECTORS

THE TRANSFORMERS™ Vol. 1, No. 72, November, 1990. (ISSN: 0887-5960) Published by MARVEL COMICS, James E. Galton, President. Stan Lee, Publisher. Michael Hobson, Group Vice President, Publishing. OFFICE OF PUBLICATION: 387 PARK AVENUE SOUTH, NEW YORK, N.Y. 10016. **Second class postage is paid at New York, N.Y. and at additional mailing offices.** Published monthly. Copyright © 1990 by HASBRO. All rights reserved. Price $1.00 per copy in the U.S. and $1.25 in Canada. Subscription rate for 12 issues: U.S. $12.00, Canada $17.00, and foreign $24.00. All other material copyright © 1990 by Marvel Entertainment Group, Inc. All rights reserved. CIRCUIT BREAKER and the distinctive likenesses thereof are trademarks of Marvel Entertainment Group, Inc. Printed in the U.S.A. No similarity between any of the names, characters, persons, and/or institutions in this magazine with those of any living or dead person or institution is intended, and any such similarity which may exist is purely coincidental. This periodical may not be sold except by authorized dealers and is sold subject to the conditions that it shall not be sold or distributed with any part of its cover or markings removed, nor in a mutilated condition. The Transformers, the logo, Autobot, Decepticon, Nebulon, all characters, groups, and their distinctive likenesses are trademarks of HASBRO and/or its subsidiaries, and are used with permission. **POSTMASTER: SEND ALL ADDRESS CHANGES TO TRANSFORMERS, c/o MARVEL COMICS, 9TH FLOOR, 387 PARK AVENUE SOUTH, NEW YORK, N.Y. 10016.**

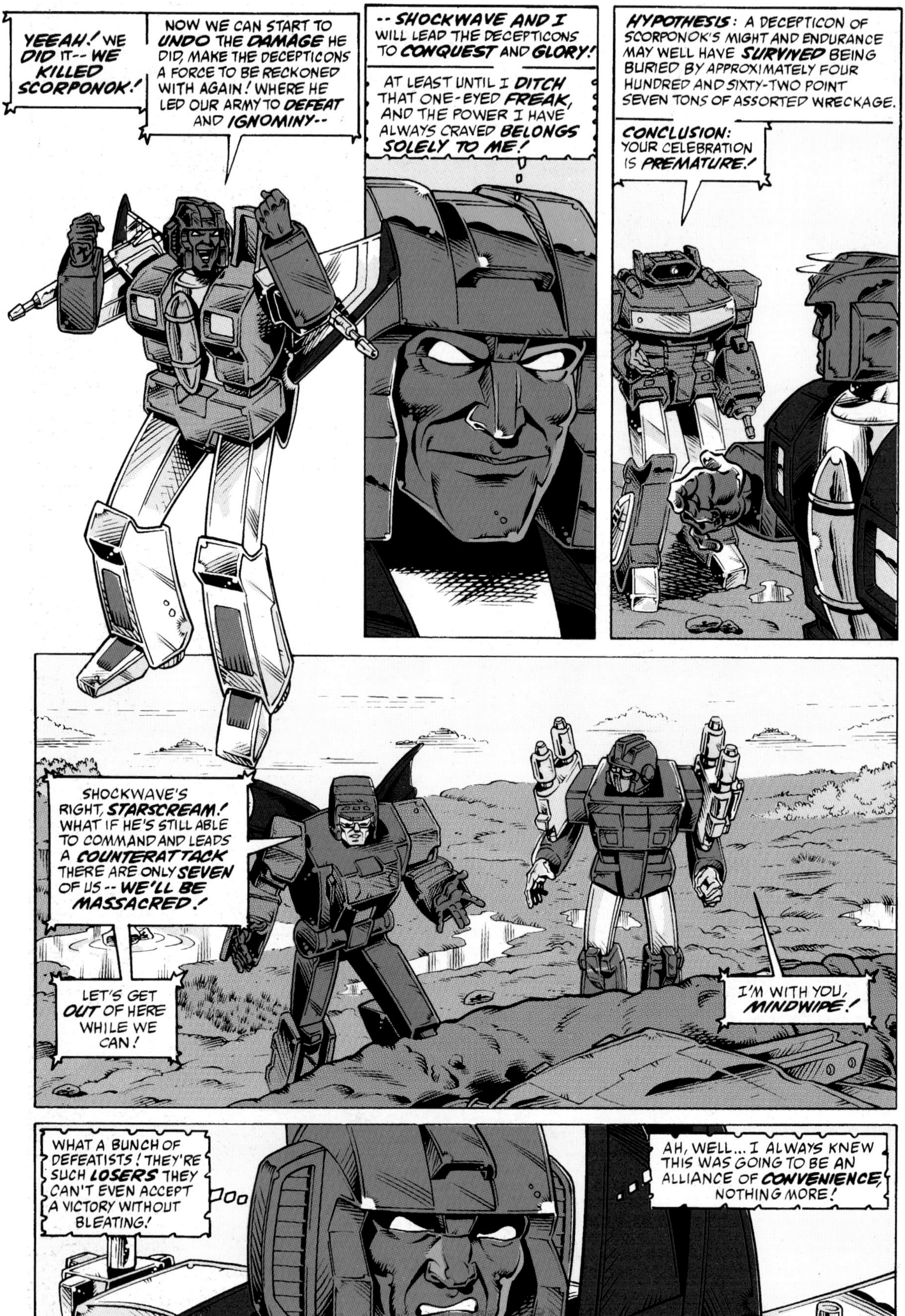
YEEAH! WE DID IT-- WE KILLED SCORPONOK!
NOW WE CAN START TO UNDO THE DAMAGE HE DID, MAKE THE DECEPTICONS A FORCE TO BE RECKONED WITH AGAIN! WHERE HE LED OUR ARMY TO DEFEAT AND IGNOMINY--
--SHOCKWAVE AND I WILL LEAD THE DECEPTICONS TO CONQUEST AND GLORY!
AT LEAST UNTIL I DITCH THAT ONE-EYED FREAK, AND THE POWER I HAVE ALWAYS CRAVED BELONGS SOLELY TO ME!
HYPOTHESIS: A DECEPTICON OF SCORPONOK'S MIGHT AND ENDURANCE MAY WELL HAVE SURVIVED BEING BURIED BY APPROXIMATELY FOUR HUNDRED AND SIXTY-TWO POINT SEVEN TONS OF ASSORTED WRECKAGE.
CONCLUSION: YOUR CELEBRATION IS PREMATURE!
SHOCKWAVE'S RIGHT, STARSCREAM! WHAT IF HE'S STILL ABLE TO COMMAND AND LEADS A COUNTERATTACK THERE ARE ONLY SEVEN OF US -- WE'LL BE MASSACRED!
LET'S GET OUT OF HERE WHILE WE CAN!
I'M WITH YOU, MINDWIPE!
WHAT A BUNCH OF DEFEATISTS! THEY'RE SUCH LOSERS THEY CAN'T EVEN ACCEPT A VICTORY WITHOUT BLEATING!
AH, WELL... I ALWAYS KNEW THIS WAS GOING TO BE AN ALLIANCE OF CONVENIENCE, NOTHING MORE!

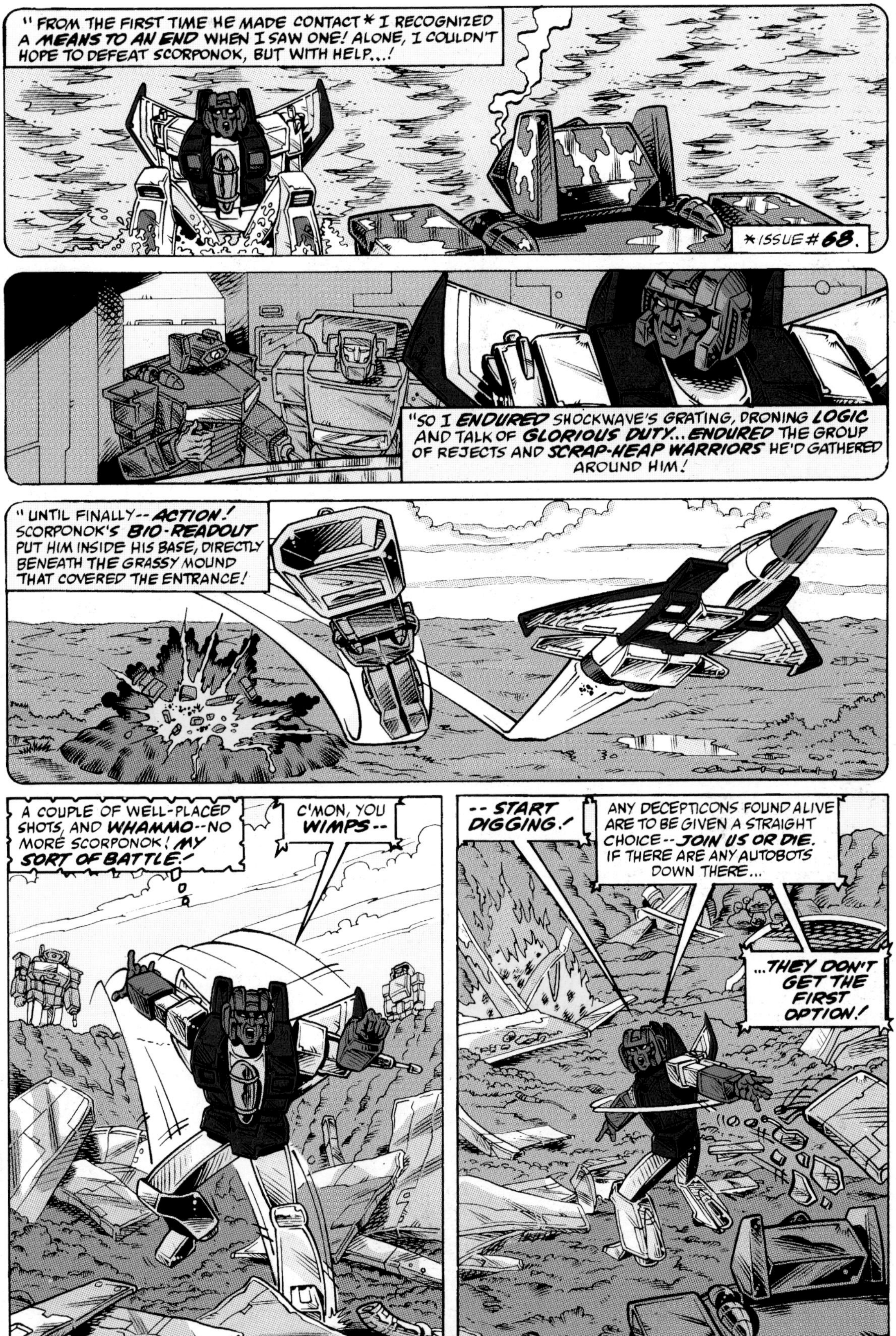
"FROM THE FIRST TIME HE MADE CONTACT* I RECOGNIZED A MEANS TO AN END WHEN I SAW ONE! ALONE, I COULDN'T HOPE TO DEFEAT SCORPONOK, BUT WITH HELP...!
*ISSUE #68.
"SO I ENDURED SHOCKWAVE'S GRATING, DRONING LOGIC AND TALK OF GLORIOUS DUTY... ENDURED THE GROUP OF REJECTS AND SCRAP-HEAP WARRIORS HE'D GATHERED AROUND HIM!
"UNTIL FINALLY--ACTION! SCORPONOK'S BIO-READOUT PUT HIM INSIDE HIS BASE, DIRECTLY BENEATH THE GRASSY MOUND THAT COVERED THE ENTRANCE!
A COUPLE OF WELL-PLACED SHOTS, AND WHAMMO--NO MORE SCORPONOK! MY SORT OF BATTLE!
C'MON, YOU WIMPS--
--START DIGGING!
ANY DECEPTICONS FOUND ALIVE ARE TO BE GIVEN A STRAIGHT CHOICE--JOIN US OR DIE. IF THERE ARE ANY AUTOBOTS DOWN THERE...
...THEY DON'T GET THE FIRST OPTION!

YESS! THAT'S MORE LIKE IT! I COULD QUITE GROW TO LIKE GIVING ORDERS! AT LAST-- IT'S ALL HERE FOR THE TAKING!

I JUST HAVE TO REACH OUT--

-- AND GRAB IT?

KRUNK!

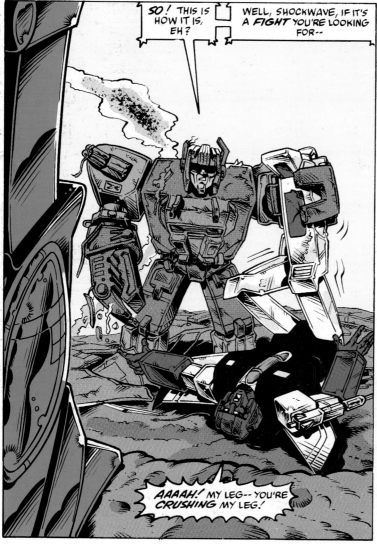

SO! THIS IS HOW IT IS, EH?

WELL, SHOCKWAVE, IF IT'S A FIGHT YOU'RE LOOKING FOR--

AAAAH! MY LEG-- YOU'RE CRUSHING MY LEG!

-- YOU'VE GOT IT!

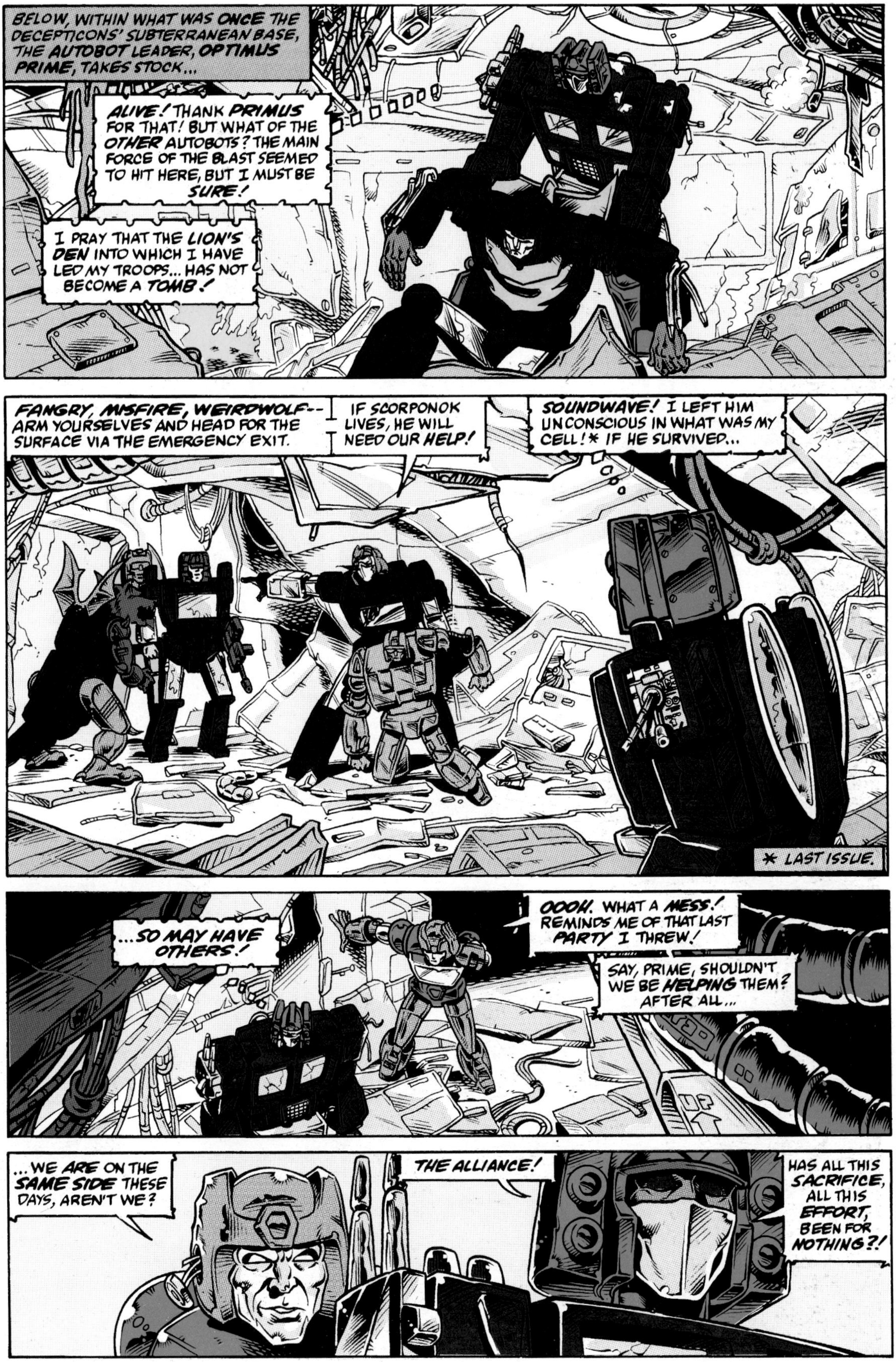
BELOW, WITHIN WHAT WAS ONCE THE DECEPTICONS' SUBTERRANEAN BASE, THE AUTOBOT LEADER, OPTIMUS PRIME, TAKES STOCK...
ALIVE! THANK PRIMUS FOR THAT! BUT WHAT OF THE OTHER AUTOBOTS? THE MAIN FORCE OF THE BLAST SEEMED TO HIT HERE, BUT I MUST BE SURE!
I PRAY THAT THE LION'S DEN INTO WHICH I HAVE LED MY TROOPS... HAS NOT BECOME A TOMB!
FANGRY, MISFIRE, WEIRDWOLF-- ARM YOURSELVES AND HEAD FOR THE SURFACE VIA THE EMERGENCY EXIT.
IF SCORPONOK LIVES, HE WILL NEED OUR HELP!
SOUNDWAVE! I LEFT HIM UNCONSCIOUS IN WHAT WAS MY CELL!* IF HE SURVIVED...
* LAST ISSUE.
...SO MAY HAVE OTHERS!
OOOH. WHAT A MESS! REMINDS ME OF THAT LAST PARTY I THREW!
SAY, PRIME, SHOULDN'T WE BE HELPING THEM? AFTER ALL...
...WE ARE ON THE SAME SIDE THESE DAYS, AREN'T WE?
THE ALLIANCE!
HAS ALL THIS SACRIFICE, ALL THIS EFFORT, BEEN FOR NOTHING?!

"WE WERE *SO CLOSE*-- SO CLOSE TO A *TRUCE!* THOUGH SCORPONOK INITIALLY *RENEGED* ON HIS WORD, USED THE AUTOBOT SURRENDER TO ANCHOR HIS OWN POSITION AS DECEPTI-CON LEADER...

"...HE FINALLY SAW THAT I WAS *RIGHT*, THAT ONLY *TOGETHER*, UNITED AS ONE, COULD WE BATTLE THE AWE-SOME THREAT OF THE CHAOS-BRINGER, *UNICRON!*

AND NOW *THIS!* WHOEVER IS DOING THE ATTACKING, IT HAS LEFT THE ALLIANCE, AND-- ULTIMATELY-- *OUR FATE*, ON DECIDELY *SHAKY* GROUND!

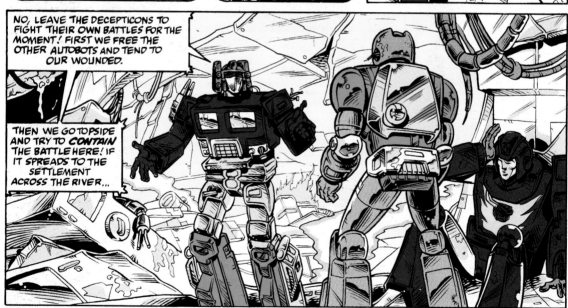

NO, LEAVE THE DECEPTICONS TO FIGHT THEIR OWN BATTLES FOR THE MOMENT! FIRST WE FREE THE OTHER AUTOBOTS AND TEND TO OUR WOUNDED.

THEN WE GO TOPSIDE AND TRY TO *CONTAIN* THE BATTLE HERE! IF IT SPREADS TO THE SETTLEMENT ACROSS THE RIVER...

"...I DREAD TO THINK HOW MANY HUMAN LIVES WILL BE LOST!"

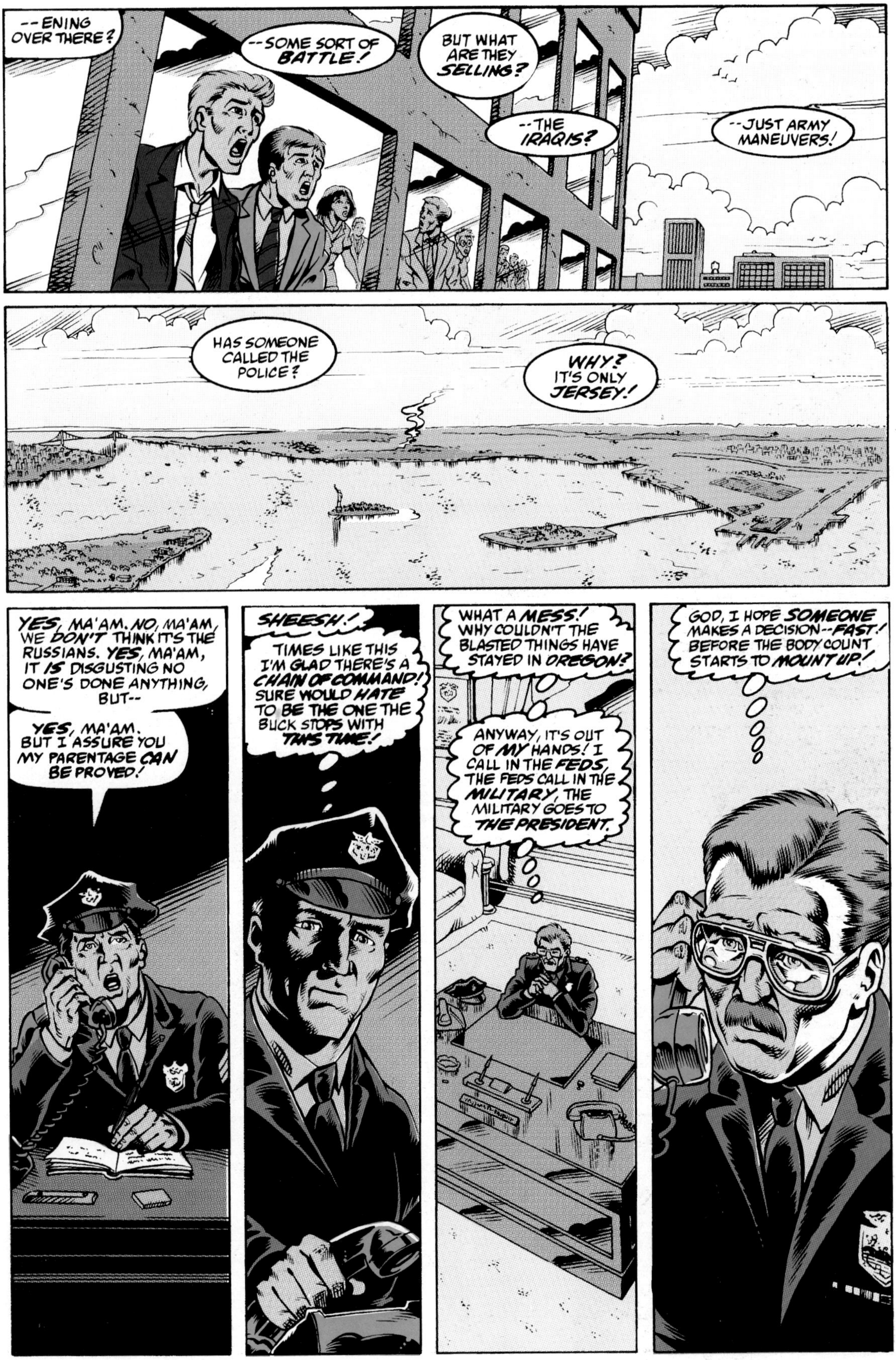
--ENING OVER THERE?
--SOME SORT OF BATTLE!
BUT WHAT ARE THEY SELLING?
--THE IRAQIS?
--JUST ARMY MANEUVERS!
HAS SOMEONE CALLED THE POLICE?
WHY? IT'S ONLY JERSEY!
YES, MA'AM. NO, MA'AM, WE DON'T THINK IT'S THE RUSSIANS. YES, MA'AM, IT IS DISGUSTING NO ONE'S DONE ANYTHING, BUT--
YES, MA'AM. BUT I ASSURE YOU MY PARENTAGE CAN BE PROVED!
SHEESH!
TIMES LIKE THIS I'M GLAD THERE'S A CHAIN OF COMMAND! SURE WOULD HATE TO BE THE ONE THE BUCK STOPS WITH THIS TIME!
WHAT A MESS! WHY COULDN'T THE BLASTED THINGS HAVE STAYED IN OREGON?
ANYWAY, IT'S OUT OF MY HANDS! I CALL IN THE FEDS, THE FEDS CALL IN THE MILITARY, THE MILITARY GOES TO THE PRESIDENT.
GOD, I HOPE SOMEONE MAKES A DECISION--FAST! BEFORE THE BODY COUNT STARTS TO MOUNT UP!

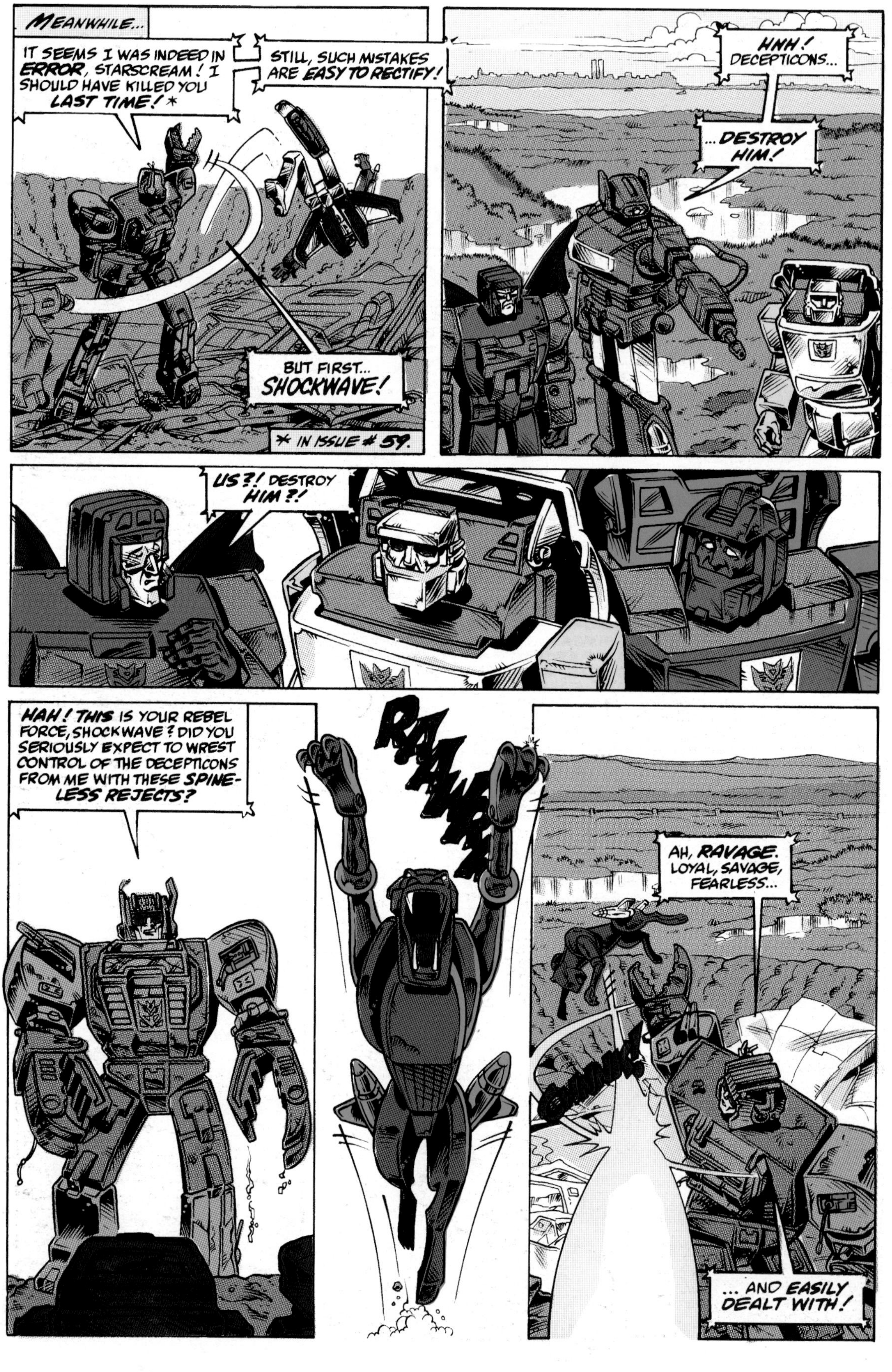
MEANWHILE...
IT SEEMS I WAS INDEED IN ERROR, STARSCREAM! I SHOULD HAVE KILLED YOU LAST TIME! *
STILL, SUCH MISTAKES ARE EASY TO RECTIFY!
BUT FIRST... SHOCKWAVE!
* IN ISSUE # 59.
HNH! DECEPTICONS...
... DESTROY HIM!
US?! DESTROY HIM?!
HAH! THIS IS YOUR REBEL FORCE, SHOCKWAVE? DID YOU SERIOUSLY EXPECT TO WREST CONTROL OF THE DECEPTICONS FROM ME WITH THESE SPINE-LESS REJECTS?
RAAWRR
AH, RAVAGE. LOYAL, SAVAGE, FEARLESS...
... AND EASILY DEALT WITH!

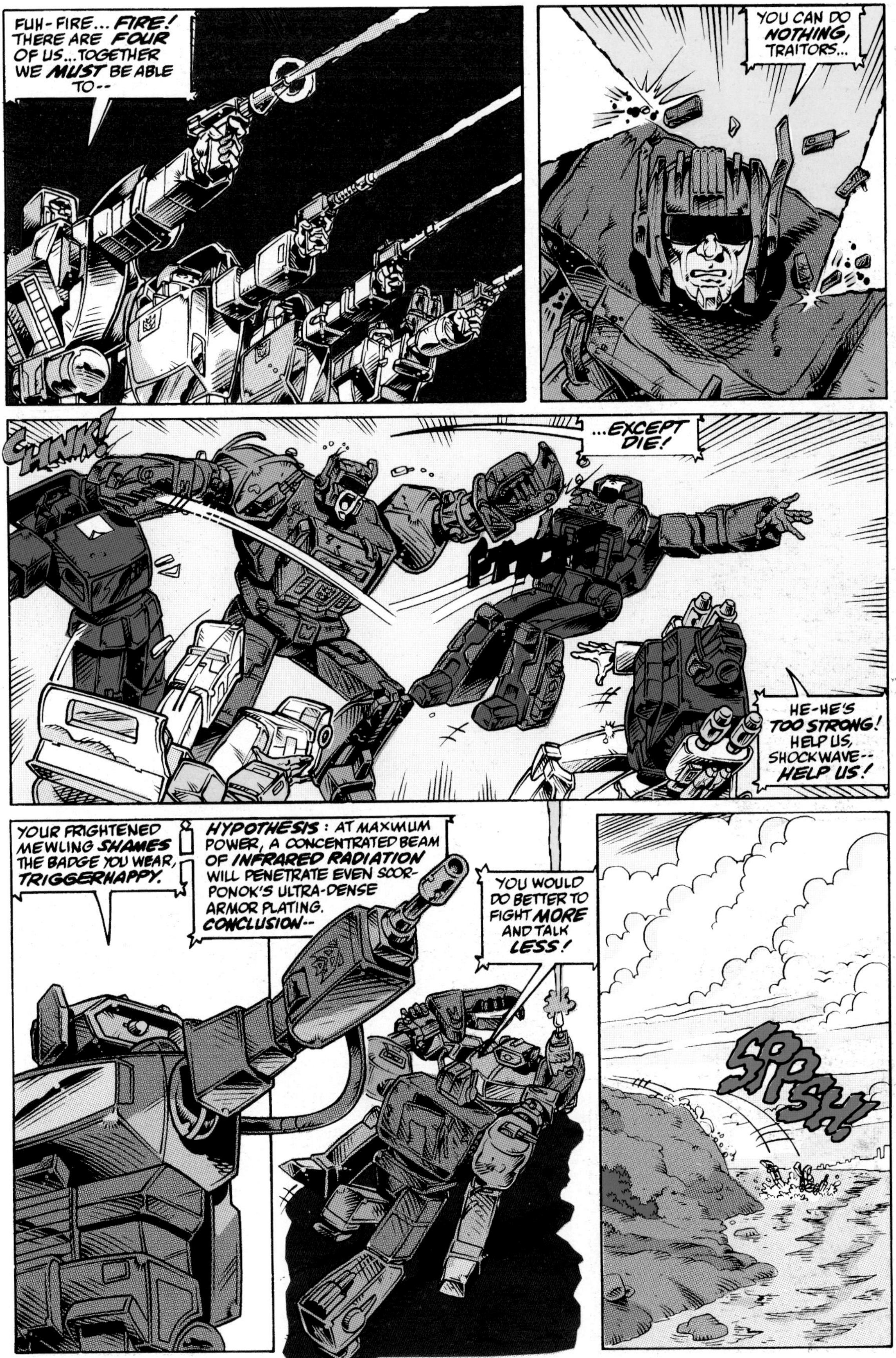
FUH-FIRE... FIRE! THERE ARE FOUR OF US... TOGETHER WE MUST BE ABLE TO--
YOU CAN DO NOTHING, TRAITORS...
CLINK!
...EXCEPT DIE!
HE-HE'S TOO STRONG! HELP US, SHOCKWAVE-- HELP US!
YOUR FRIGHTENED MEWLING SHAMES THE BADGE YOU WEAR, TRIGGERHAPPY.
HYPOTHESIS: AT MAXIMUM POWER, A CONCENTRATED BEAM OF INFRARED RADIATION WILL PENETRATE EVEN SCORPONOK'S ULTRA-DENSE ARMOR PLATING. CONCLUSION--
YOU WOULD DO BETTER TO FIGHT MORE AND TALK LESS!
SPPSH!

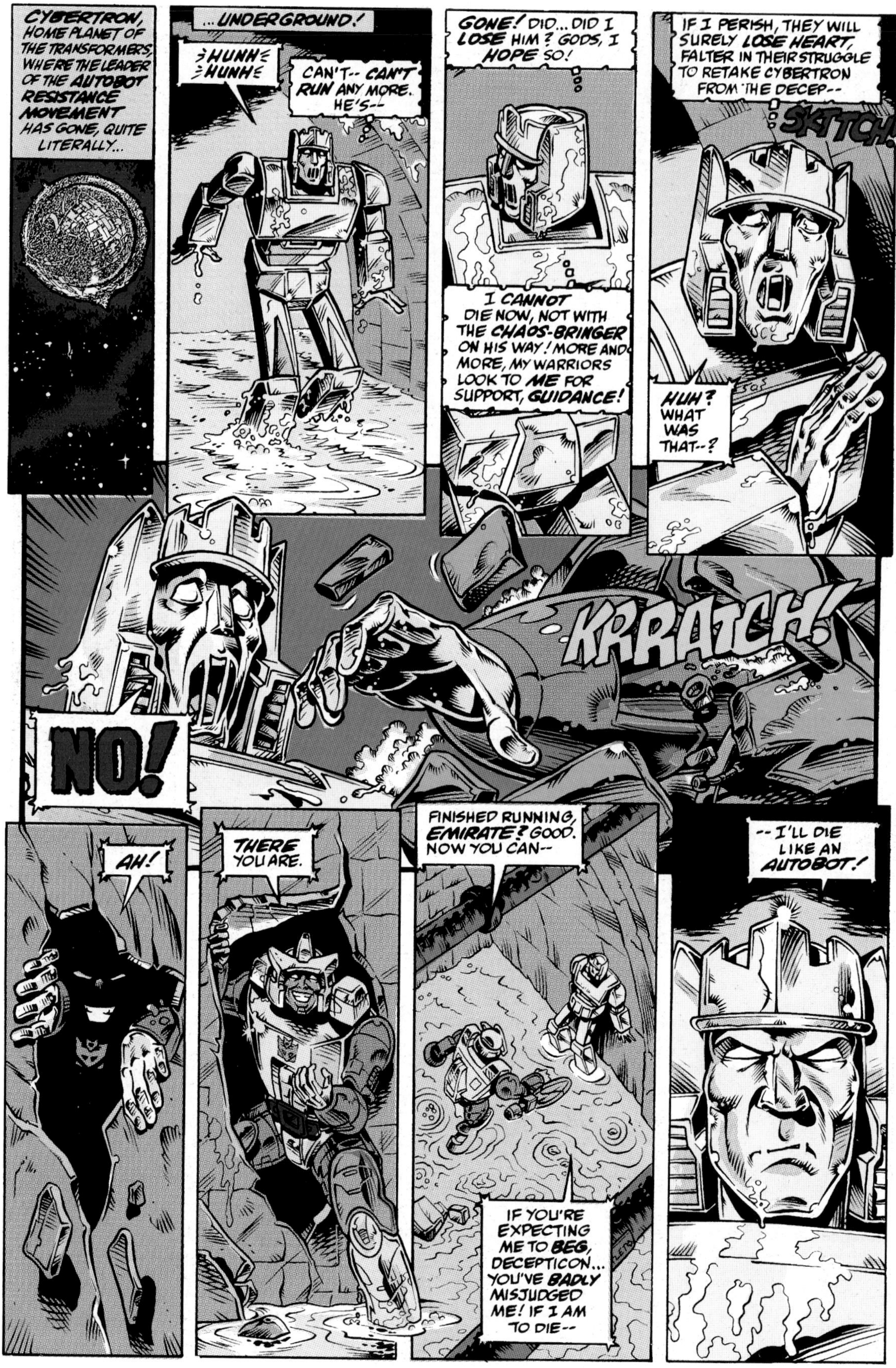
CYBERTRON, HOME PLANET OF THE TRANSFORMERS, WHERE THE LEADER OF THE AUTOBOT RESISTANCE MOVEMENT HAS GONE, QUITE LITERALLY...
...UNDERGROUND!
HUNH HUNH
CAN'T-- CAN'T RUN ANY MORE. HE'S--
GONE! DID... DID I LOSE HIM? GODS, I HOPE SO!
I CANNOT DIE NOW, NOT WITH THE CHAOS-BRINGER ON HIS WAY! MORE AND MORE, MY WARRIORS LOOK TO ME FOR SUPPORT, GUIDANCE!
IF I PERISH, THEY WILL SURELY LOSE HEART, FALTER IN THEIR STRUGGLE TO RETAKE CYBERTRON FROM THE DECEP--
SKTTCH!
HUH? WHAT WAS THAT--?
KRRATCH!
NO!
AH!
THERE YOU ARE.
FINISHED RUNNING, EMIRATE? GOOD. NOW YOU CAN--
IF YOU'RE EXPECTING ME TO BEG, DECEPTICON... YOU'VE BADLY MISJUDGED ME! IF I AM TO DIE--
--I'LL DIE LIKE AN AUTOBOT!

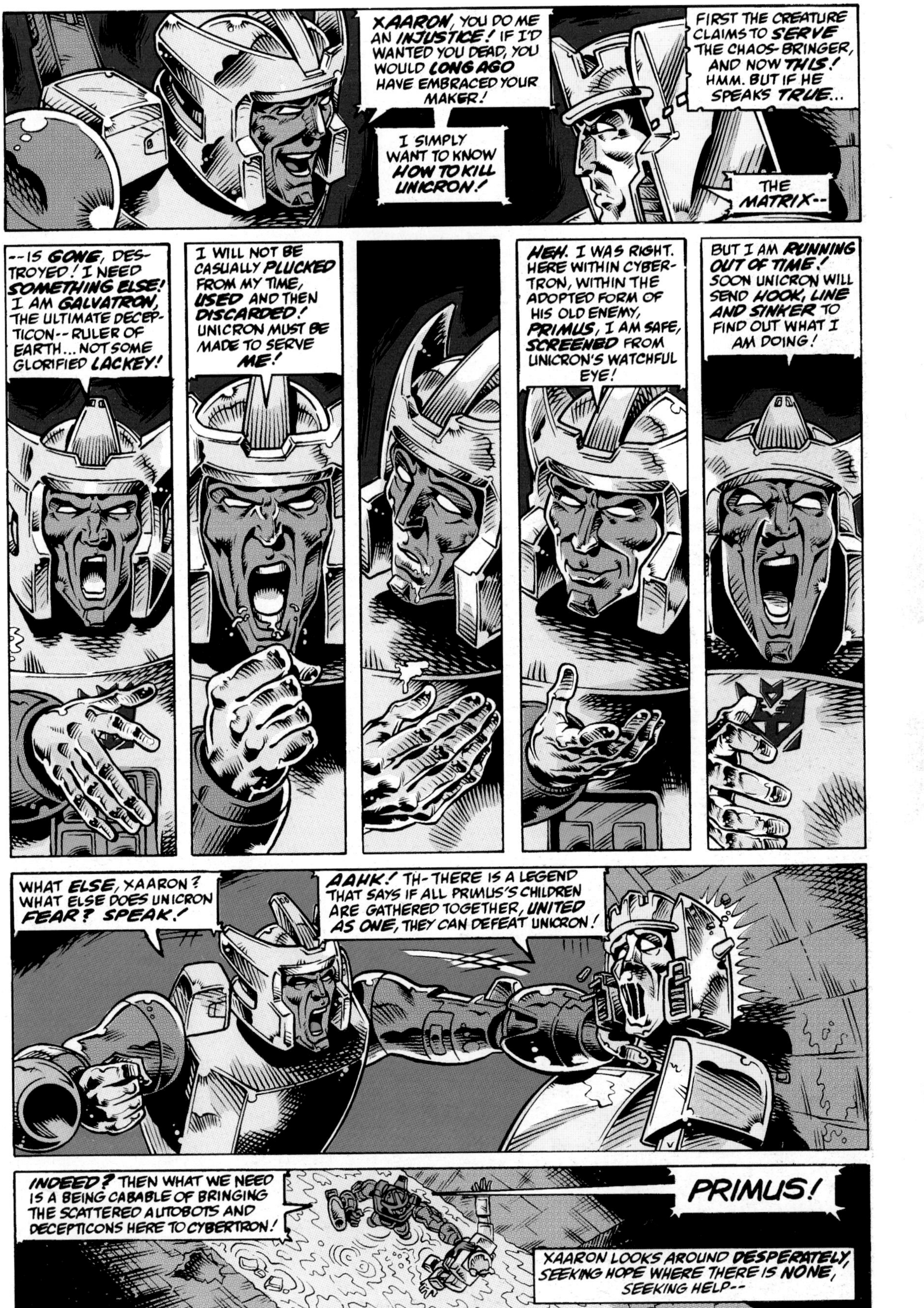
XAARON, YOU DO ME AN INJUSTICE! IF I'D WANTED YOU DEAD, YOU WOULD LONG AGO HAVE EMBRACED YOUR MAKER!
I SIMPLY WANT TO KNOW HOW TO KILL UNICRON!
FIRST THE CREATURE CLAIMS TO SERVE THE CHAOS-BRINGER, AND NOW THIS! HMM. BUT IF HE SPEAKS TRUE...
THE MATRIX--
--IS GONE, DESTROYED! I NEED SOMETHING ELSE! I AM GALVATRON, THE ULTIMATE DECEPTICON--RULER OF EARTH... NOT SOME GLORIFIED LACKEY!
I WILL NOT BE CASUALLY PLUCKED FROM MY TIME, USED AND THEN DISCARDED! UNICRON MUST BE MADE TO SERVE ME!
HEH. I WAS RIGHT. HERE WITHIN CYBERTRON, WITHIN THE ADOPTED FORM OF HIS OLD ENEMY, PRIMUS, I AM SAFE, SCREENED FROM UNICRON'S WATCHFUL EYE!
BUT I AM RUNNING OUT OF TIME! SOON UNICRON WILL SEND HOOK, LINE AND SINKER TO FIND OUT WHAT I AM DOING!
WHAT ELSE, XAARON? WHAT ELSE DOES UNICRON FEAR? SPEAK!
AAHK! TH-THERE IS A LEGEND THAT SAYS IF ALL PRIMUS'S CHILDREN ARE GATHERED TOGETHER, UNITED AS ONE, THEY CAN DEFEAT UNICRON!
INDEED? THEN WHAT WE NEED IS A BEING CABABLE OF BRINGING THE SCATTERED AUTOBOTS AND DECEPTICONS HERE TO CYBERTRON!
PRIMUS!
XAARON LOOKS AROUND DESPERATELY, SEEKING HOPE WHERE THERE IS NONE, SEEKING HELP--

-- WHEN HE KNOWS *NO ONE'S OUT THERE* TO GIVE IT!

HYDRUS FOUR...

I TELL YA, *GRIMLOCK* -- I FEEL *STRONG ENOUGH* TO TAKE ON THE ENTIRE DECEPTICON ARMY *SINGLE-HANDED!*

THIS *NUCLEON* STUFF YOU USED TO RESTORE US IS *SOMETHING ELSE!* WE'RE BACK -- *LEANER, MEANER AND BADDER THAN EVER!*

ME GLAD YOU HAPPY, *SNARL.* BEEN TOO LONG SINCE *DINOBOTS* WERE TOGETHER! NOW WE *SHOW* OPTIMUS PRIME -- KICK UNICRON'S TAIL ACROSS UNIVERSE!

AND ME SHOW PRIME HE *WRONG* TO SAY NOT USE NUCLEON. HE WEAK -- SAY IT DANGEROUS, *UNPREDICTABLE!*

I BRING BACK ENOUGH NUCLEON TO GIVE LIFE TO *ALL* DE-ACTIVATED AUTOBOTS, WHEN HE SEE HOW POWERFUL *WE* ARE HE *HAVE* TO --

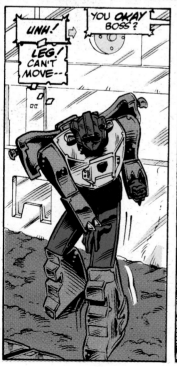

UNH!

LEG! CAN'T MOVE --

YOU *OKAY* BOSS?

OF COURSE, *SLAG!* FINISH HOOKING UP CONTAINMENT UNIT TO SHUTTLECRAFT AND WE GET OFF THIS *SLIME PIT* OF A PLANET!

WHAT DUMB ROBOT SAY ABOUT *EFFECT* OF NUCLEON?

TIME WILL TELL...

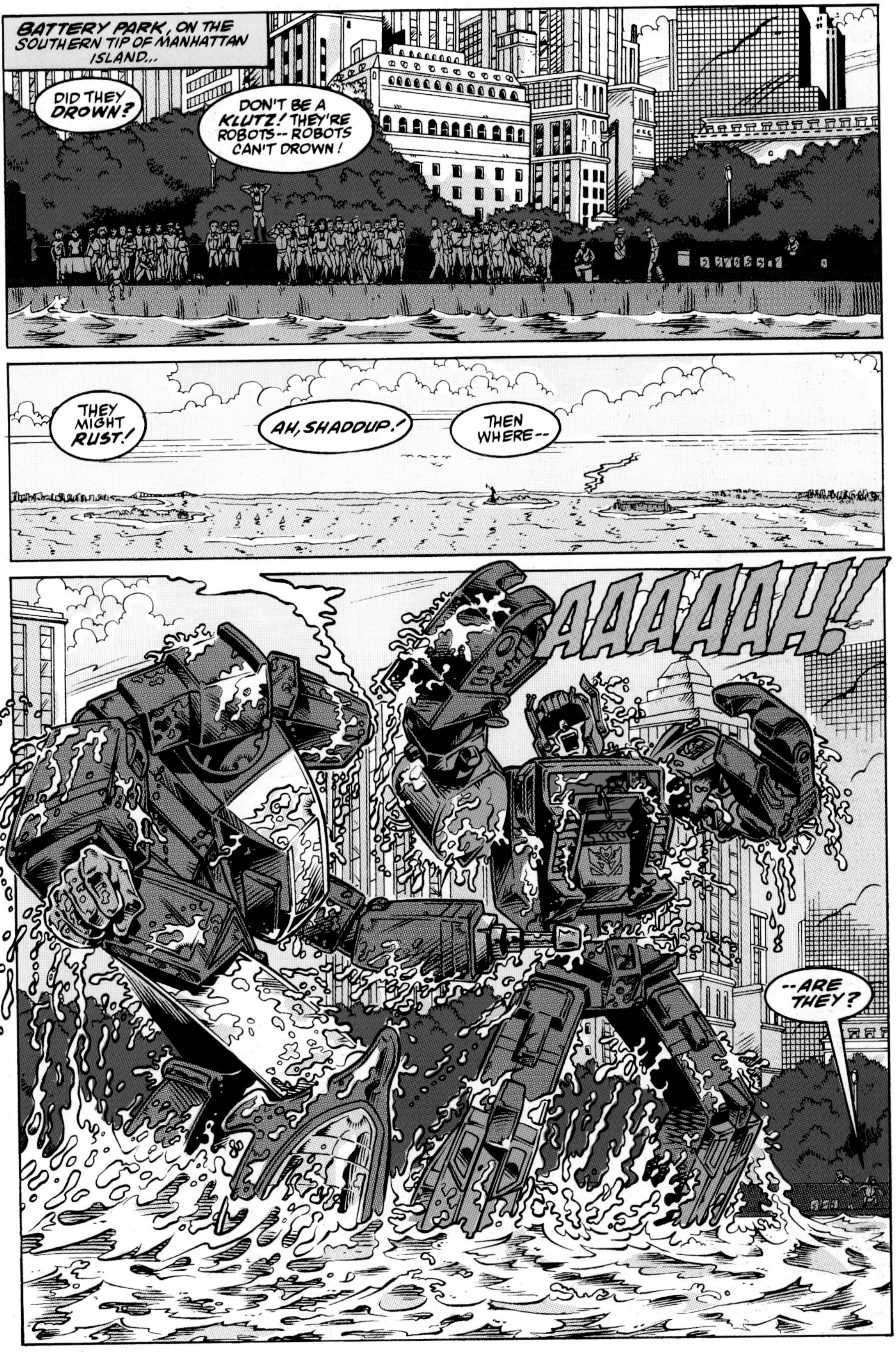
BATTERY PARK, ON THE SOUTHERN TIP OF MANHATTAN ISLAND...
DID THEY DROWN?
DON'T BE A KLUTZ! THEY'RE ROBOTS-- ROBOTS CAN'T DROWN!
THEY MIGHT RUST!
AH, SHADDUP!
THEN WHERE--
AAAAAH!!
--ARE THEY?

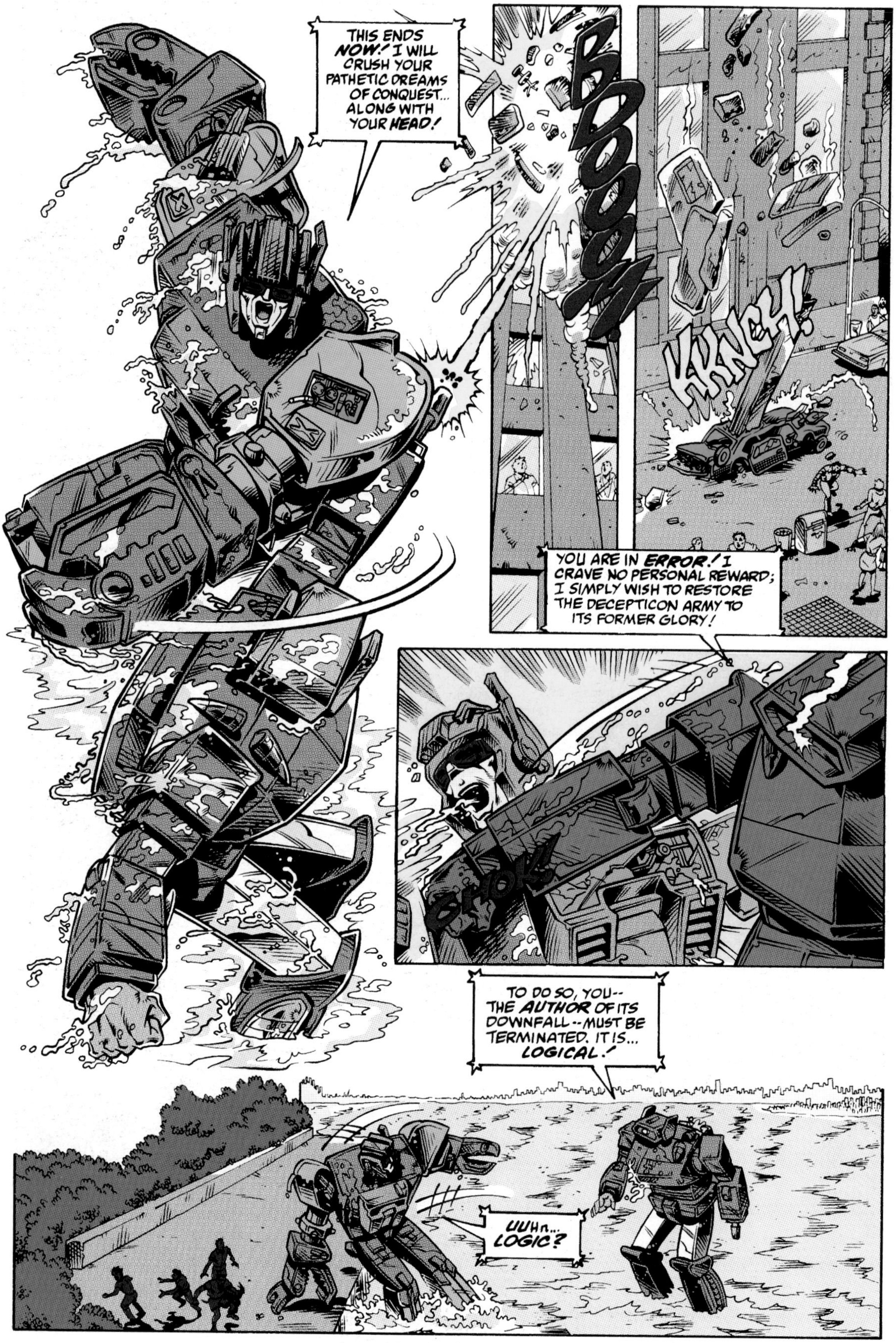
THIS ENDS NOW! I WILL CRUSH YOUR PATHETIC DREAMS OF CONQUEST... ALONG WITH YOUR HEAD!
BOOOOM!
KKRNCH!
YOU ARE IN ERROR! I CRAVE NO PERSONAL REWARD; I SIMPLY WISH TO RESTORE THE DECEPTICON ARMY TO ITS FORMER GLORY!
CHOK!
TO DO SO, YOU-- THE AUTHOR OF ITS DOWNFALL--MUST BE TERMINATED. IT IS... LOGICAL!
UUHn... LOGIC?

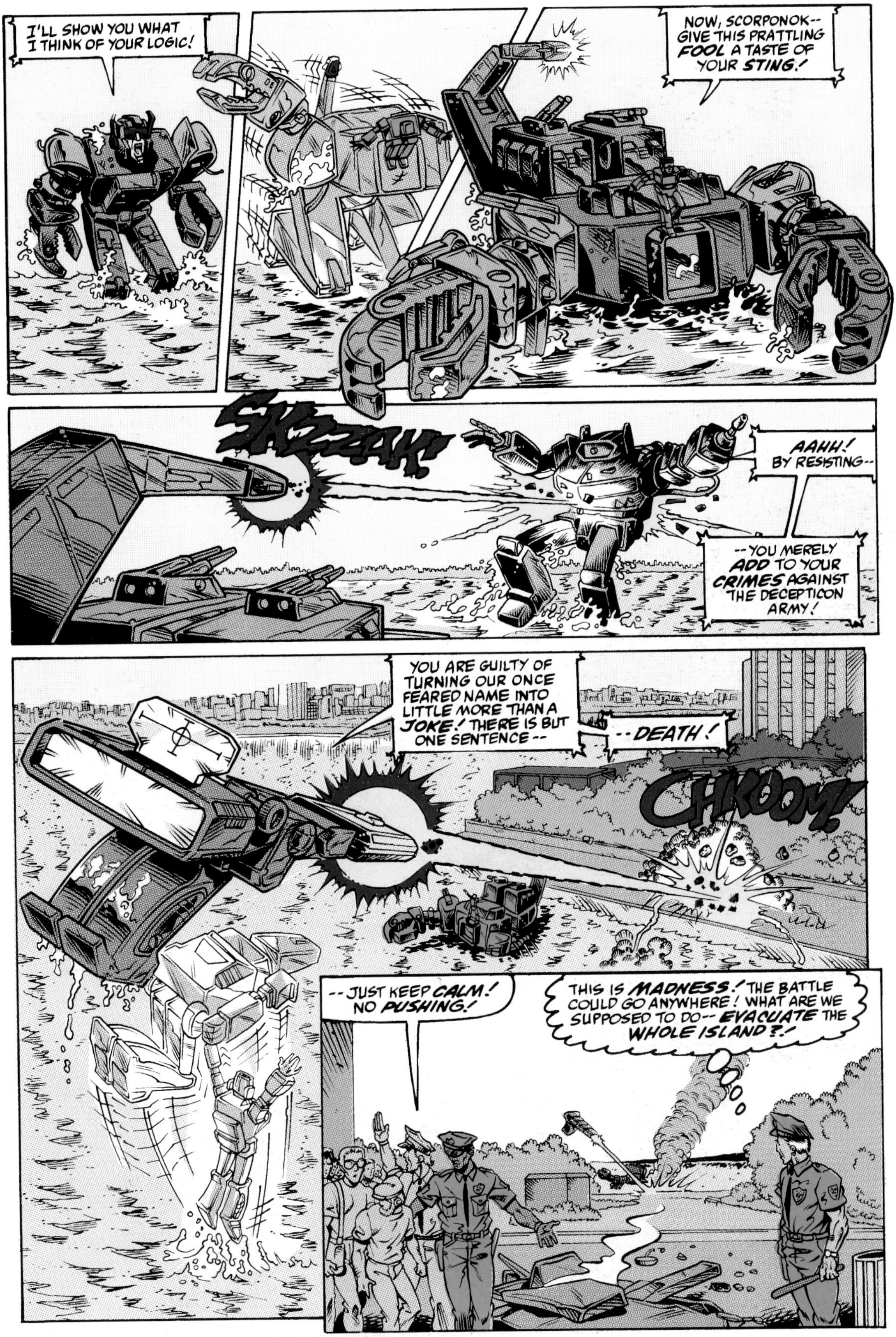
I'LL SHOW YOU WHAT I THINK OF YOUR LOGIC!
NOW, SCORPONOK-- GIVE THIS PRATTLING FOOL A TASTE OF YOUR STING!
SKZZZAK!
AAHH! BY RESISTING--
--YOU MERELY ADD TO YOUR CRIMES AGAINST THE DECEPTICON ARMY!
YOU ARE GUILTY OF TURNING OUR ONCE FEARED NAME INTO LITTLE MORE THAN A JOKE! THERE IS BUT ONE SENTENCE --
--DEATH!
CHROOM!
--JUST KEEP CALM! NO PUSHING!
THIS IS MADNESS! THE BATTLE COULD GO ANYWHERE! WHAT ARE WE SUPPOSED TO DO-- EVACUATE THE WHOLE ISLAND?!

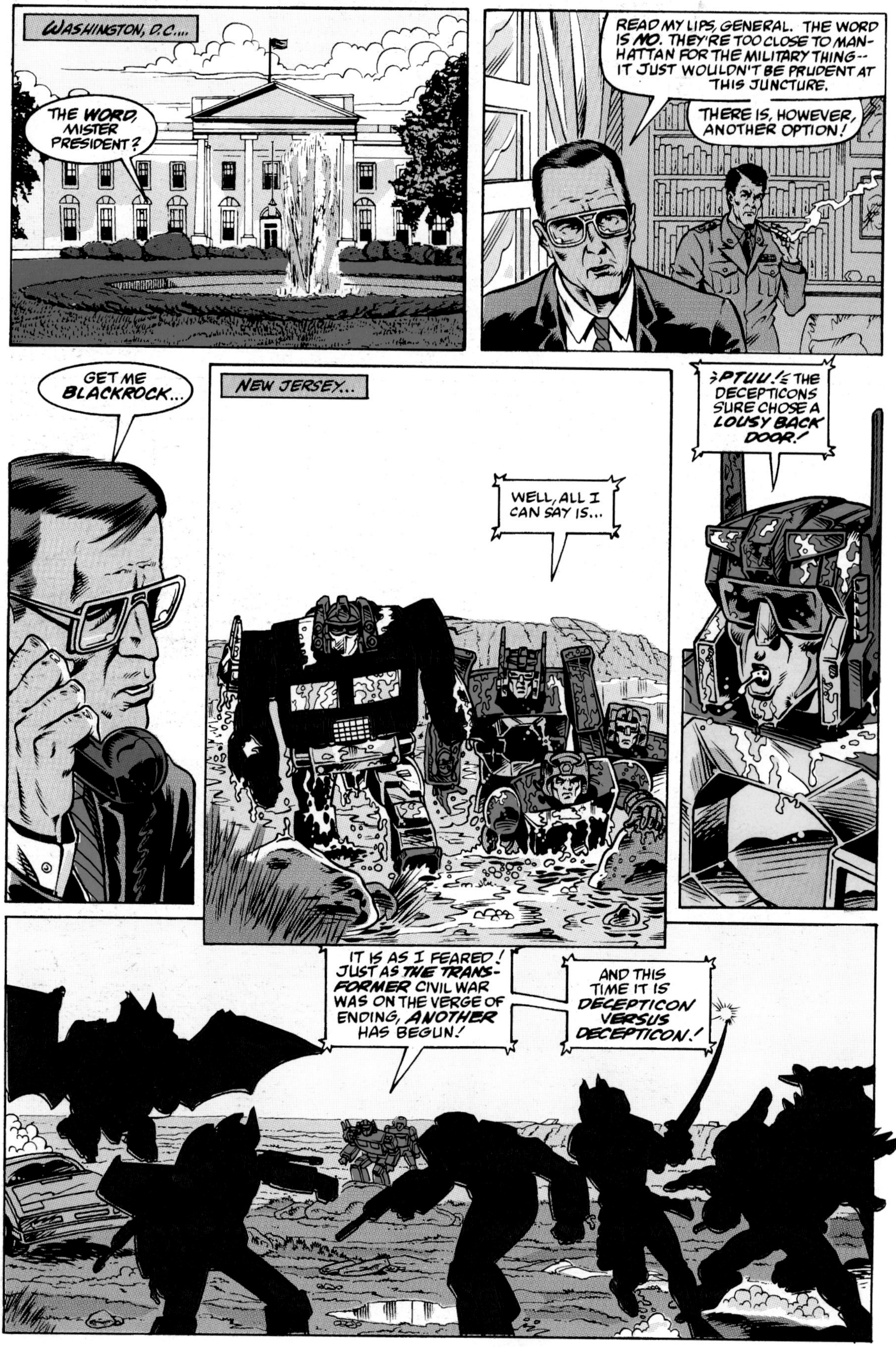
WASHINGTON, D.C....
THE WORD, MISTER PRESIDENT?
READ MY LIPS, GENERAL. THE WORD IS NO. THEY'RE TOO CLOSE TO MANHATTAN FOR THE MILITARY THING -- IT JUST WOULDN'T BE PRUDENT AT THIS JUNCTURE.
THERE IS, HOWEVER, ANOTHER OPTION!
GET ME BLACKROCK...
NEW JERSEY...
WELL, ALL I CAN SAY IS...
PTUU! THE DECEPTICONS SURE CHOSE A LOUSY BACK DOOR!
IT IS AS I FEARED! JUST AS THE TRANSFORMER CIVIL WAR WAS ON THE VERGE OF ENDING, ANOTHER HAS BEGUN!
AND THIS TIME IT IS DECEPTICON VERSUS DECEPTICON!

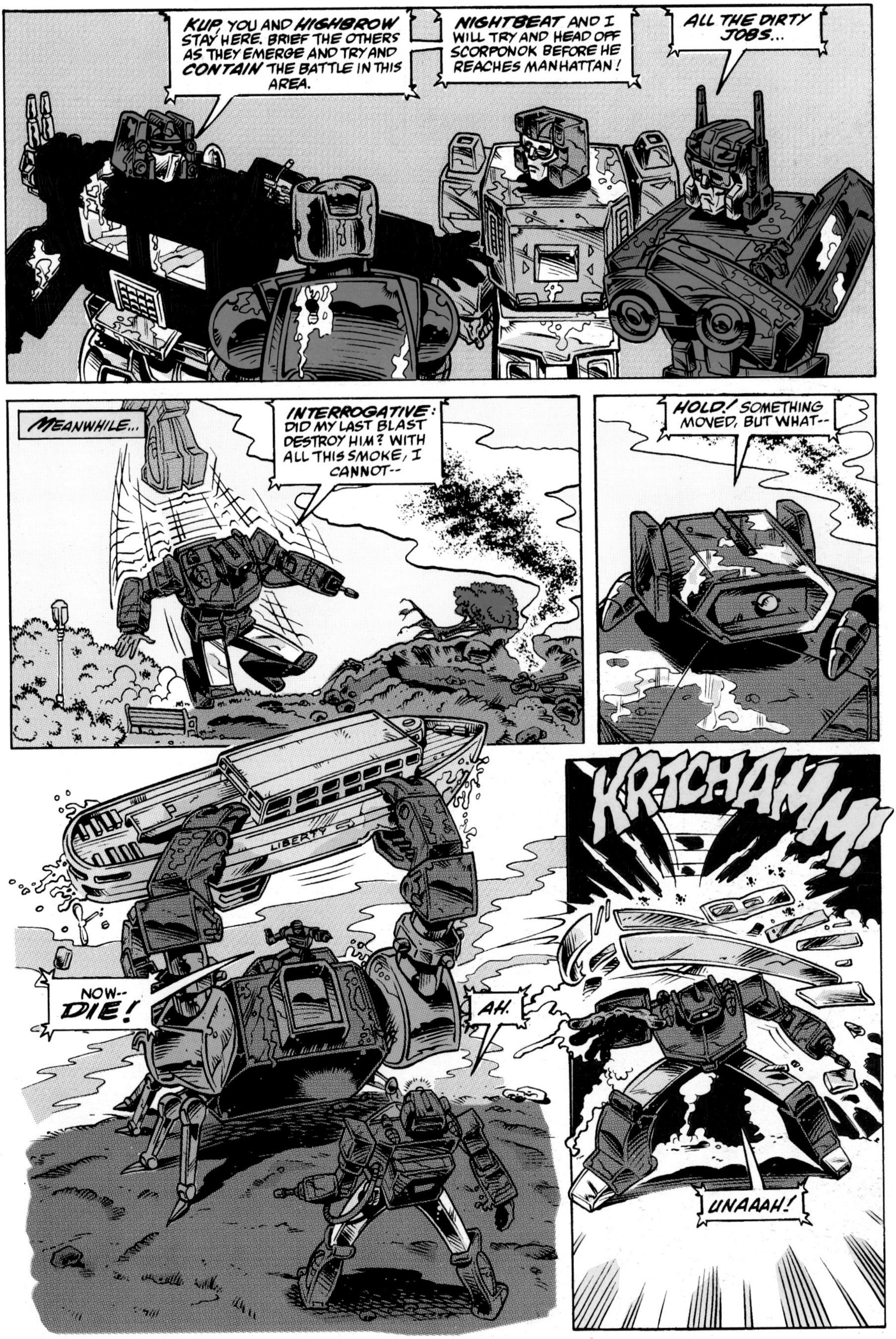
KUP, YOU AND HIGHBROW STAY HERE. BRIEF THE OTHERS AS THEY EMERGE AND TRY AND CONTAIN THE BATTLE IN THIS AREA.
NIGHTBEAT AND I WILL TRY AND HEAD OFF SCORPONOK BEFORE HE REACHES MANHATTAN!
ALL THE DIRTY JOBS...
MEANWHILE...
INTERROGATIVE: DID MY LAST BLAST DESTROY HIM? WITH ALL THIS SMOKE, I CANNOT--
HOLD! SOMETHING MOVED, BUT WHAT--
LIBERTY
NOW-- DIE!
AH.
KRTCHAMM!
UNAAAH!

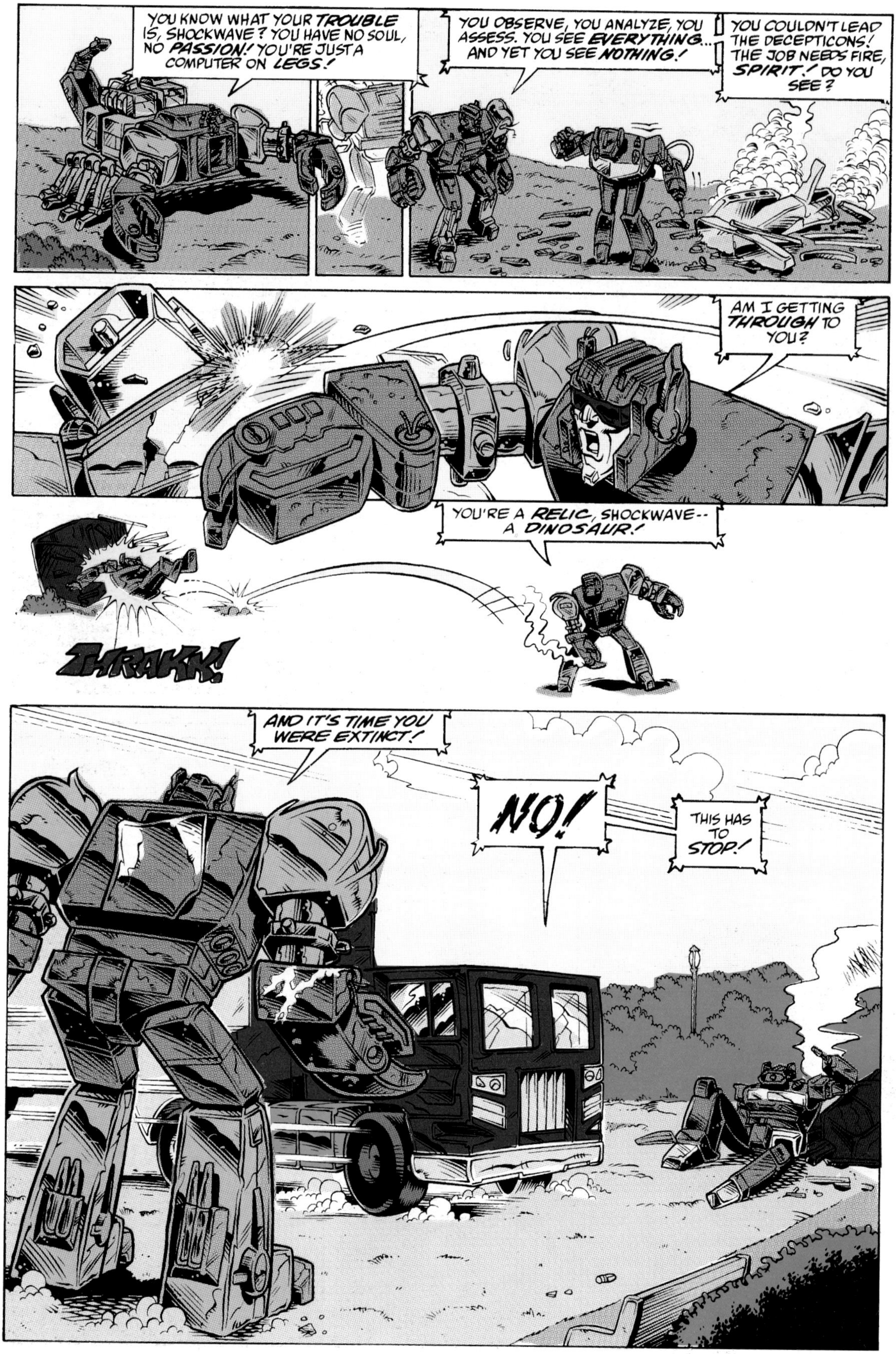

YOU KNOW WHAT YOUR TROUBLE IS, SHOCKWAVE? YOU HAVE NO SOUL, NO PASSION! YOU'RE JUST A COMPUTER ON LEGS!
YOU OBSERVE, YOU ANALYZE, YOU ASSESS. YOU SEE EVERYTHING... AND YET YOU SEE NOTHING!
YOU COULDN'T LEAD THE DECEPTICONS! THE JOB NEEDS FIRE, SPIRIT! DO YOU SEE?
AM I GETTING THROUGH TO YOU?
YOU'RE A RELIC, SHOCKWAVE-- A DINOSAUR!
THRAKK!
AND IT'S TIME YOU WERE EXTINCT!
NO!
THIS HAS TO STOP!

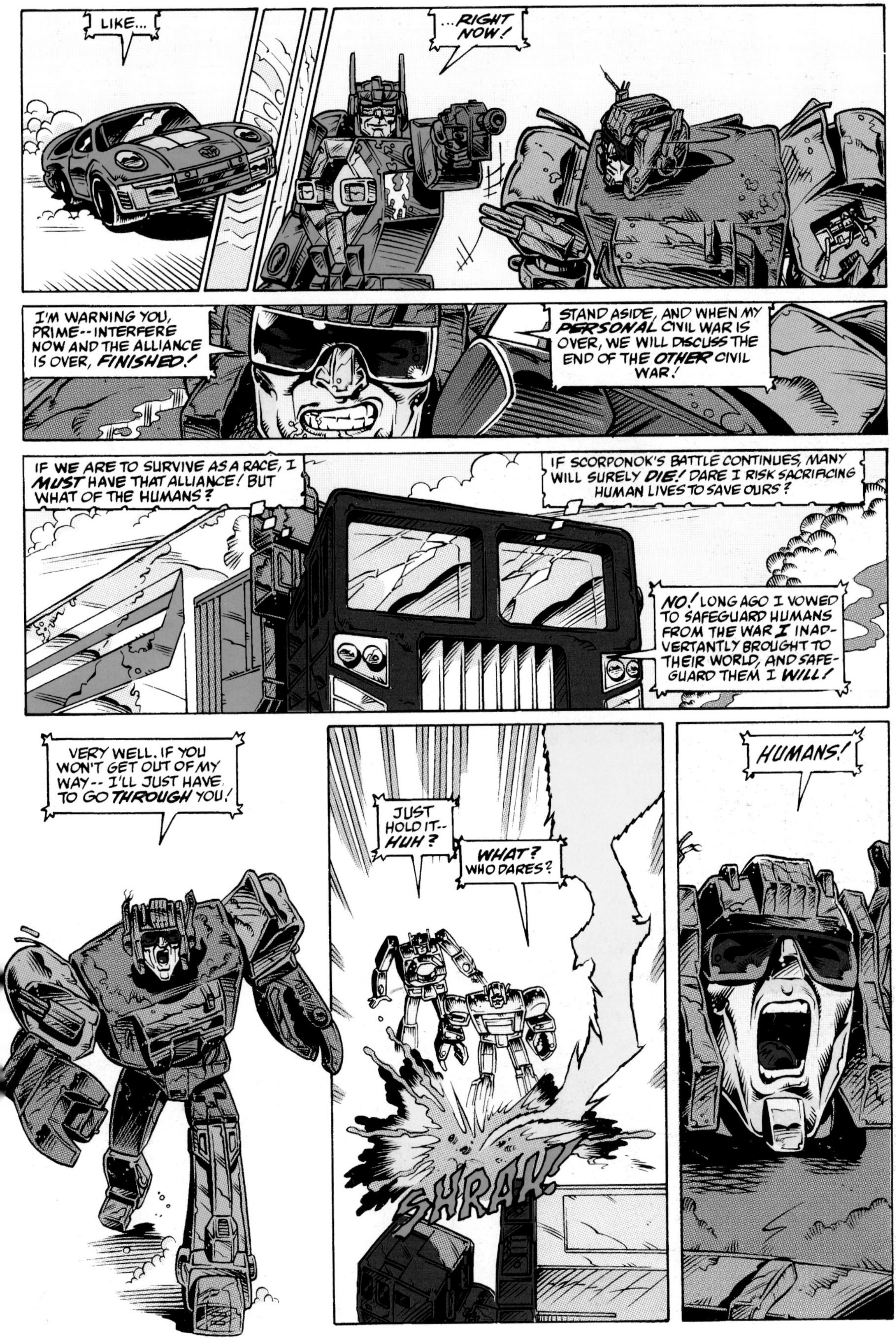

LIKE...
...RIGHT NOW!
I'M WARNING YOU, PRIME--INTERFERE NOW AND THE ALLIANCE IS OVER, FINISHED!
STAND ASIDE, AND WHEN MY PERSONAL CIVIL WAR IS OVER, WE WILL DISCUSS THE END OF THE OTHER CIVIL WAR!
IF WE ARE TO SURVIVE AS A RACE, I MUST HAVE THAT ALLIANCE! BUT WHAT OF THE HUMANS?
IF SCORPONOK'S BATTLE CONTINUES, MANY WILL SURELY DIE! DARE I RISK SACRIFICING HUMAN LIVES TO SAVE OURS?
NO! LONG AGO I VOWED TO SAFEGUARD HUMANS FROM THE WAR I INADVERTANTLY BROUGHT TO THEIR WORLD, AND SAFEGUARD THEM I WILL!
VERY WELL. IF YOU WON'T GET OUT OF MY WAY-- I'LL JUST HAVE TO GO THROUGH YOU!
JUST HOLD IT-- HUH?
WHAT? WHO DARES?
SHRAK!
HUMANS!

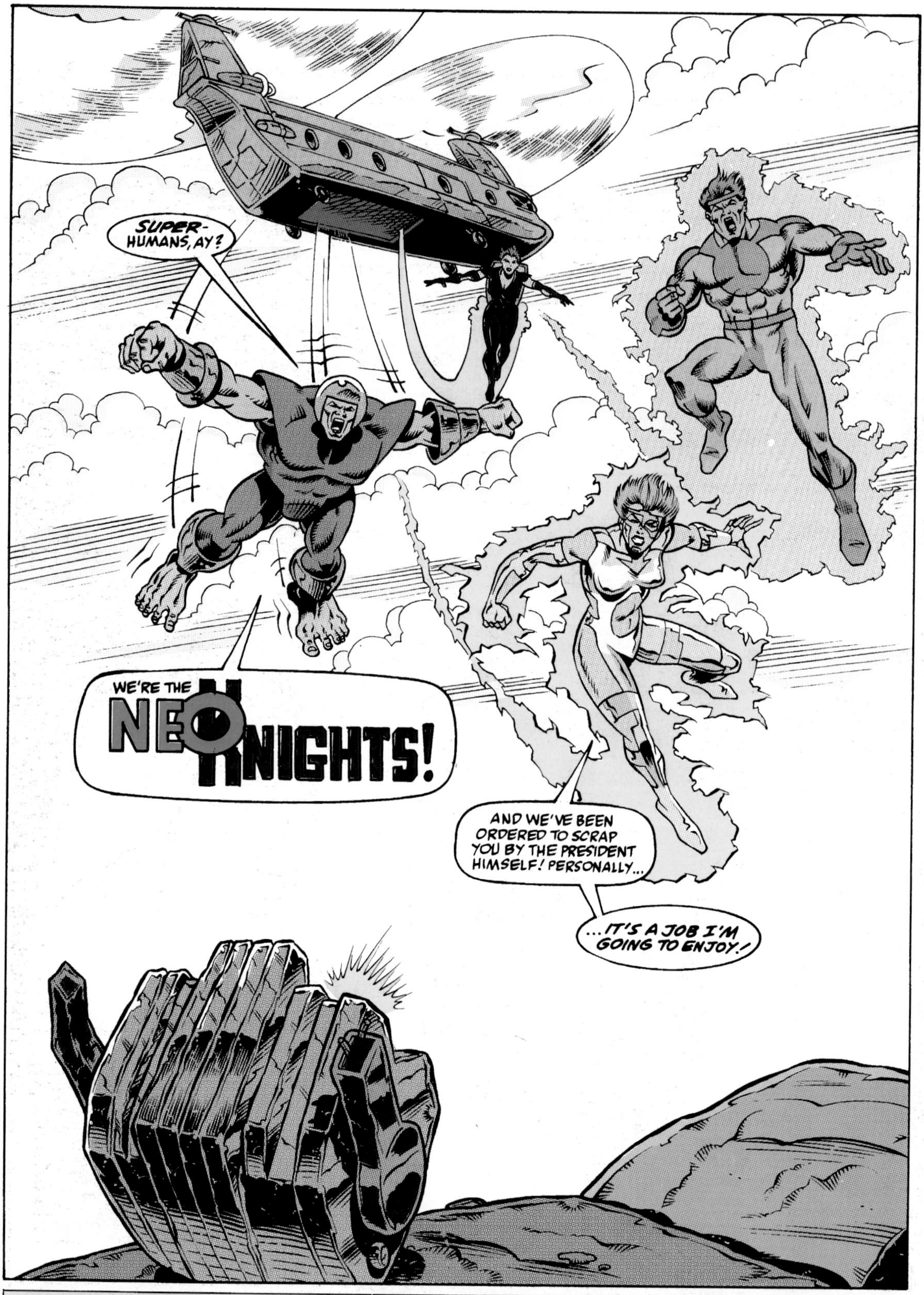
SUPER-HUMANS, AY?
WE'RE THE NEO KNIGHTS!
AND WE'VE BEEN ORDERED TO SCRAP YOU BY THE PRESIDENT HIMSELF! PERSONALLY...
...IT'S A JOB I'M GOING TO ENJOY!

NEXT ISSUE: UNICRON'S ON THE LAST LEG OF HIS JOURNEY TO CYBERTRON, AND THAT MEANS THAT JUST ABOUT EVERYONE IS **OUT OF TIME!**

They **were** the dream--mechanical beings able to transform their bodies into vehicles, machinery and weapons; a last line of defense against the chaos-bringer, **Unicron**! They **are** at war, heroic **Autobot** pitted against evil **Decepticon**, both on their homeworld, the metal planet called **Cybertron**, and here on our **Earth**. They **are** the galaxy's last hope, they **are**-- TRANSFORMERS

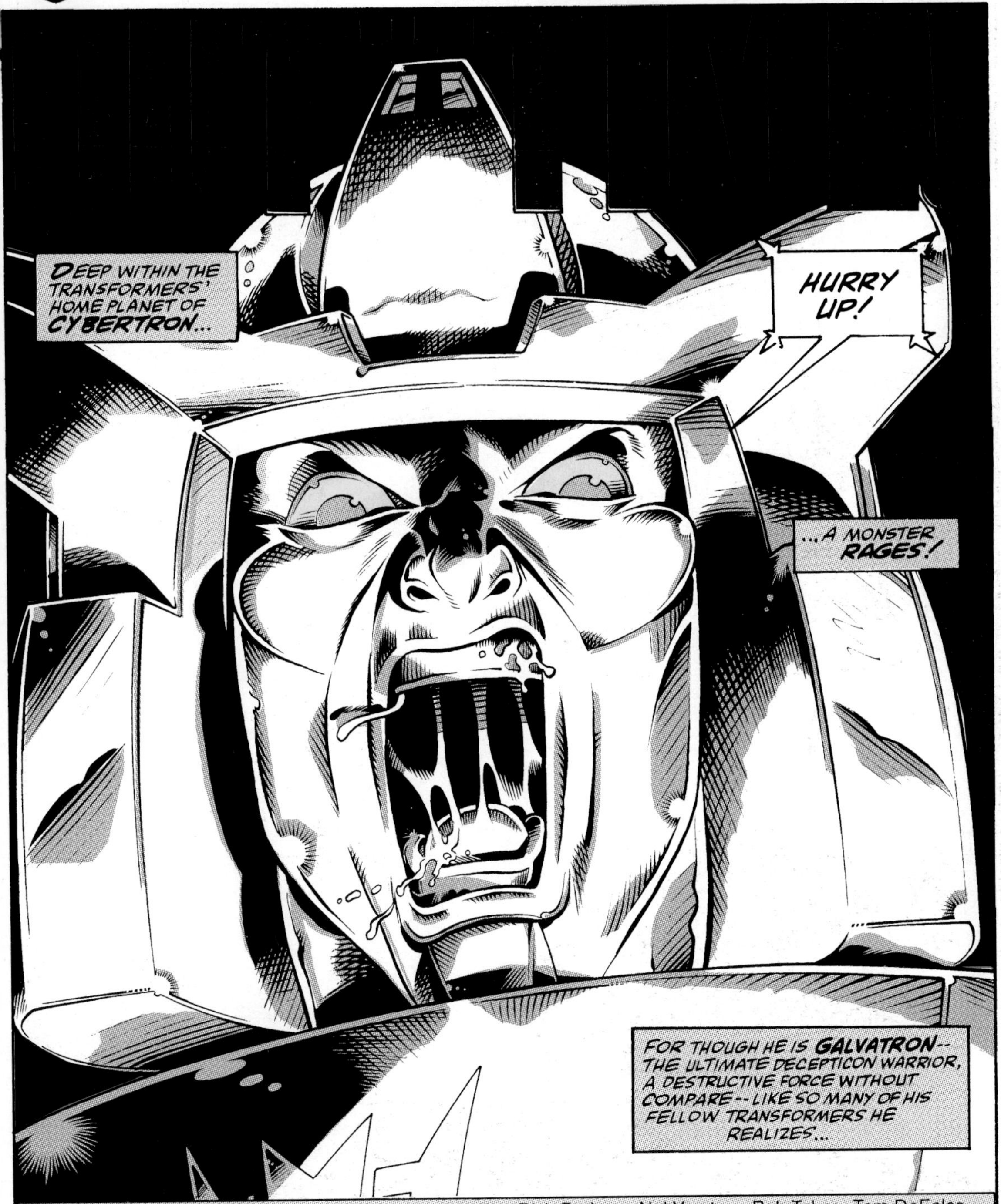

DEEP WITHIN THE TRANSFORMERS' HOME PLANET OF CYBERTRON...
HURRY UP!
...A MONSTER RAGES!
FOR THOUGH HE IS GALVATRON-- THE ULTIMATE DECEPTICON WARRIOR, A DESTRUCTIVE FORCE WITHOUT COMPARE-- LIKE SO MANY OF HIS FELLOW TRANSFORMERS HE REALIZES...

Simon Furman	Andrew Wildman	Stephen Baskerville	Rick Parker	Nel Yomtov	Rob Tokar	Tom DeFalco
WRITER	PENCILER	INKER	LETTERER	COLORIST	EDITOR	EDITOR IN CHIEF

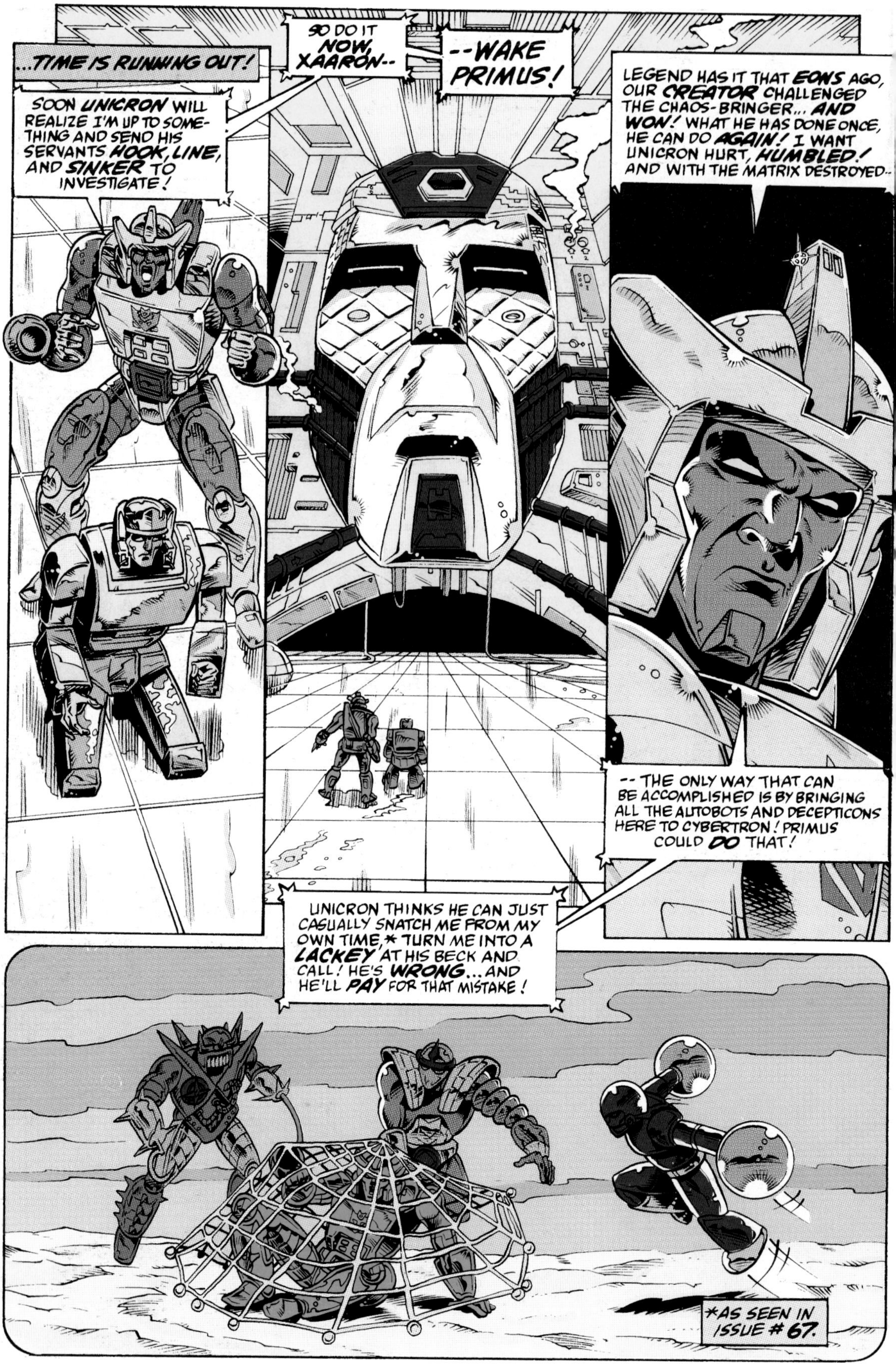
...TIME IS RUNNING OUT!
SOON UNICRON WILL REALIZE I'M UP TO SOMETHING AND SEND HIS SERVANTS HOOK, LINE, AND SINKER TO INVESTIGATE!
SO DO IT NOW, XAARON--
--WAKE PRIMUS!
LEGEND HAS IT THAT EONS AGO, OUR CREATOR CHALLENGED THE CHAOS-BRINGER... AND WON! WHAT HE HAS DONE ONCE, HE CAN DO AGAIN! I WANT UNICRON HURT, HUMBLED! AND WITH THE MATRIX DESTROYED...
--THE ONLY WAY THAT CAN BE ACCOMPLISHED IS BY BRINGING ALL THE AUTOBOTS AND DECEPTICONS HERE TO CYBERTRON! PRIMUS COULD DO THAT!
UNICRON THINKS HE CAN JUST CASUALLY SNATCH ME FROM MY OWN TIME,* TURN ME INTO A LACKEY AT HIS BECK AND CALL! HE'S WRONG... AND HE'LL PAY FOR THAT MISTAKE!
*AS SEEN IN ISSUE #67.

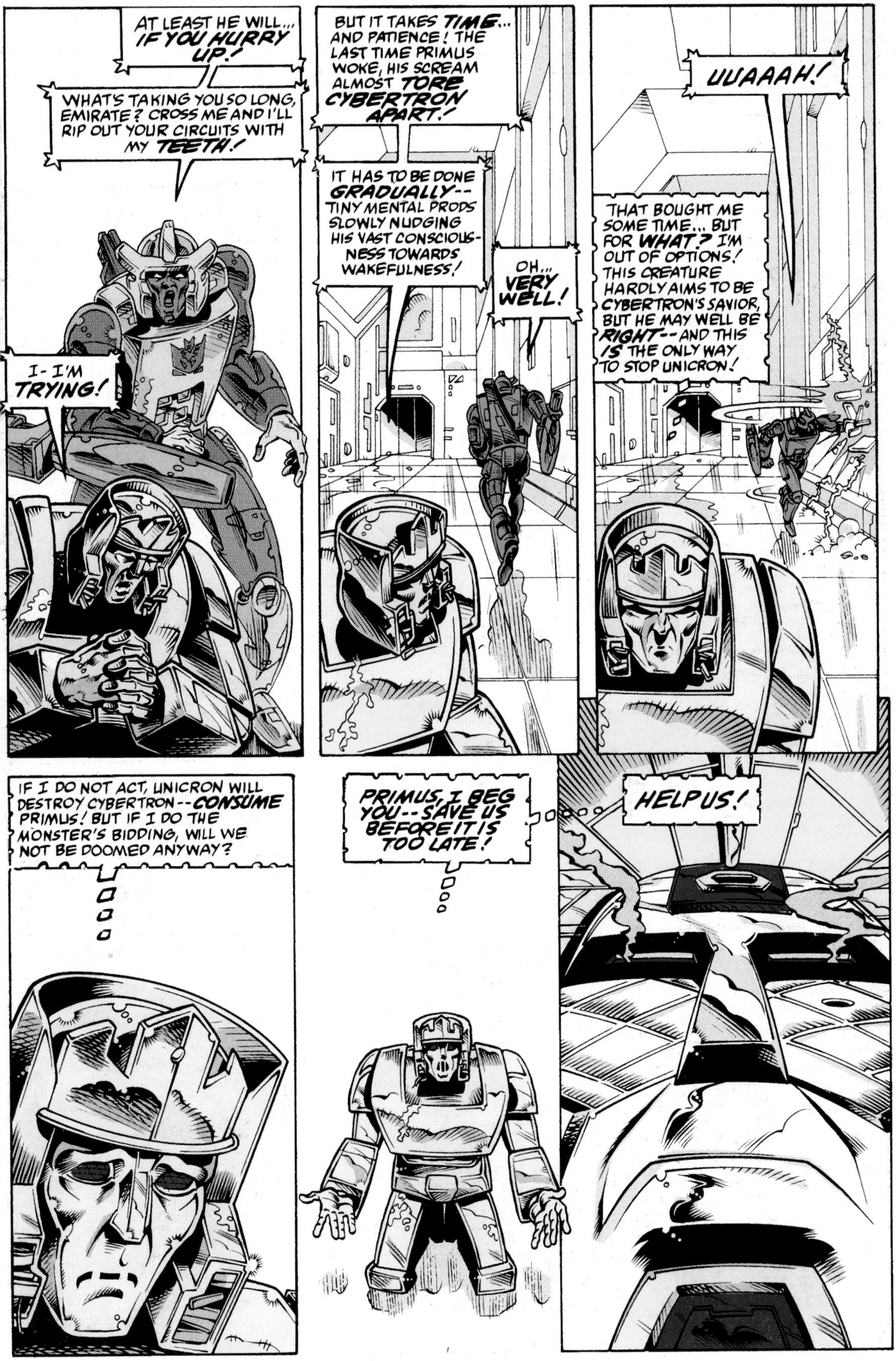

AT LEAST HE WILL... IF YOU HURRY UP!
WHAT'S TAKING YOU SO LONG, EMIRATE? CROSS ME AND I'LL RIP OUT YOUR CIRCUITS WITH MY TEETH!
I- I'M TRYING!
BUT IT TAKES TIME... AND PATIENCE! THE LAST TIME PRIMUS WOKE, HIS SCREAM ALMOST TORE CYBERTRON APART!
IT HAS TO BE DONE GRADUALLY-- TINY MENTAL PRODS SLOWLY NUDGING HIS VAST CONSCIOUSNESS TOWARDS WAKEFULNESS!
OH... VERY WELL!
UUAAAH!
THAT BOUGHT ME SOME TIME... BUT FOR WHAT? I'M OUT OF OPTIONS! THIS CREATURE HARDLY AIMS TO BE CYBERTRON'S SAVIOR, BUT HE MAY WELL BE RIGHT-- AND THIS IS THE ONLY WAY TO STOP UNICRON!
IF I DO NOT ACT, UNICRON WILL DESTROY CYBERTRON--CONSUME PRIMUS! BUT IF I DO THE MONSTER'S BIDDING, WILL WE NOT BE DOOMED ANYWAY?
PRIMUS, I BEG YOU--SAVE US BEFORE IT IS TOO LATE!
HELP US!

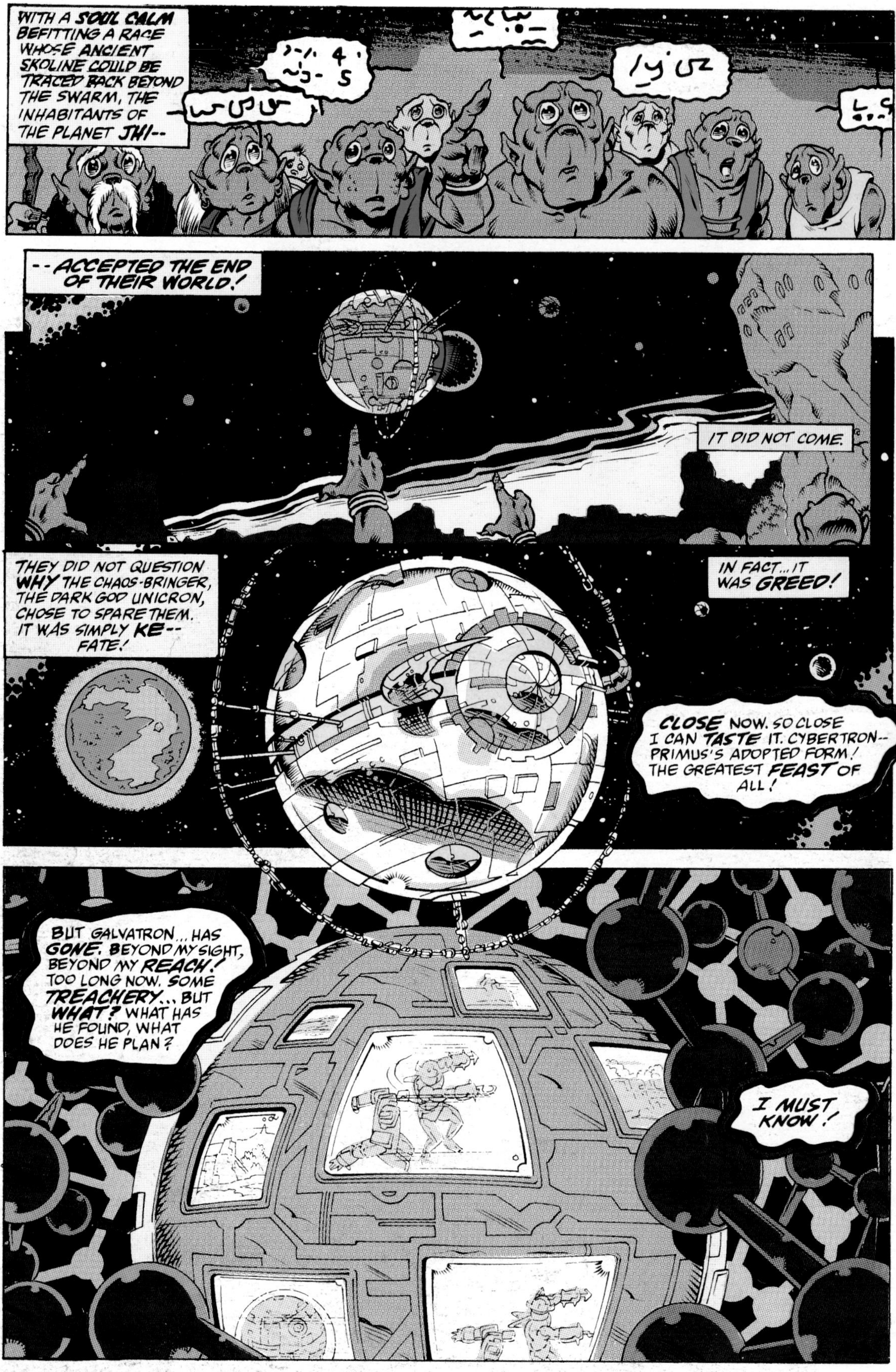
WITH A SOUL CALM BEFITTING A RACE WHOSE ANCIENT SKOLINE COULD BE TRACED BACK BEYOND THE SWARM, THE INHABITANTS OF THE PLANET JHI--
--ACCEPTED THE END OF THEIR WORLD!
IT DID NOT COME.
THEY DID NOT QUESTION WHY THE CHAOS-BRINGER, THE DARK GOD UNICRON, CHOSE TO SPARE THEM. IT WAS SIMPLY KE--FATE!
IN FACT... IT WAS GREED!
CLOSE NOW. SO CLOSE I CAN TASTE IT. CYBERTRON--PRIMUS'S ADOPTED FORM! THE GREATEST FEAST OF ALL!
BUT GALVATRON... HAS GONE. BEYOND MY SIGHT, BEYOND MY REACH! TOO LONG NOW. SOME TREACHERY... BUT WHAT? WHAT HAS HE FOUND, WHAT DOES HE PLAN?
I MUST KNOW!

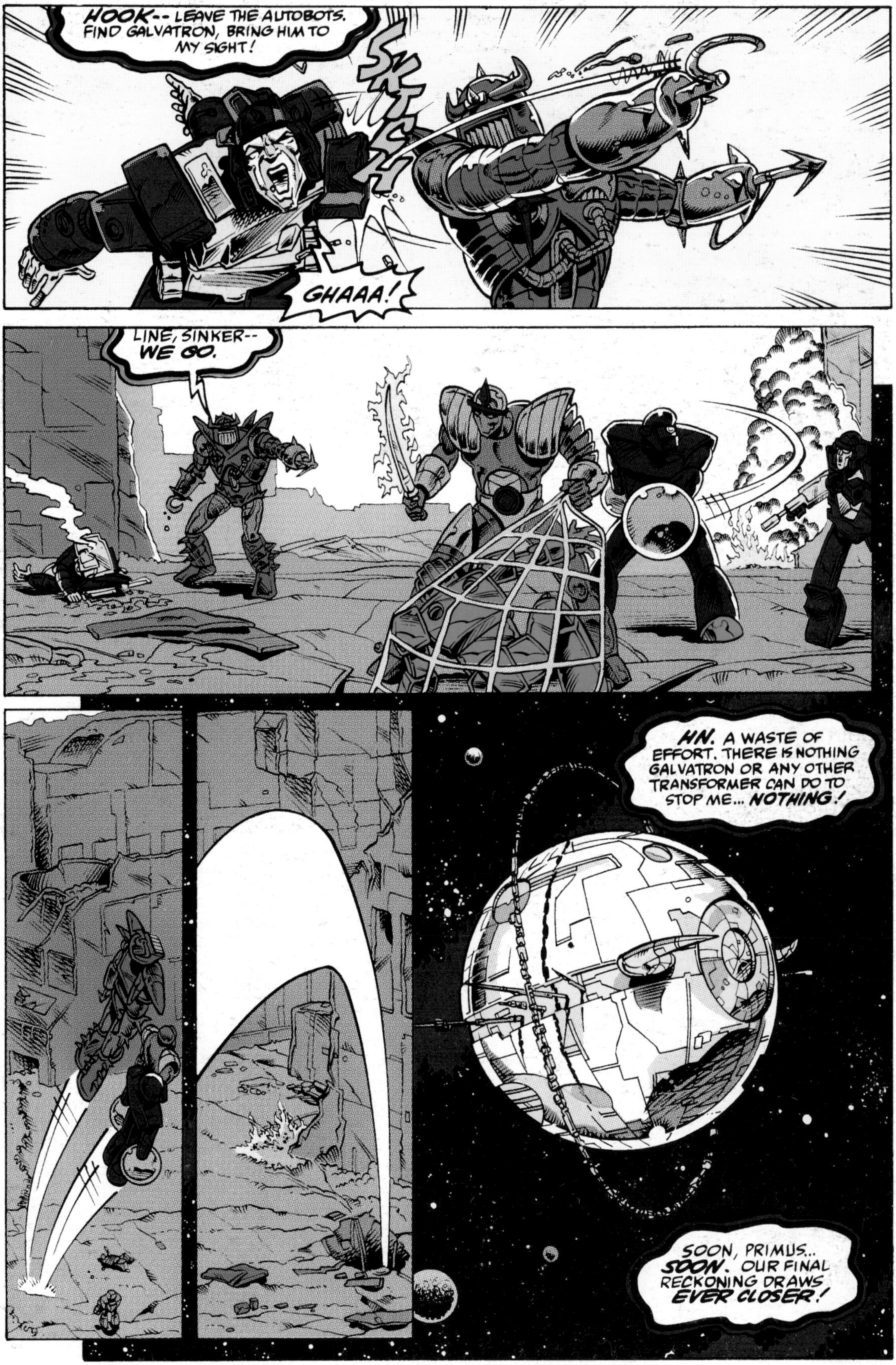
HOOK-- LEAVE THE AUTOBOTS. FIND GALVATRON, BRING HIM TO MY SIGHT!
SKTCH
GHAAA!
LINE, SINKER-- WE GO.
HN. A WASTE OF EFFORT. THERE IS NOTHING GALVATRON OR ANY OTHER TRANSFORMER CAN DO TO STOP ME... NOTHING!
SOON, PRIMUS... SOON. OUR FINAL RECKONING DRAWS EVER CLOSER!

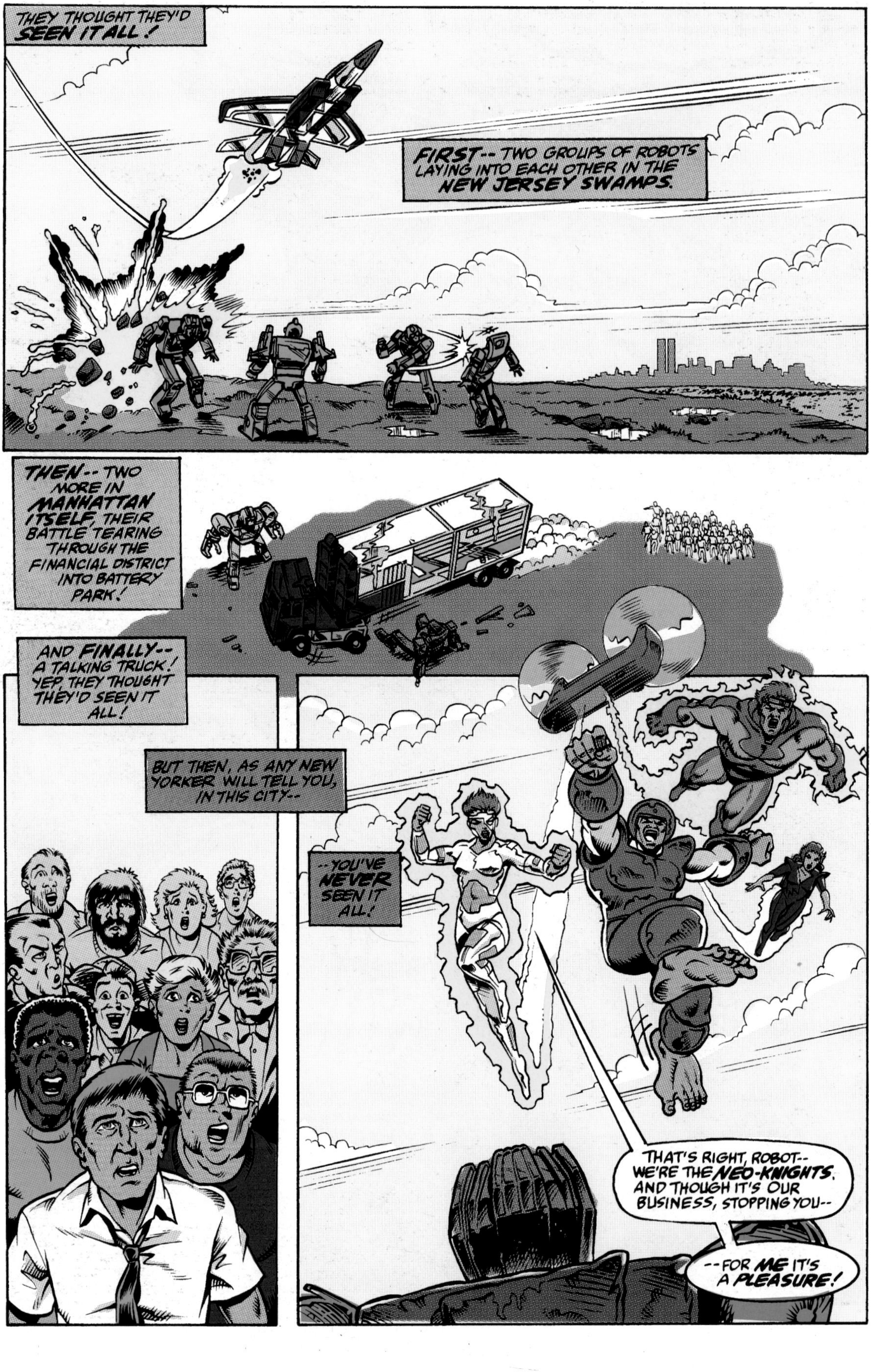
THEY THOUGHT THEY'D SEEN IT ALL!
FIRST-- TWO GROUPS OF ROBOTS LAYING INTO EACH OTHER IN THE NEW JERSEY SWAMPS.
THEN-- TWO MORE IN MANHATTAN ITSELF, THEIR BATTLE TEARING THROUGH THE FINANCIAL DISTRICT INTO BATTERY PARK!
AND FINALLY-- A TALKING TRUCK! YEP. THEY THOUGHT THEY'D SEEN IT ALL!
BUT THEN, AS ANY NEW YORKER WILL TELL YOU, IN THIS CITY--
--YOU'VE NEVER SEEN IT ALL!
THAT'S RIGHT, ROBOT-- WE'RE THE NEO-KNIGHTS. AND THOUGH IT'S OUR BUSINESS, STOPPING YOU--
--FOR ME IT'S A PLEASURE!

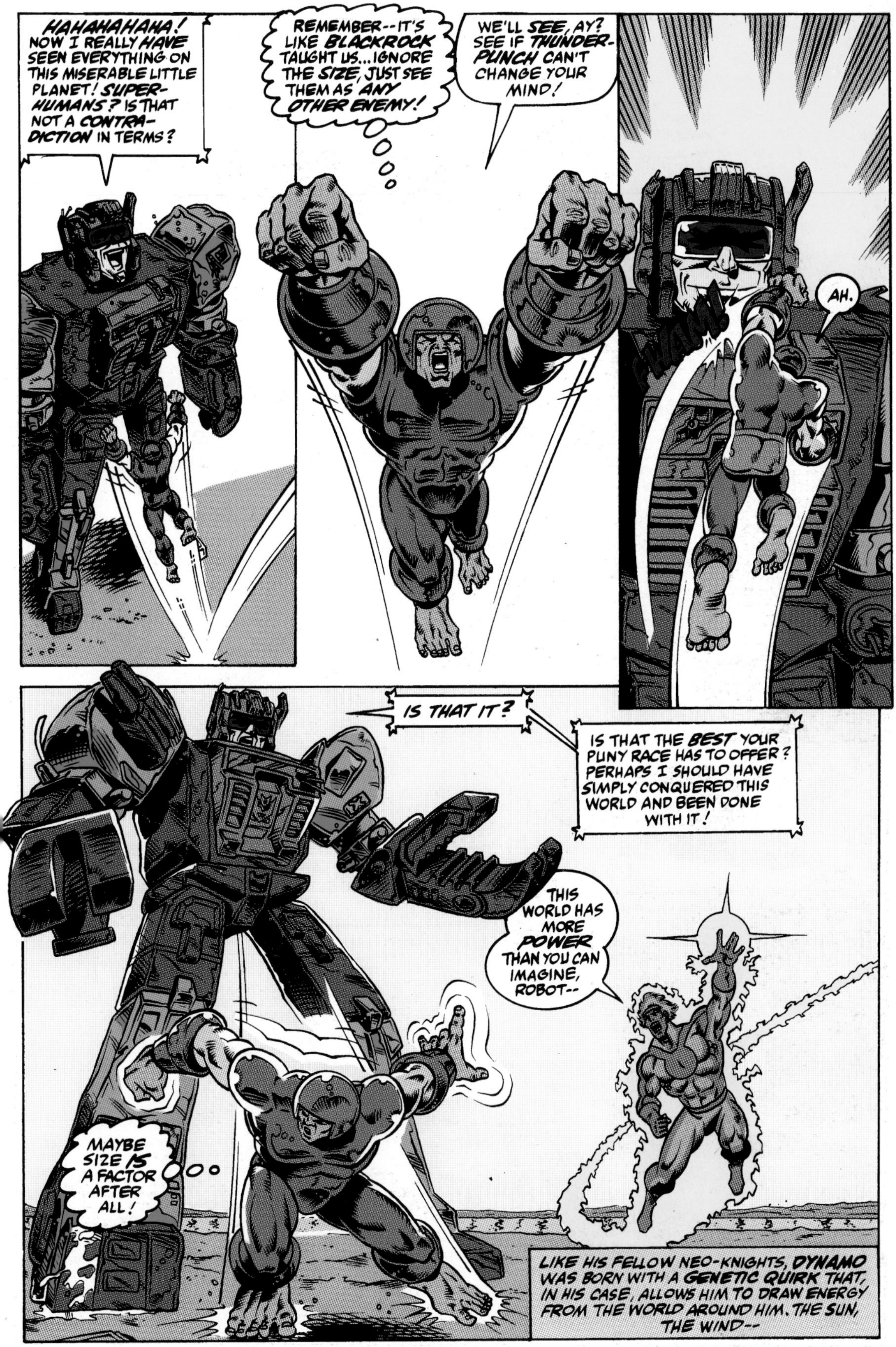
HAHAHAHAHA! NOW I REALLY HAVE SEEN EVERYTHING ON THIS MISERABLE LITTLE PLANET! SUPER-HUMANS? IS THAT NOT A CONTRA-DICTION IN TERMS?
REMEMBER--IT'S LIKE BLACKROCK TAUGHT US...IGNORE THE SIZE, JUST SEE THEM AS ANY OTHER ENEMY!
WE'LL SEE, AY? SEE IF THUNDER-PUNCH CAN'T CHANGE YOUR MIND!
FWAM!
AH.
IS THAT IT?
IS THAT THE BEST YOUR PUNY RACE HAS TO OFFER? PERHAPS I SHOULD HAVE SIMPLY CONQUERED THIS WORLD AND BEEN DONE WITH IT!
THIS WORLD HAS MORE POWER THAN YOU CAN IMAGINE, ROBOT--
MAYBE SIZE IS A FACTOR AFTER ALL!
LIKE HIS FELLOW NEO-KNIGHTS, DYNAMO WAS BORN WITH A GENETIC QUIRK THAT, IN HIS CASE, ALLOWS HIM TO DRAW ENERGY FROM THE WORLD AROUND HIM. THE SUN, THE WIND--

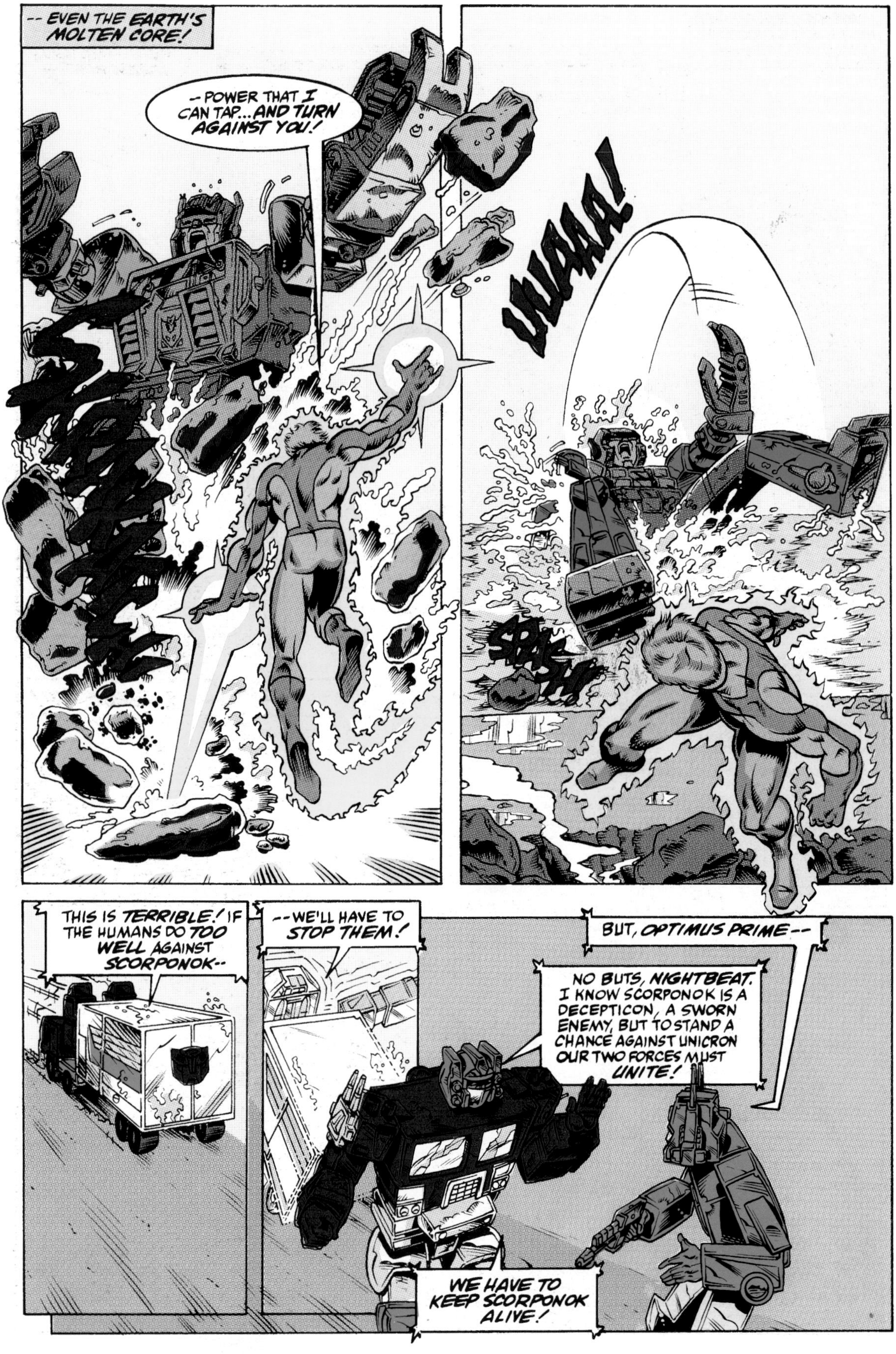
-- EVEN THE EARTH'S MOLTEN CORE!
-- POWER THAT I CAN TAP... AND TURN AGAINST YOU!
UWAAA!
SPLASH!
THIS IS TERRIBLE! IF THE HUMANS DO TOO WELL AGAINST SCORPONOK--
--WE'LL HAVE TO STOP THEM!
BUT, OPTIMUS PRIME--
NO BUTS, NIGHTBEAT. I KNOW SCORPONOK IS A DECEPTICON, A SWORN ENEMY, BUT TO STAND A CHANCE AGAINST UNICRON OUR TWO FORCES MUST UNITE!
WE HAVE TO KEEP SCORPONOK ALIVE!

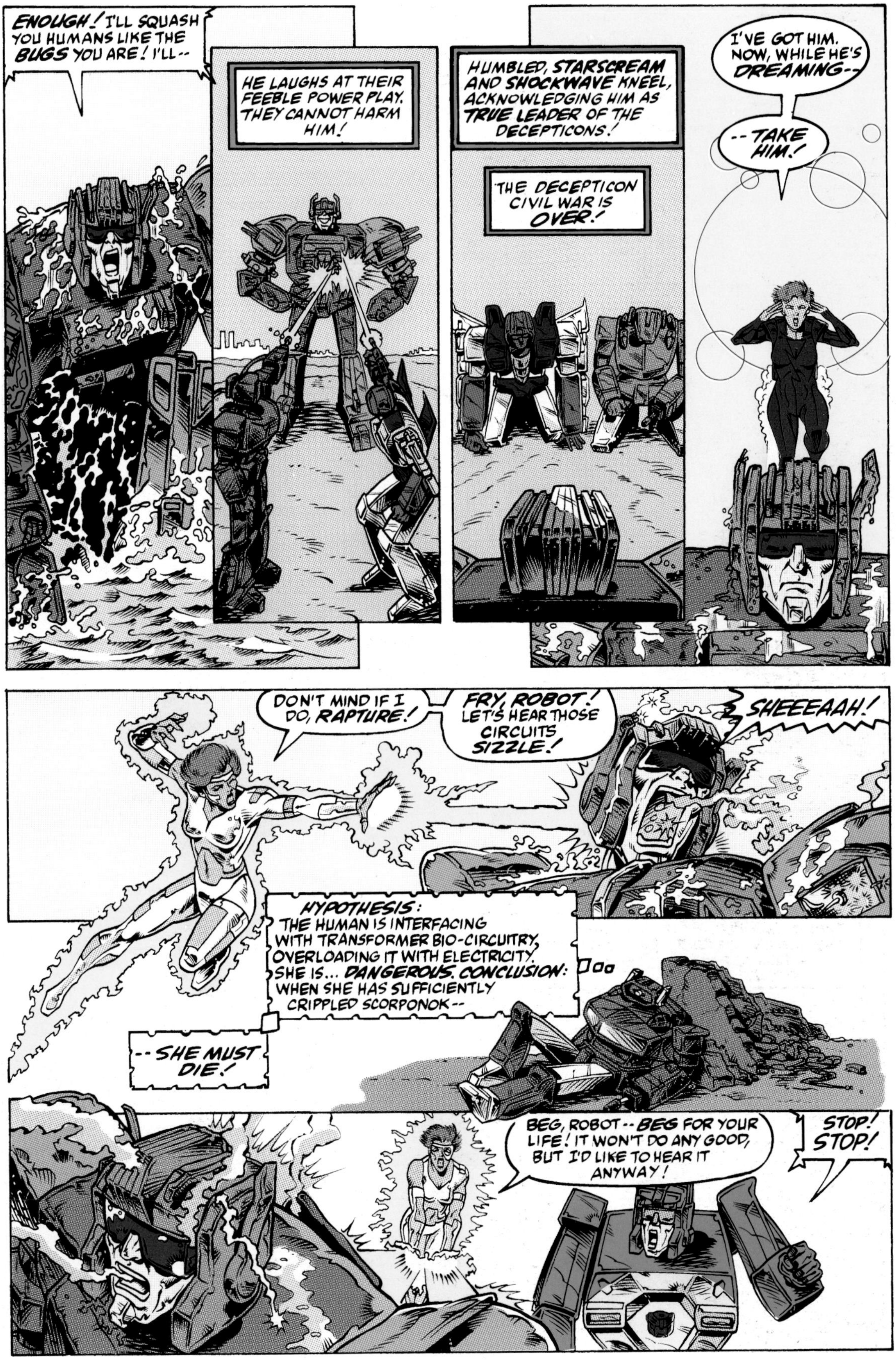
ENOUGH! I'LL SQUASH YOU HUMANS LIKE THE BUGS YOU ARE! I'LL--
HE LAUGHS AT THEIR FEEBLE POWER PLAY. THEY CANNOT HARM HIM!
HUMBLED, STARSCREAM AND SHOCKWAVE KNEEL, ACKNOWLEDGING HIM AS TRUE LEADER OF THE DECEPTICONS!
THE DECEPTICON CIVIL WAR IS OVER!
I'VE GOT HIM. NOW, WHILE HE'S DREAMING--
--TAKE HIM!
DON'T MIND IF I DO, RAPTURE!
FRY, ROBOT! LET'S HEAR THOSE CIRCUITS SIZZLE!
SHEEEAAH!
HYPOTHESIS: THE HUMAN IS INTERFACING WITH TRANSFORMER BIO-CIRCUITRY, OVERLOADING IT WITH ELECTRICITY. SHE IS... DANGEROUS. CONCLUSION: WHEN SHE HAS SUFFICIENTLY CRIPPLED SCORPONOK--
--SHE MUST DIE!
BEG, ROBOT--BEG FOR YOUR LIFE! IT WON'T DO ANY GOOD, BUT I'D LIKE TO HEAR IT ANYWAY!
STOP! STOP!

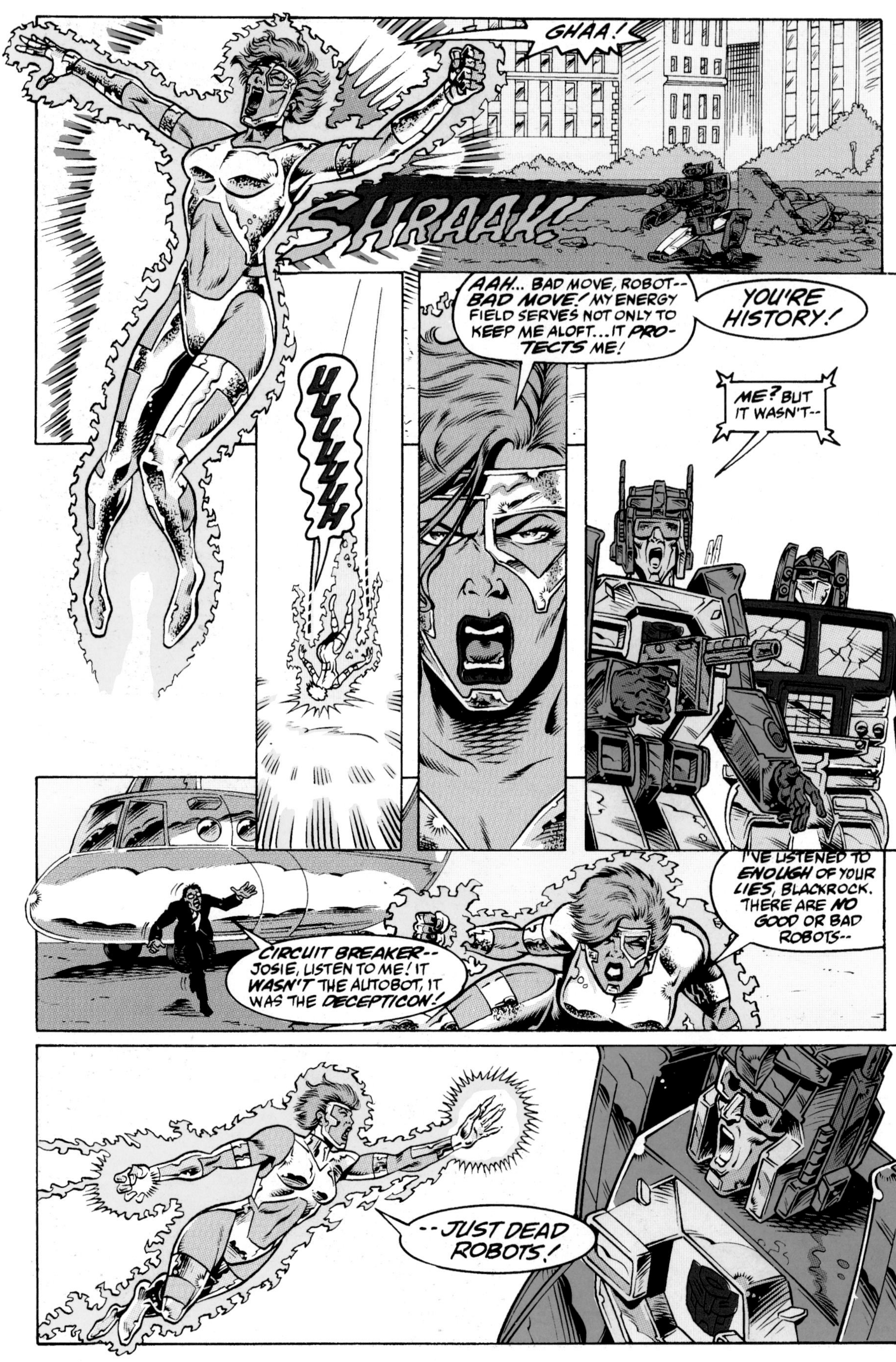
GHAA!
SHRAAK!
UUUUUHH
AAH... BAD MOVE, ROBOT-- BAD MOVE! MY ENERGY FIELD SERVES NOT ONLY TO KEEP ME ALOFT... IT PROTECTS ME!
YOU'RE HISTORY!
ME? BUT IT WASN'T--
CIRCUIT BREAKER-- JOSIE, LISTEN TO ME! IT WASN'T THE AUTOBOT, IT WAS THE DECEPTICON!
I'VE LISTENED TO ENOUGH OF YOUR LIES, BLACKROCK. THERE ARE NO GOOD OR BAD ROBOTS--
--JUST DEAD ROBOTS!

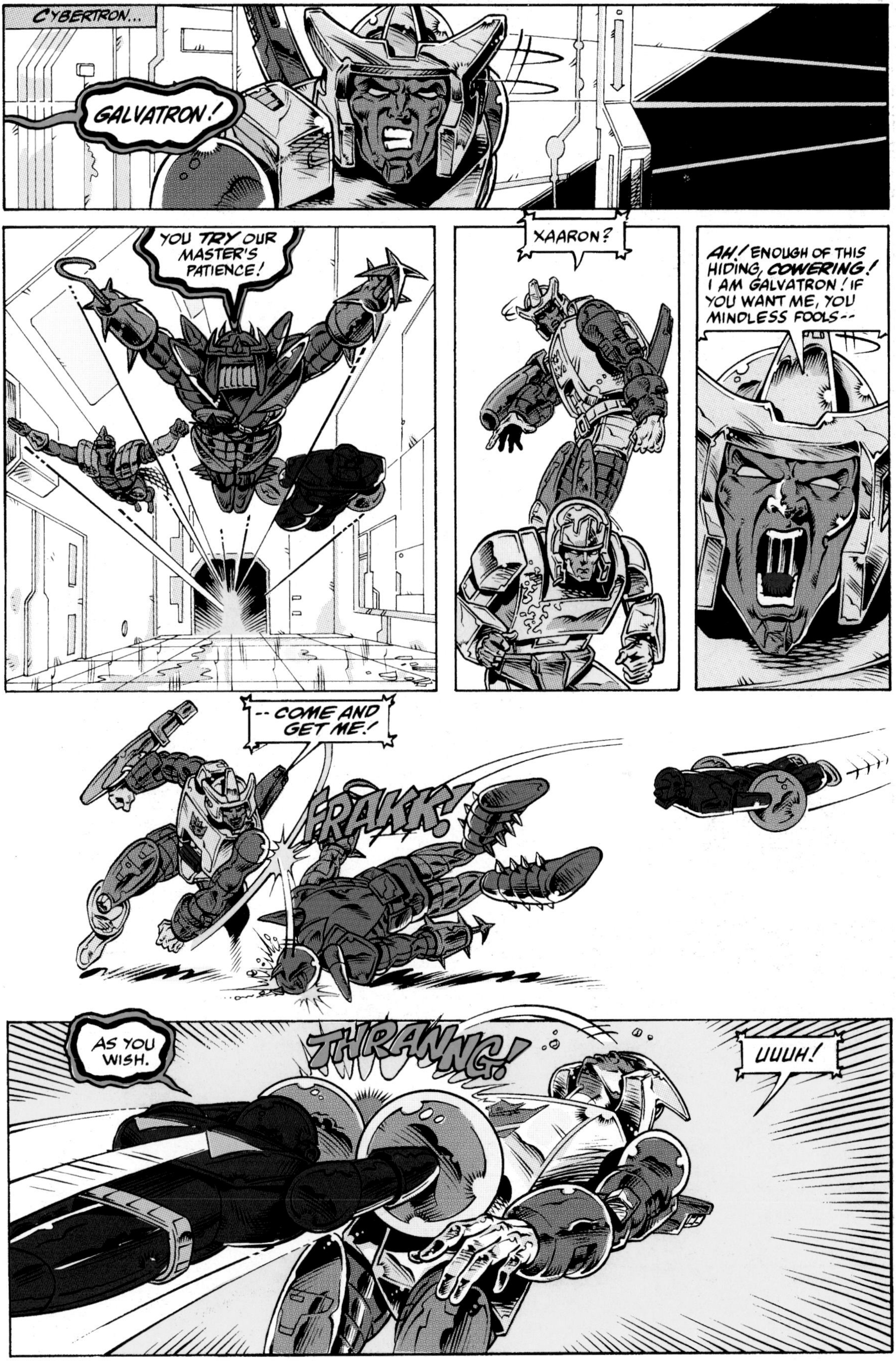
CYBERTRON...
GALVATRON!
YOU TRY OUR MASTER'S PATIENCE!
XAARON?
AH! ENOUGH OF THIS HIDING, COWERING! I AM GALVATRON! IF YOU WANT ME, YOU MINDLESS FOOLS--
--COME AND GET ME!
FRAKK!
AS YOU WISH.
THRANNG!
UUUH!

IS MINE!

FSHH!

NO!

CHAK!

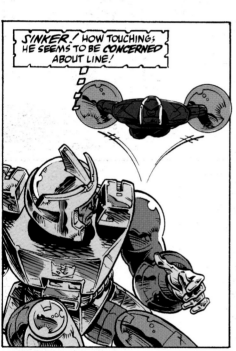

SINKER! HOW TOUCHING; HE SEEMS TO BE CONCERNED ABOUT LINE!

PERHAPS THEN I SHOULD BRING THESE TWO DEAR FRIENDS...

CHUNNCH!

...CLOSER TOGETHER!

TO THINK THAT I ALLOWED YOU THREE TO BEST ME WHEN LAST WE FOUGHT!

IT IS TIME TO EDUCATE YOU--

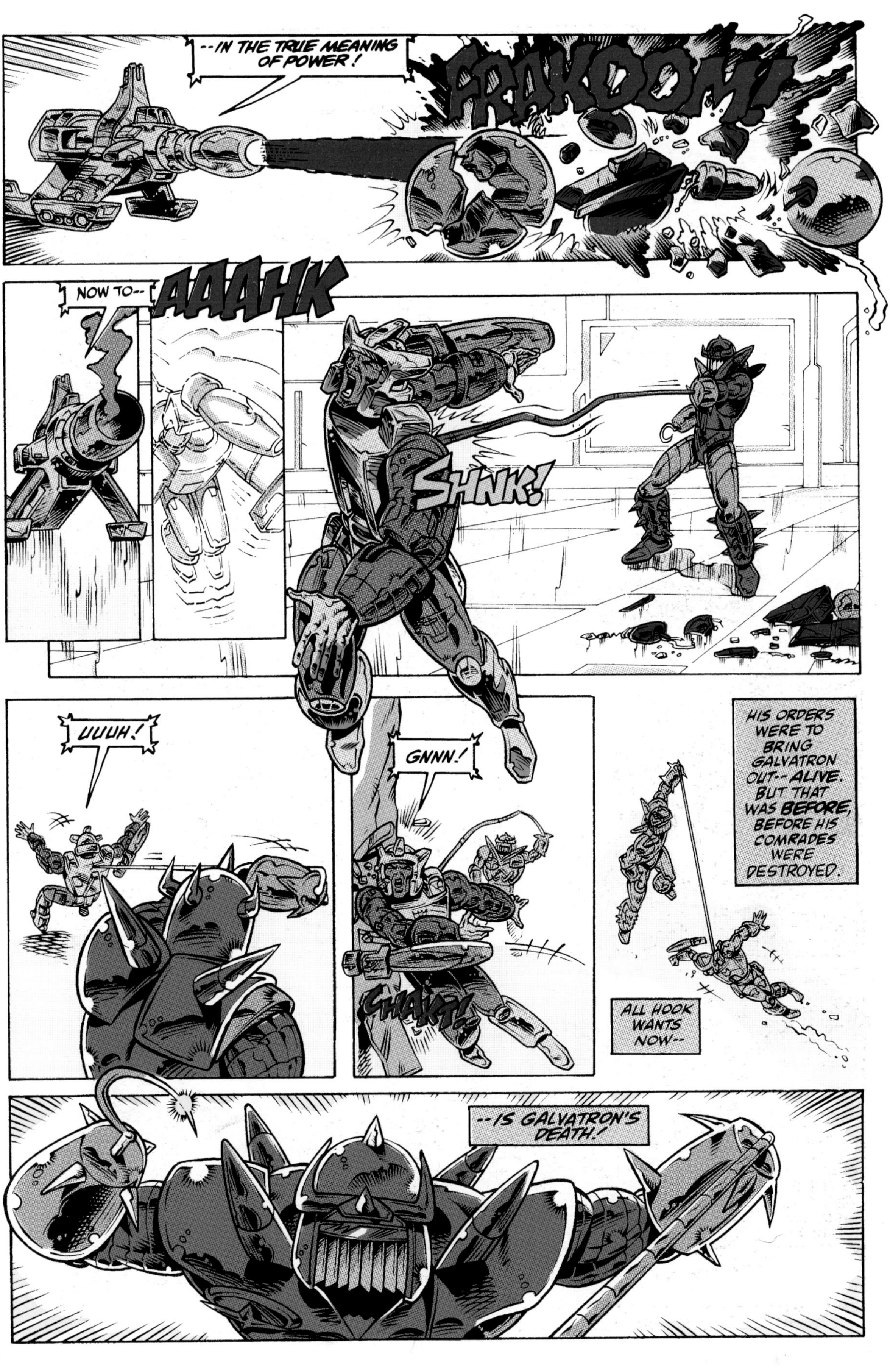
--IN THE TRUE MEANING OF POWER!
FRAKOOM!
NOW TO--
AAAHK
SHNK!
UUUH!
GNNN!
CHAKT!
HIS ORDERS WERE TO BRING GALVATRON OUT-- ALIVE. BUT THAT WAS BEFORE, BEFORE HIS COMRADES WERE DESTROYED.
ALL HOOK WANTS NOW--
--IS GALVATRON'S DEATH!

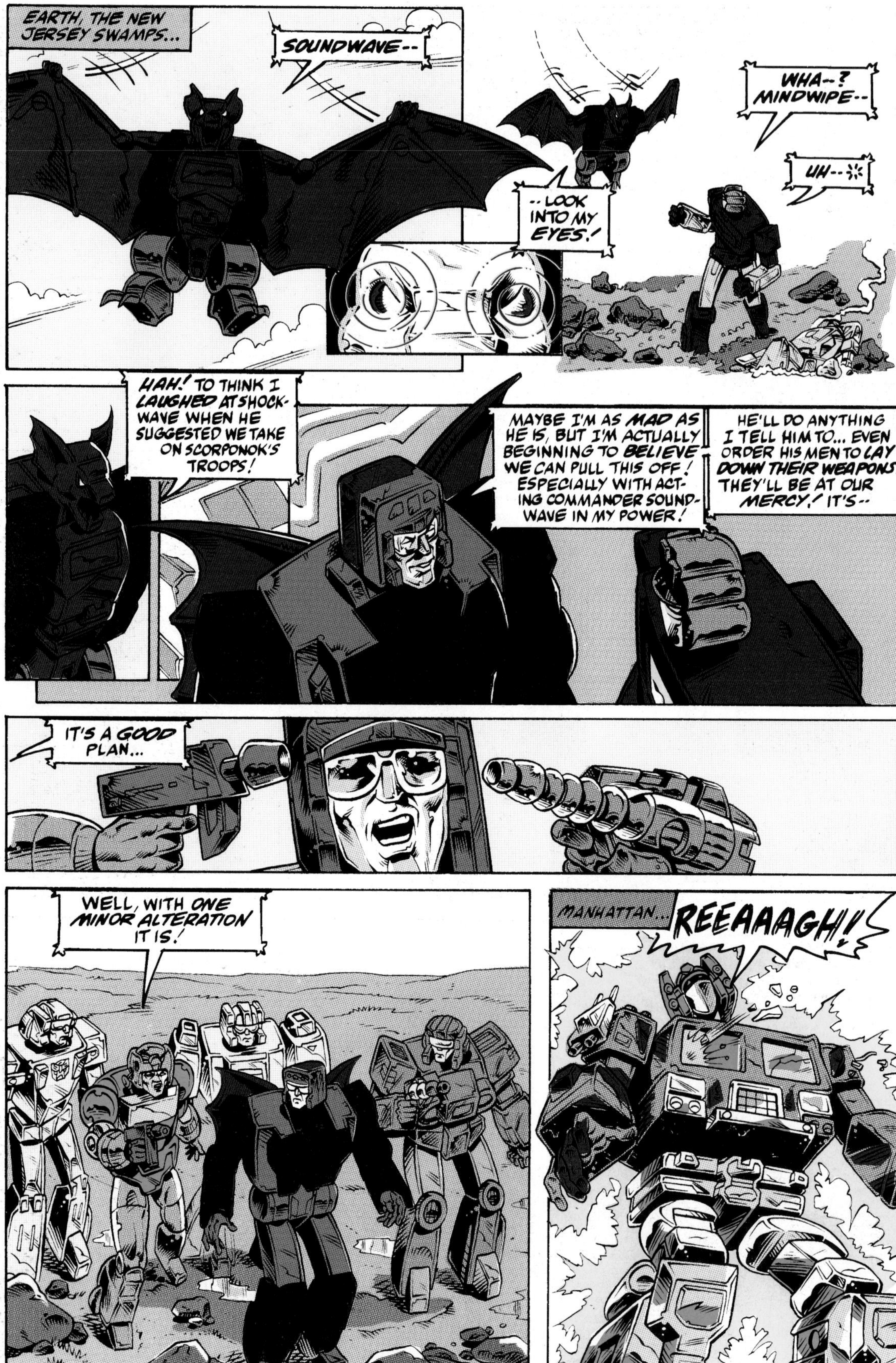
EARTH, THE NEW JERSEY SWAMPS...
SOUNDWAVE--
..LOOK INTO MY EYES!
WHA--? MINDWIPE--
UH--
HAH! TO THINK I LAUGHED AT SHOCKWAVE WHEN HE SUGGESTED WE TAKE ON SCORPONOK'S TROOPS!
MAYBE I'M AS MAD AS HE IS, BUT I'M ACTUALLY BEGINNING TO BELIEVE WE CAN PULL THIS OFF! ESPECIALLY WITH ACTING COMMANDER SOUNDWAVE IN MY POWER!
HE'LL DO ANYTHING I TELL HIM TO... EVEN ORDER HIS MEN TO LAY DOWN THEIR WEAPONS! THEY'LL BE AT OUR MERCY! IT'S--
IT'S A GOOD PLAN...
WELL, WITH ONE MINOR ALTERATION IT IS!
MANHATTAN...
REEAAAAGH!!

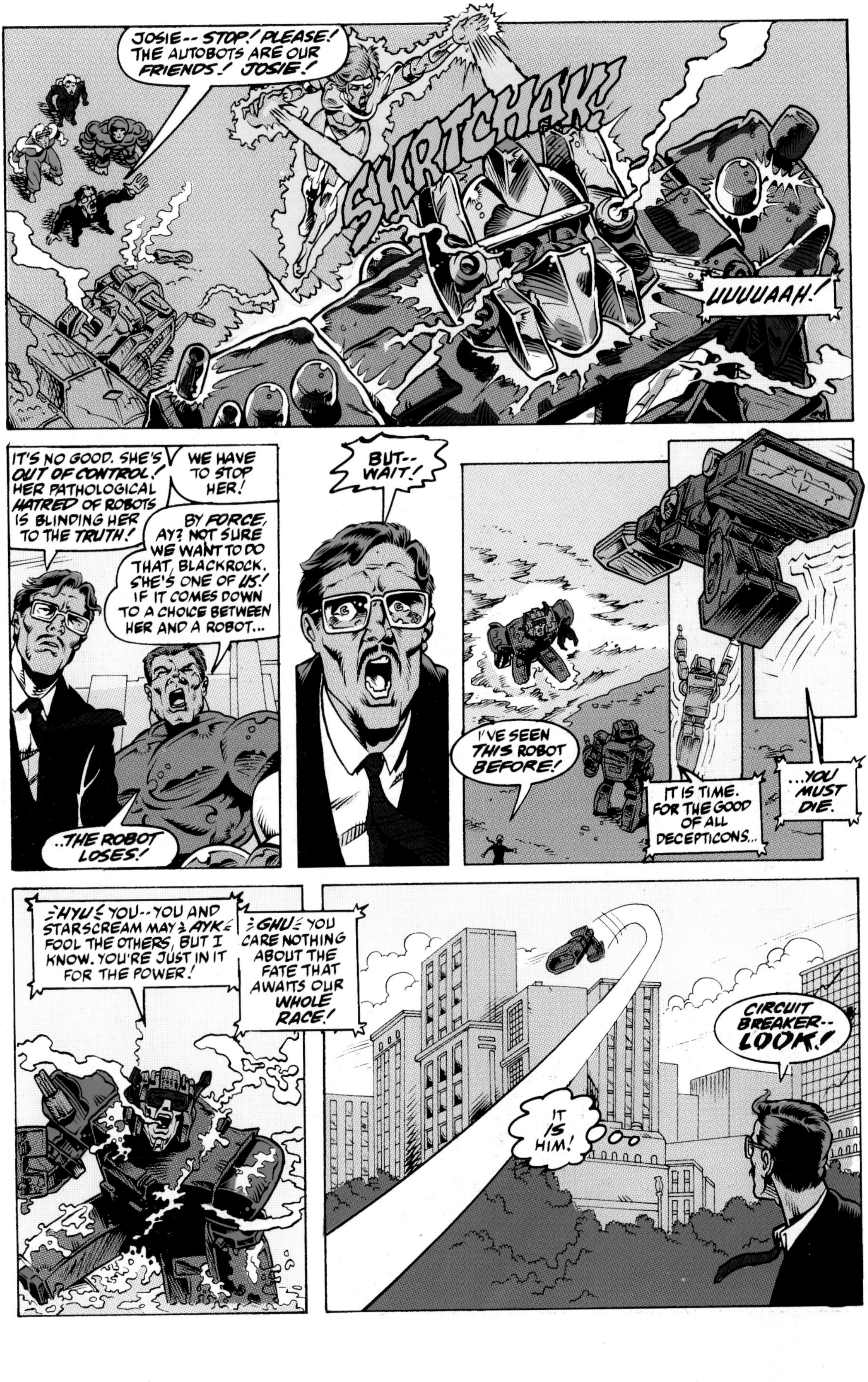
JOSIE-- STOP! PLEASE! THE AUTOBOTS ARE OUR FRIENDS! JOSIE!
SKRTCHAK!
UUUUAAH!
IT'S NO GOOD. SHE'S OUT OF CONTROL! HER PATHOLOGICAL HATRED OF ROBOTS IS BLINDING HER TO THE TRUTH!
WE HAVE TO STOP HER!
BY FORCE, AY? NOT SURE WE WANT TO DO THAT, BLACKROCK. SHE'S ONE OF US! IF IT COMES DOWN TO A CHOICE BETWEEN HER AND A ROBOT...
..THE ROBOT LOSES!
BUT-- WAIT!
I'VE SEEN THIS ROBOT BEFORE!
IT IS TIME. FOR THE GOOD OF ALL DECEPTICONS...
...YOU MUST DIE.
HYU YOU-- YOU AND STARSCREAM MAY AYK FOOL THE OTHERS, BUT I KNOW. YOU'RE JUST IN IT FOR THE POWER!
GHU YOU CARE NOTHING ABOUT THE FATE THAT AWAITS OUR WHOLE RACE!
CIRCUIT BREAKER-- LOOK!
IT IS HIM!

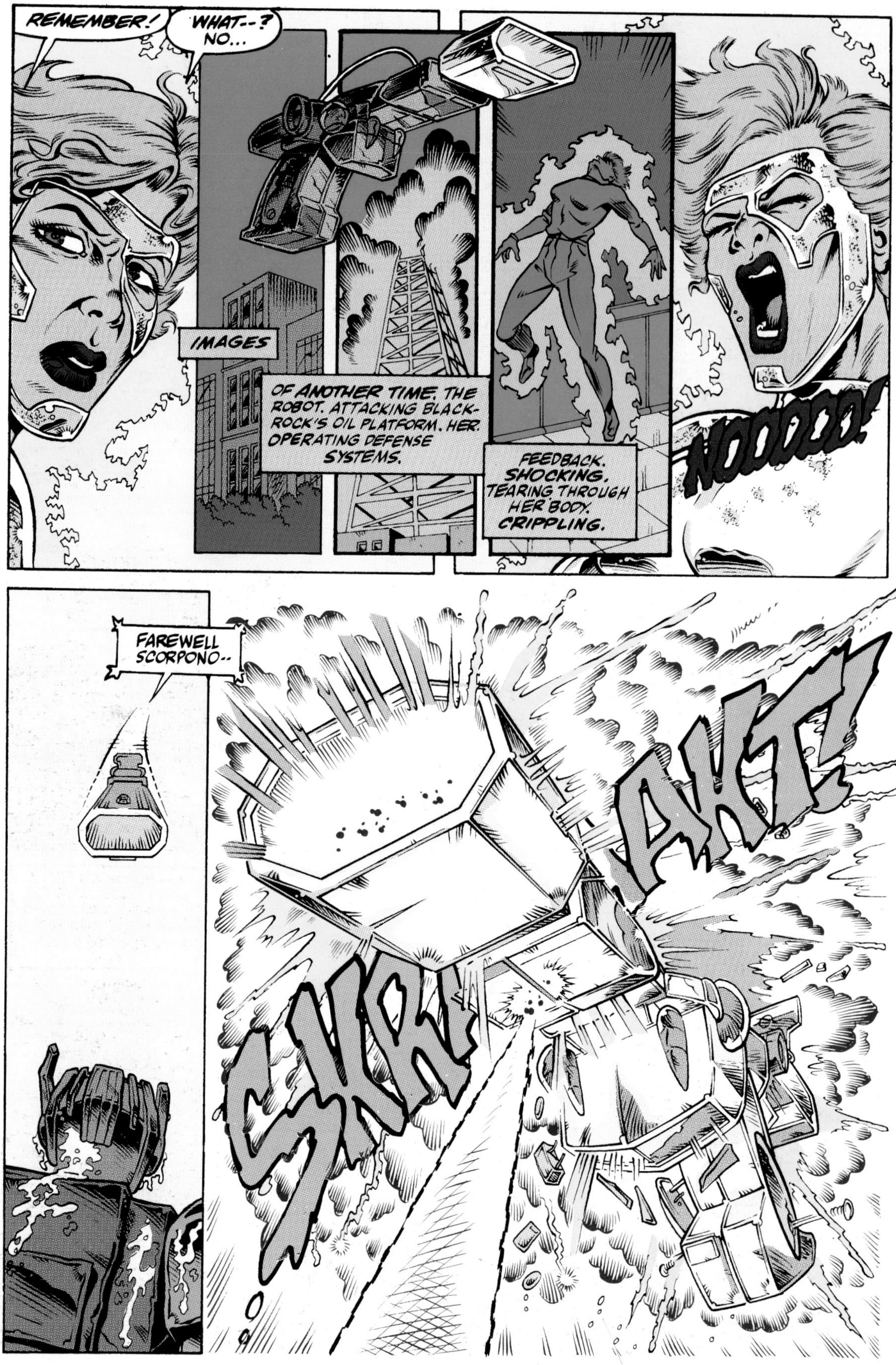
REMEMBER!
WHAT--? NO...
IMAGES
OF ANOTHER TIME. THE ROBOT. ATTACKING BLACK-ROCK'S OIL PLATFORM. HER. OPERATING DEFENSE SYSTEMS.
FEEDBACK. SHOCKING. TEARING THROUGH HER BODY. CRIPPLING.
NOOOOO!
FAREWELL SCORPONO--
SKR-AKT!

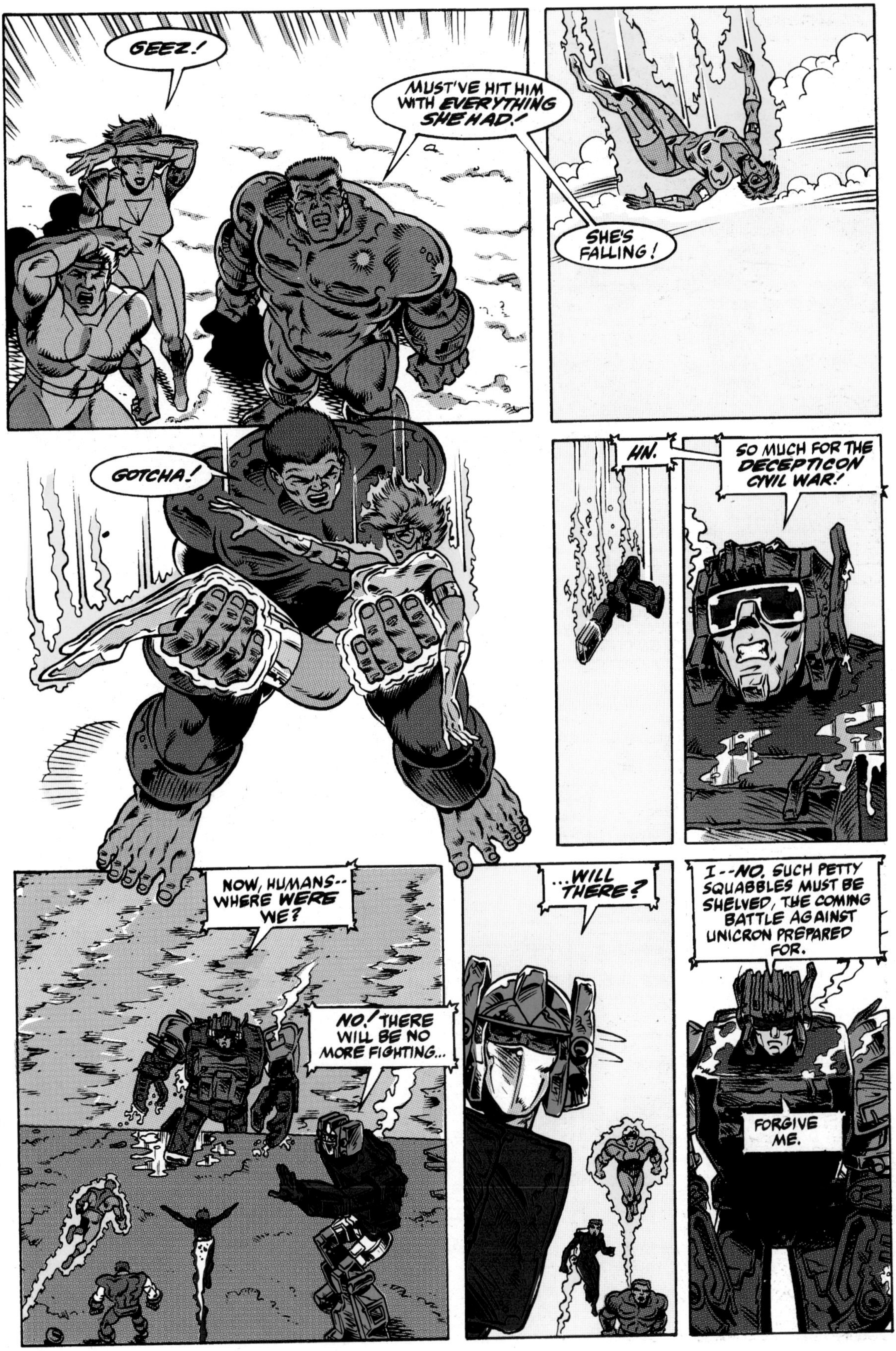
GEEZ!
MUST'VE HIT HIM WITH EVERYTHING SHE HAD!
SHE'S FALLING!
GOTCHA!
HN.
SO MUCH FOR THE DECEPTICON CIVIL WAR!
NOW, HUMANS-- WHERE WERE WE?
NO! THERE WILL BE NO MORE FIGHTING...
...WILL THERE?
I--NO, SUCH PETTY SQUABBLES MUST BE SHELVED, THE COMING BATTLE AGAINST UNICRON PREPARED FOR.
FORGIVE ME.

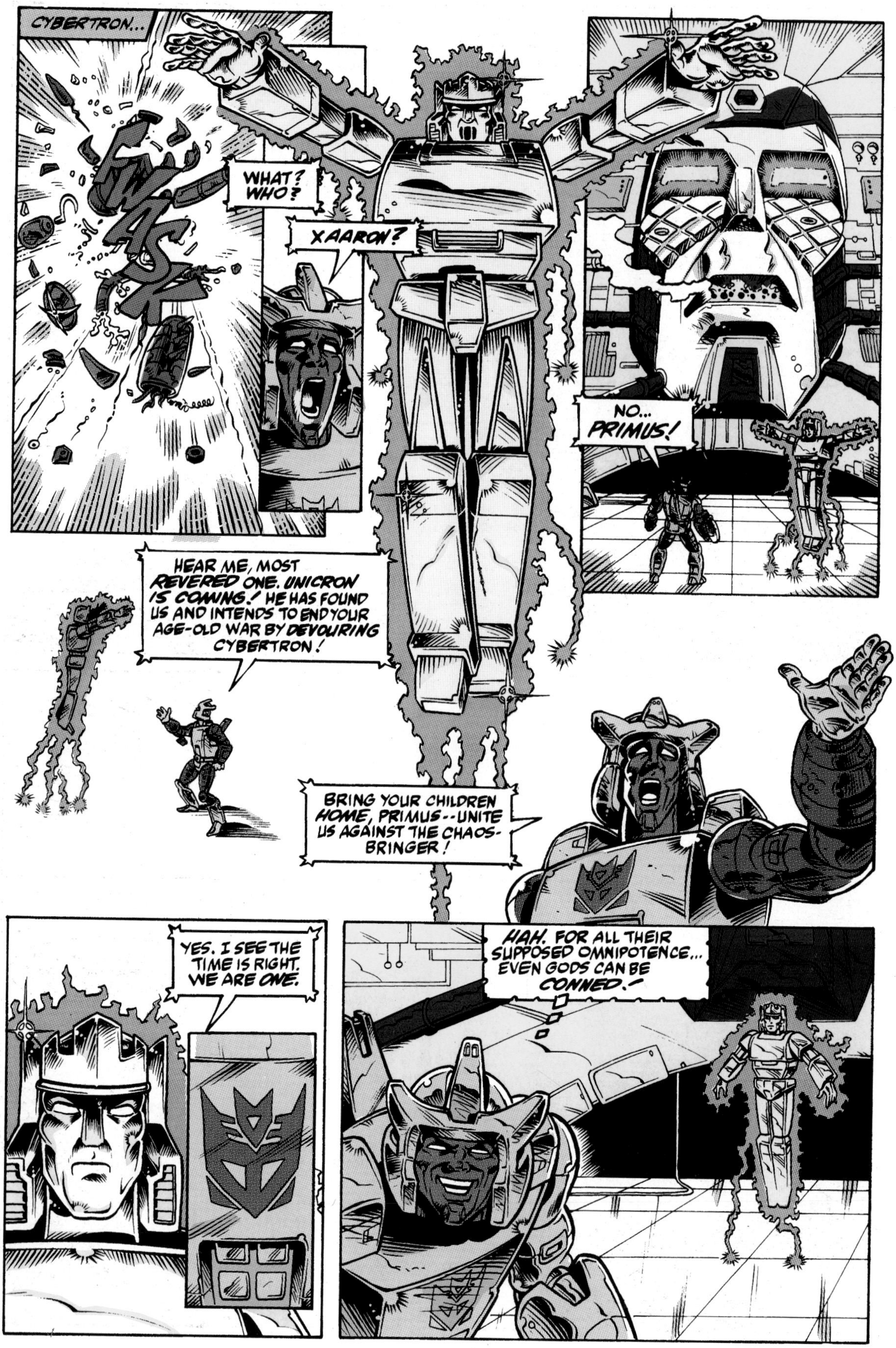
CYBERTRON...
CHHASSH
WHAT? WHO?
XAARON?
NO... PRIMUS!
HEAR ME, MOST REVERED ONE. UNICRON IS COMING! HE HAS FOUND US AND INTENDS TO END YOUR AGE-OLD WAR BY DEVOURING CYBERTRON!
BRING YOUR CHILDREN HOME, PRIMUS--UNITE US AGAINST THE CHAOS-BRINGER!
YES. I SEE THE TIME IS RIGHT. WE ARE ONE.
HAH. FOR ALL THEIR SUPPOSED OMNIPOTENCE... EVEN GODS CAN BE CONNED.!

ARE YOU SURE ABOUT THIS, SOUNDWAVE? SIDING WITH THE AUTOBOTS?
YES. I AM SURE.
FOR THE GOOD OF ALL TRANSFORMERS WE MUST UNITE OUR FORCES.
HEH. NOW IF ONLY WE COULD HYPNOTIZE ALL DECE--
PRIME? ARE YOU INJURED? THE HUMAN, SHE DID YOU PERMANENT DAMAGE?
UHH... NO. IT'S--
THEY... JUST VANISHED! ALL OF THEM!
NO, LOOK. THIS ONE'S STI--
AWW, MAN... HOW'M I SUPPOSED TO WRITE THIS ONE UP?

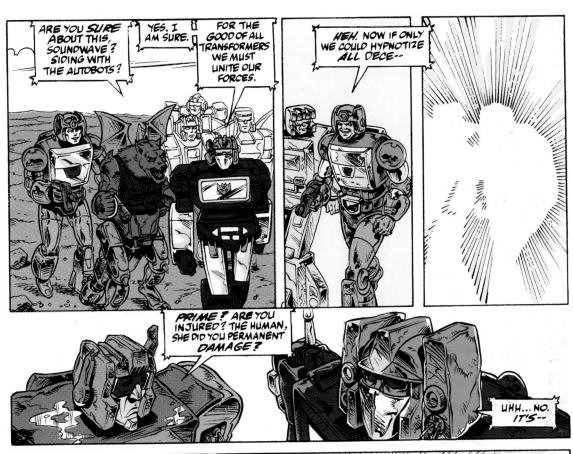

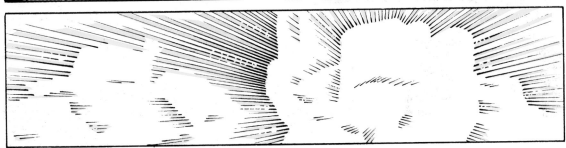

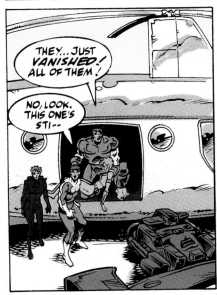

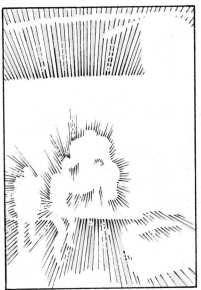

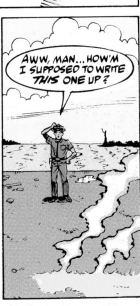

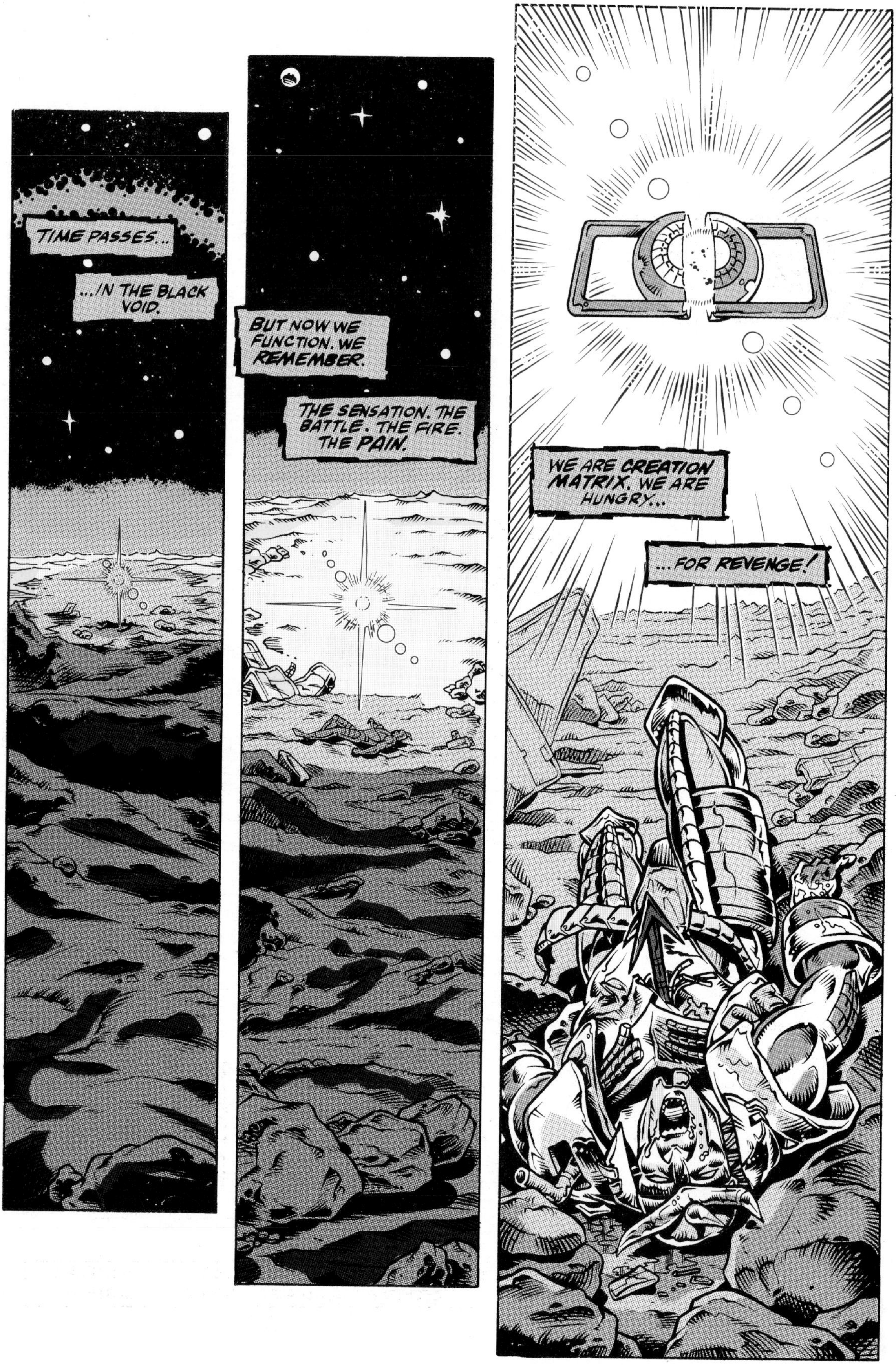

TIME PASSES...
...IN THE BLACK VOID.
BUT NOW WE FUNCTION. WE REMEMBER.
THE SENSATION. THE BATTLE. THE FIRE. THE PAIN.
WE ARE CREATION MATRIX. WE ARE HUNGRY...
...FOR REVENGE!

 EVERY *PLANET*, WHOLE GALAXIES, EVEN THE STUFF OF *SPACE* ITSELF -- GONE, DESTROYED... *CONSUMED!*

LEAVING ONLY--

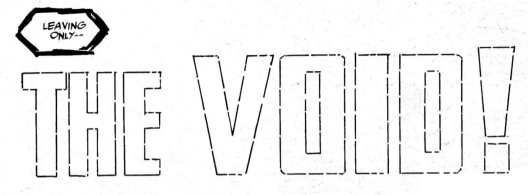

THE VOID!

Simon Furman	Andrew Wildman	Stephen Baskerville	Rick Parker	Nel Yomtov	Rob Tokar	Tom DeFalco
WRITER	PENCILER	INKER	LETTERER	COLORIST	NOBODY	NOTHING

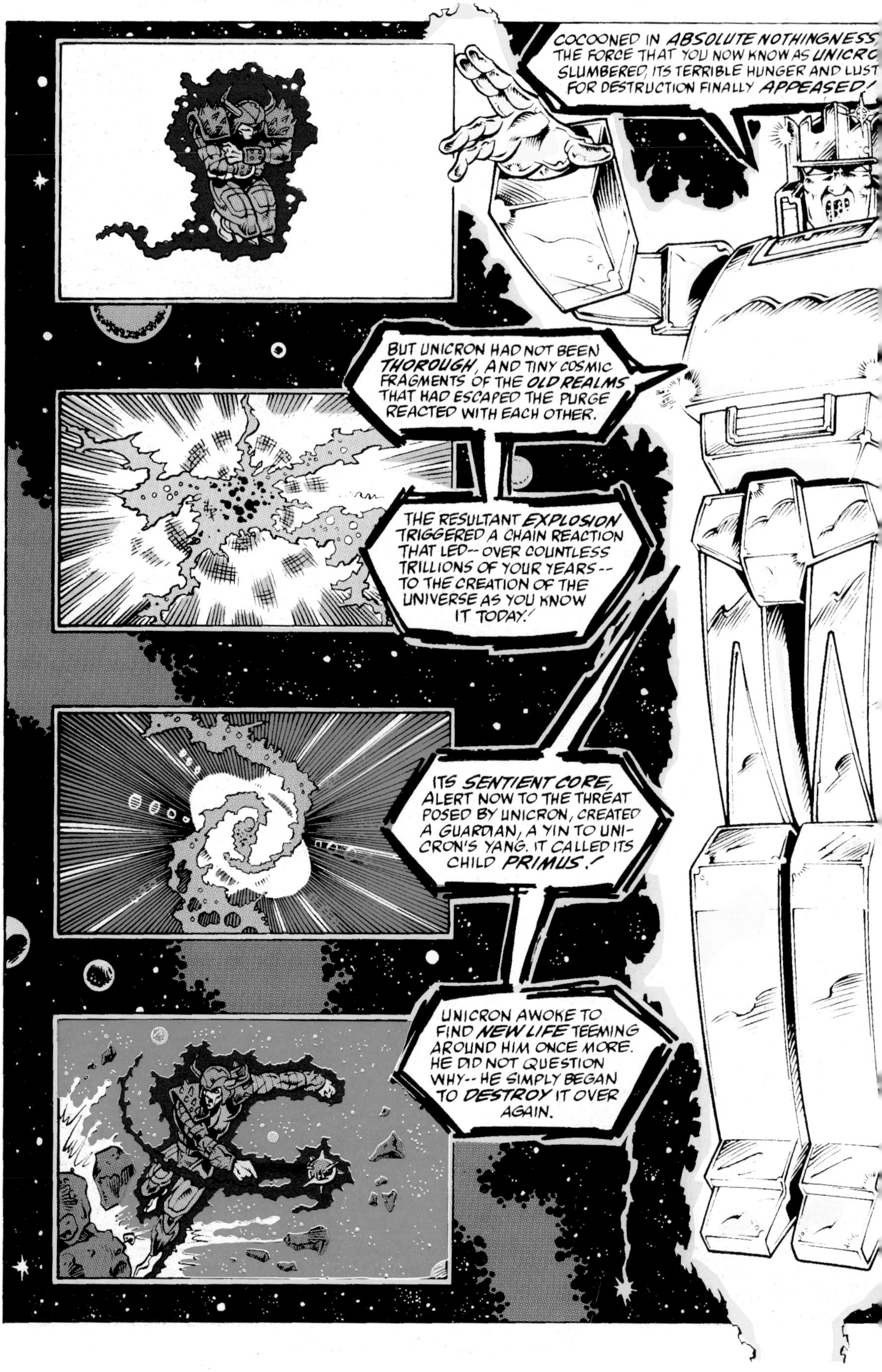
COCOONED IN ABSOLUTE NOTHINGNESS THE FORCE THAT YOU NOW KNOW AS UNICRON SLUMBERED, ITS TERRIBLE HUNGER AND LUST FOR DESTRUCTION FINALLY APPEASED!
BUT UNICRON HAD NOT BEEN THOROUGH, AND TINY COSMIC FRAGMENTS OF THE OLD REALMS THAT HAD ESCAPED THE PURGE REACTED WITH EACH OTHER.
THE RESULTANT EXPLOSION TRIGGERED A CHAIN REACTION THAT LED-- OVER COUNTLESS TRILLIONS OF YOUR YEARS -- TO THE CREATION OF THE UNIVERSE AS YOU KNOW IT TODAY!
ITS SENTIENT CORE, ALERT NOW TO THE THREAT POSED BY UNICRON, CREATED A GUARDIAN, A YIN TO UNICRON'S YANG. IT CALLED ITS CHILD PRIMUS!
UNICRON AWOKE TO FIND NEW LIFE TEEMING AROUND HIM ONCE MORE. HE DID NOT QUESTION WHY-- HE SIMPLY BEGAN TO DESTROY IT OVER AGAIN.

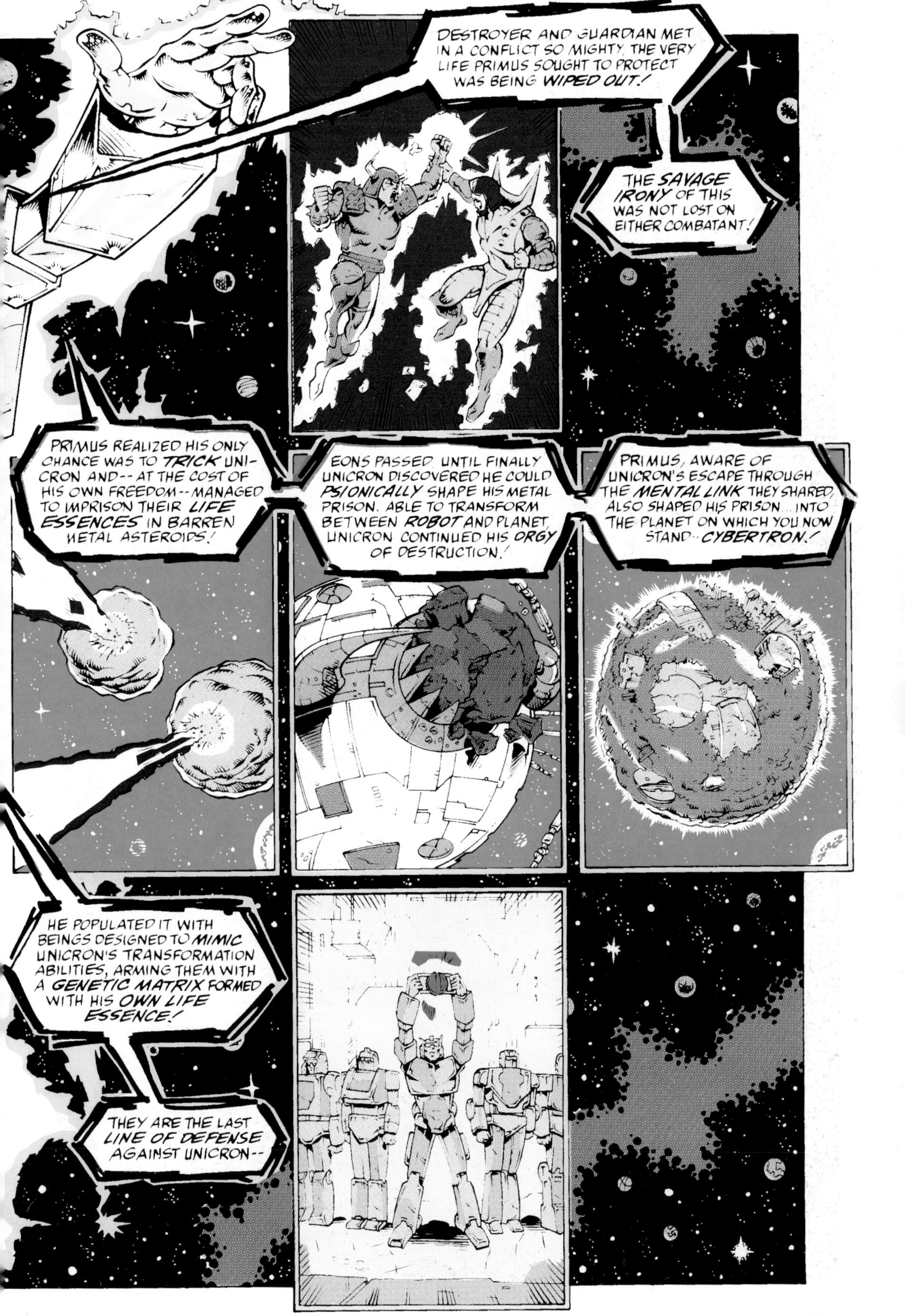
DESTROYER AND GUARDIAN MET IN A CONFLICT SO MIGHTY, THE VERY LIFE PRIMUS SOUGHT TO PROTECT WAS BEING WIPED OUT!
THE SAVAGE IRONY OF THIS WAS NOT LOST ON EITHER COMBATANT!
PRIMUS REALIZED HIS ONLY CHANCE WAS TO TRICK UNICRON AND-- AT THE COST OF HIS OWN FREEDOM--MANAGED TO IMPRISON THEIR LIFE ESSENCES IN BARREN METAL ASTEROIDS!
EONS PASSED, UNTIL FINALLY UNICRON DISCOVERED HE COULD PSIONICALLY SHAPE HIS METAL PRISON. ABLE TO TRANSFORM BETWEEN ROBOT AND PLANET, UNICRON CONTINUED HIS ORGY OF DESTRUCTION!
PRIMUS, AWARE OF UNICRON'S ESCAPE THROUGH THE MENTAL LINK THEY SHARED, ALSO SHAPED HIS PRISON... INTO THE PLANET ON WHICH YOU NOW STAND--CYBERTRON!
HE POPULATED IT WITH BEINGS DESIGNED TO MIMIC UNICRON'S TRANSFORMATION ABILITIES, ARMING THEM WITH A GENETIC MATRIX FORMED WITH HIS OWN LIFE ESSENCE!
THEY ARE THE LAST LINE OF DEFENSE AGAINST UNICRON--

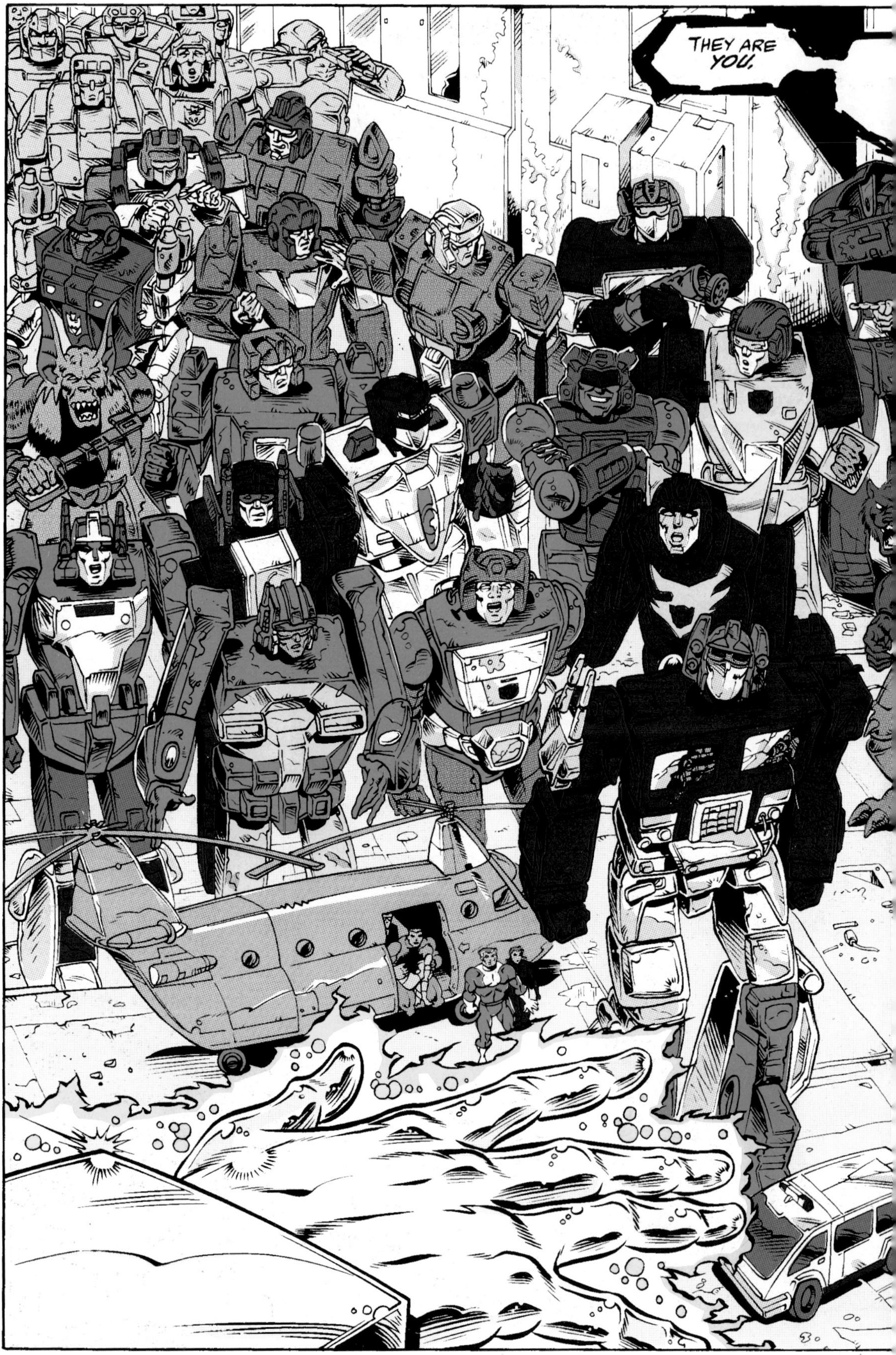
THEY ARE YOU.

THEY ARE
TRANSFORMERS

THE *CIVIL WAR* THAT SPLIT YOU INTO *AUTOBOT* AND *DECEPTICON* BROKE THE LINE. ONLY *TOGETHER*, UNITED AS ONE FORCE FOR GOOD CAN YOU STAND AGAINST THE CHAOS-BRINGER!

I SHUT MYSELF DOWN, *HID* MYSELF. BUT THE HIDING IS *OVER* ; UNICRON HAS FOUND ME. UNLESS OLD ENMITIES ARE BURIED, THE LINE RE-FORMED-- THE UNIVERSE IS *DOOMED*.

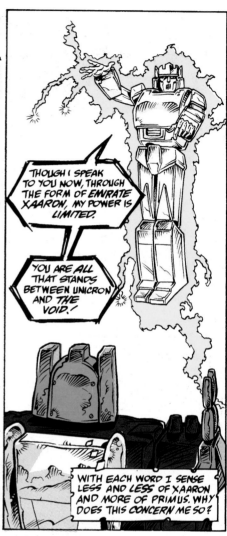

THOUGH I SPEAK TO YOU NOW, THROUGH THE FORM OF *EMIRATE XAARON*, MY POWER IS LIMITED.

YOU ARE *ALL* THAT STANDS BETWEEN UNICRON AND *THE VOID*!

WITH EACH WORD I SENSE LESS AND *LESS* OF XAARON AND *MORE* OF PRIMUS. WHY DOES THIS *CONCERN* ME SO?

WHY DOES IT FEEL SO WRONG?

OPTIMUS PRIME--

-- YOU WILL *LEAD* MY CHILDREN AGAINST UNICRON!

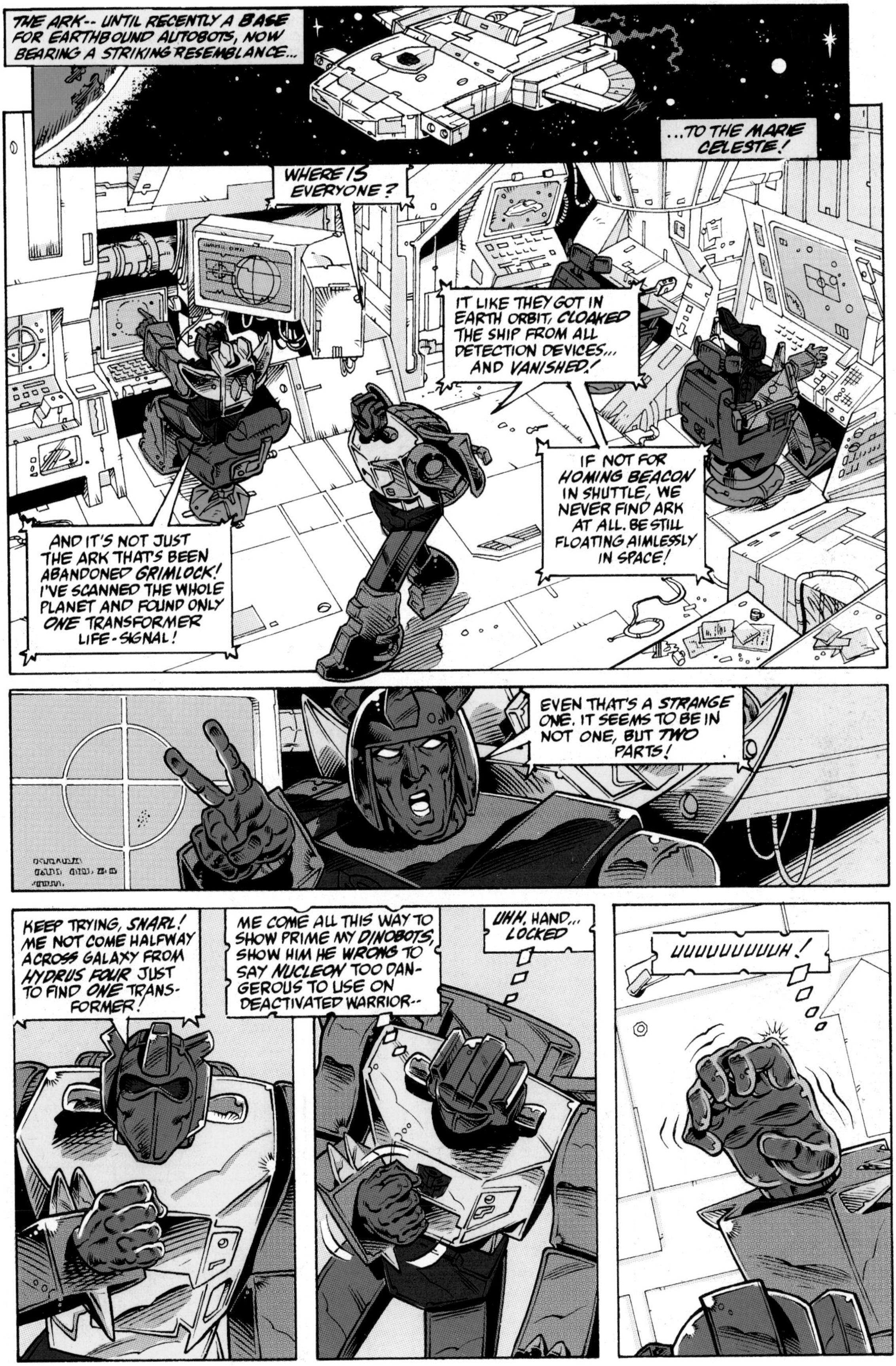
THE ARK-- UNTIL RECENTLY A BASE FOR EARTHBOUND AUTOBOTS, NOW BEARING A STRIKING RESEMBLANCE...
...TO THE MARIE CELESTE!
WHERE IS EVERYONE?
IT LIKE THEY GOT IN EARTH ORBIT, CLOAKED THE SHIP FROM ALL DETECTION DEVICES... AND VANISHED!
IF NOT FOR HOMING BEACON IN SHUTTLE, WE NEVER FIND ARK AT ALL. BE STILL FLOATING AIMLESSLY IN SPACE!
AND IT'S NOT JUST THE ARK THAT'S BEEN ABANDONED GRIMLOCK! I'VE SCANNED THE WHOLE PLANET AND FOUND ONLY ONE TRANSFORMER LIFE-SIGNAL!
EVEN THAT'S A STRANGE ONE. IT SEEMS TO BE IN NOT ONE, BUT TWO PARTS!
KEEP TRYING, SNARL! ME NOT COME HALFWAY ACROSS GALAXY FROM HYDRUS FOUR JUST TO FIND ONE TRANSFORMER!
ME COME ALL THIS WAY TO SHOW PRIME MY DINOBOTS, SHOW HIM HE WRONG TO SAY NUCLEON TOO DANGEROUS TO USE ON DEACTIVATED WARRIOR--
UHH, HAND... LOCKED
UUUUUUUUUH!

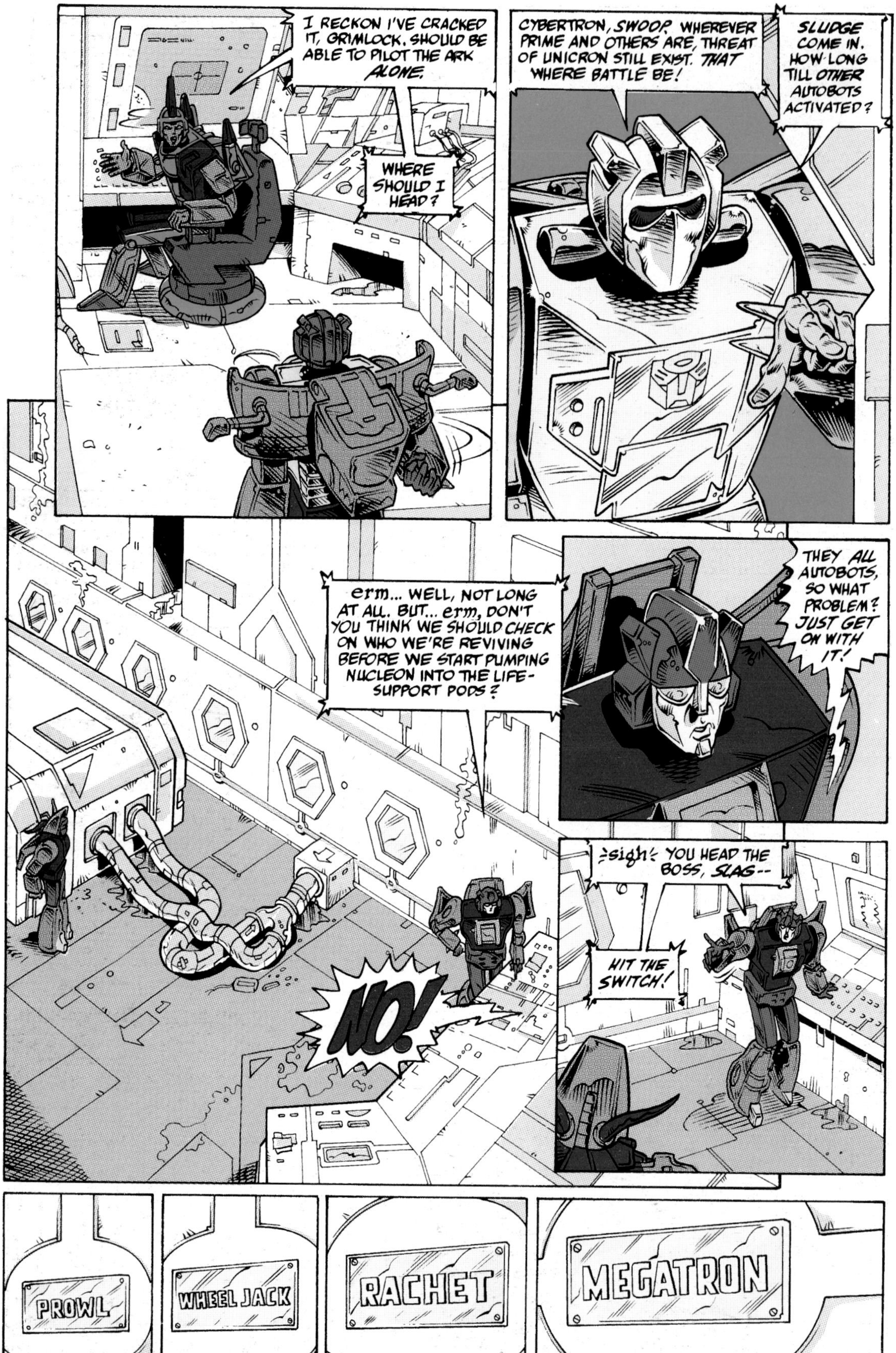
I RECKON I'VE CRACKED IT, GRIMLOCK. SHOULD BE ABLE TO PILOT THE ARK ALONE.
WHERE SHOULD I HEAD?
CYBERTRON, SWOOP. WHEREVER PRIME AND OTHERS ARE, THREAT OF UNICRON STILL EXIST. THAT WHERE BATTLE BE!
SLUDGE COME IN. HOW LONG TILL OTHER AUTOBOTS ACTIVATED?
erm... WELL, NOT LONG AT ALL. BUT... erm, DON'T YOU THINK WE SHOULD CHECK ON WHO WE'RE REVIVING BEFORE WE START PUMPING NUCLEON INTO THE LIFE-SUPPORT PODS?
THEY ALL AUTOBOTS, SO WHAT PROBLEM? JUST GET ON WITH IT!
-sigh- YOU HEAD THE BOSS, SLAG--
HIT THE SWITCH!
NO!
PROWL
WHEEL JACK
RACHET
MEGATRON

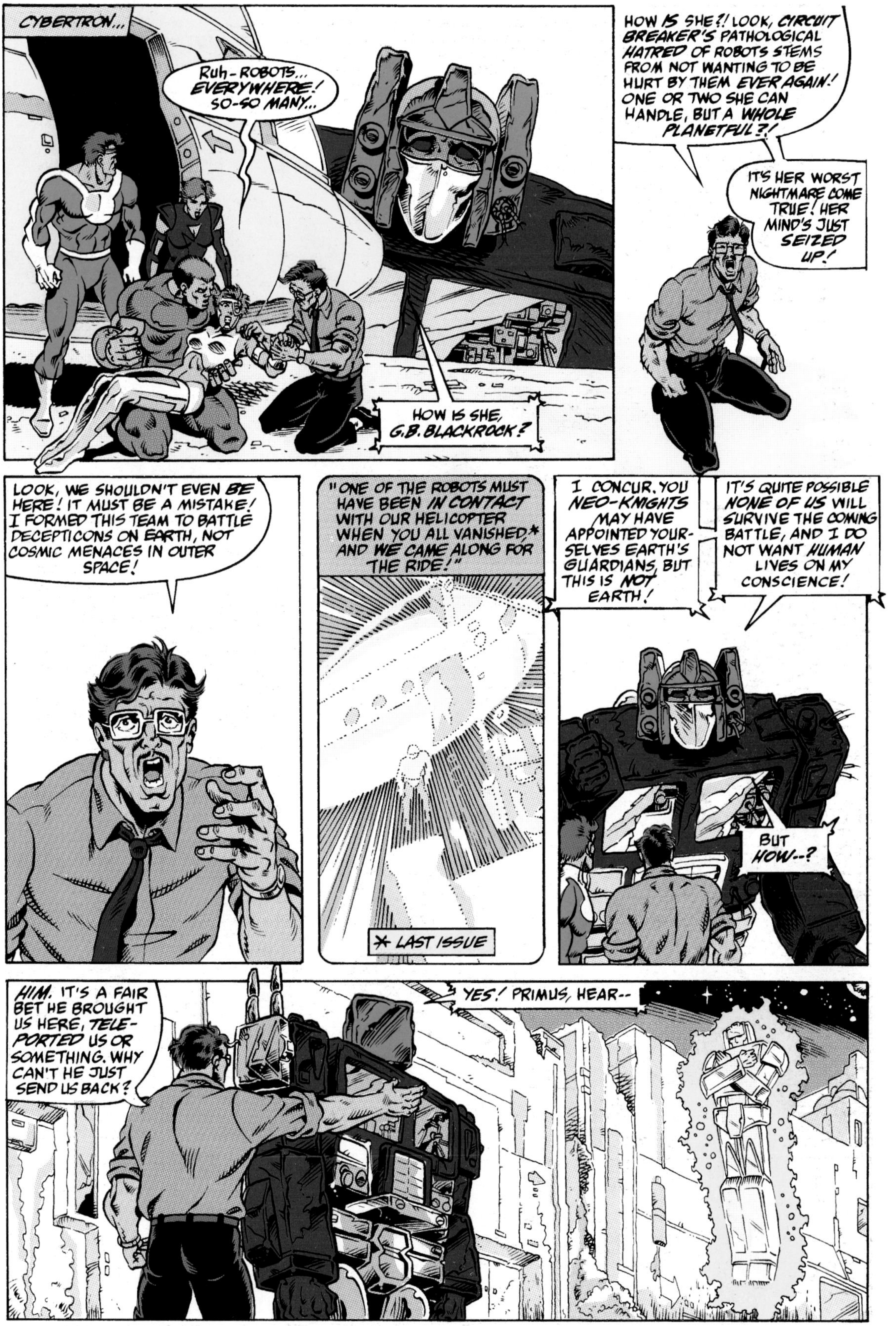
CYBERTRON...
Ruh-ROBOTS... EVERYWHERE! SO-SO MANY...
HOW IS SHE, G.B. BLACKROCK?
HOW IS SHE?! LOOK, CIRCUIT BREAKER'S PATHOLOGICAL HATRED OF ROBOTS STEMS FROM NOT WANTING TO BE HURT BY THEM EVER AGAIN! ONE OR TWO SHE CAN HANDLE, BUT A WHOLE PLANETFUL?!
IT'S HER WORST NIGHTMARE COME TRUE! HER MIND'S JUST SEIZED UP!
LOOK, WE SHOULDN'T EVEN BE HERE! IT MUST BE A MISTAKE! I FORMED THIS TEAM TO BATTLE DECEPTICONS ON EARTH, NOT COSMIC MENACES IN OUTER SPACE!
"ONE OF THE ROBOTS MUST HAVE BEEN IN CONTACT WITH OUR HELICOPTER WHEN YOU ALL VANISHED* AND WE CAME ALONG FOR THE RIDE!"
* LAST ISSUE
I CONCUR. YOU NEO-KNIGHTS MAY HAVE APPOINTED YOURSELVES EARTH'S GUARDIANS, BUT THIS IS NOT EARTH!
IT'S QUITE POSSIBLE NONE OF US WILL SURVIVE THE COMING BATTLE, AND I DO NOT WANT HUMAN LIVES ON MY CONSCIENCE!
BUT HOW--?
HIM. IT'S A FAIR BET HE BROUGHT US HERE, TELEPORTED US OR SOMETHING. WHY CAN'T HE JUST SEND US BACK?
YES! PRIMUS, HEAR--

--ME?

HAHAHA! SEEMS LIKE YOUR 'GOD' ISN'T INTERESTED IN US *MERE MORTALS*, EY?

IT WOULD SEEM NOT.

WHICH LEADS ONE TO WONDER... EXACTLY WHAT SORT OF 'GOD' THIS PRIMUS *TRULY IS!*

NEARBY...

THE LONG *SLEEP* IS OVER, THE HOUR DRAWS NEAR! OUR *TRUE LORD* APPROACHES!

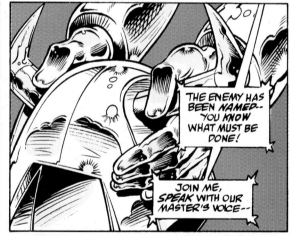

THE ENEMY HAS BEEN *NAMED*-- YOU KNOW WHAT MUST BE DONE!

JOIN ME, *SPEAK* WITH OUR MASTER'S VOICE--

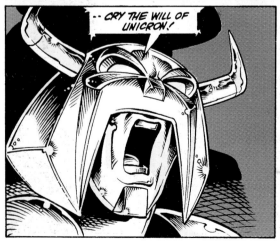

-- CRY THE WILL OF *UNICRON!*

DEATH TO OPTIMUS PRIME!

DEATH TO OPTIMUS PRIME!

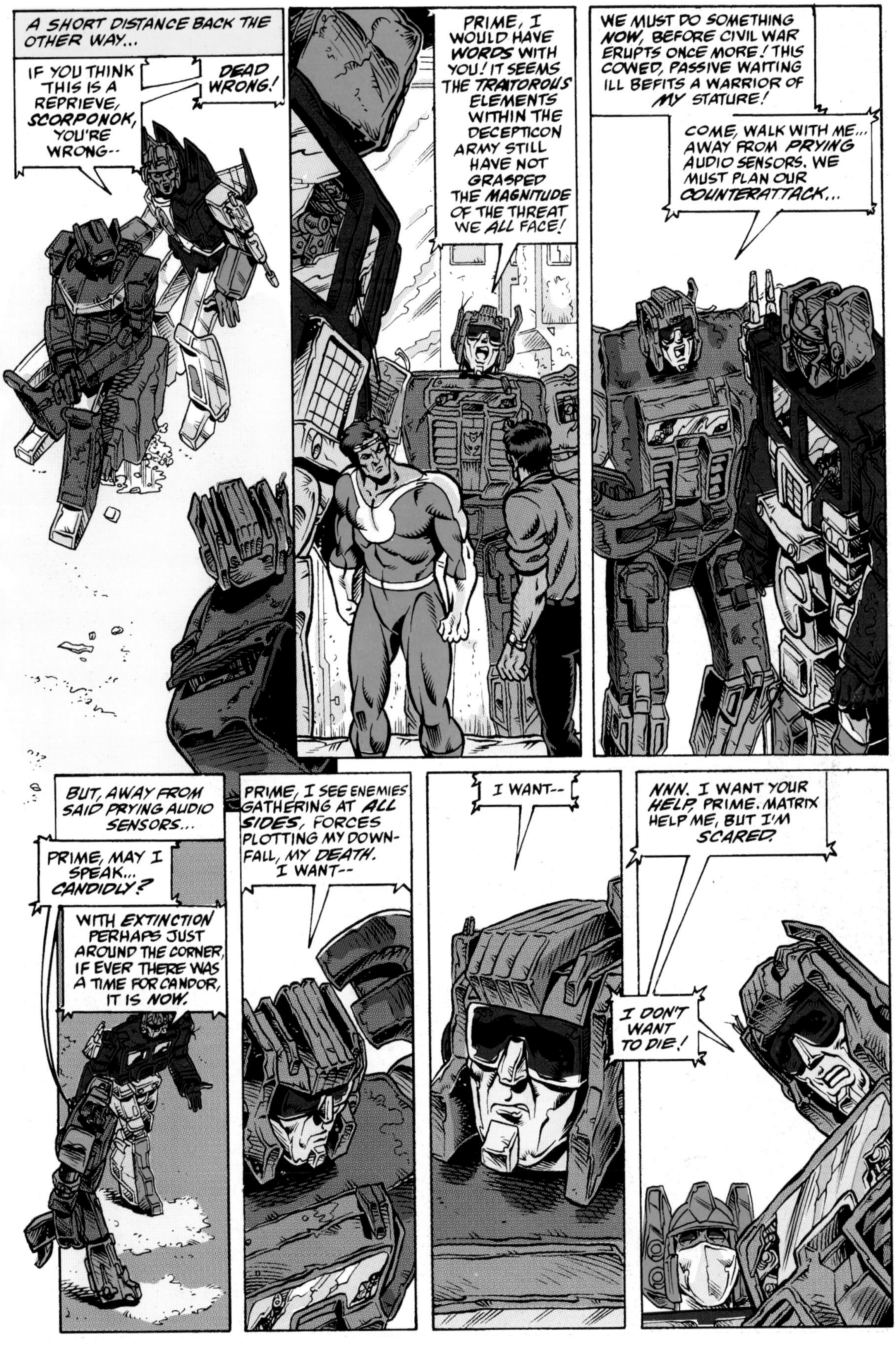
A SHORT DISTANCE BACK THE OTHER WAY...
IF YOU THINK THIS IS A REPRIEVE, SCORPONOK, YOU'RE WRONG--
DEAD WRONG!
PRIME, I WOULD HAVE WORDS WITH YOU! IT SEEMS THE TRAITOROUS ELEMENTS WITHIN THE DECEPTICON ARMY STILL HAVE NOT GRASPED THE MAGNITUDE OF THE THREAT WE ALL FACE!
WE MUST DO SOMETHING NOW, BEFORE CIVIL WAR ERUPTS ONCE MORE! THIS COWED, PASSIVE WAITING ILL BEFITS A WARRIOR OF MY STATURE!
COME, WALK WITH ME... AWAY FROM PRYING AUDIO SENSORS. WE MUST PLAN OUR COUNTERATTACK...
BUT, AWAY FROM SAID PRYING AUDIO SENSORS...
PRIME, MAY I SPEAK... CANDIDLY?
WITH EXTINCTION PERHAPS JUST AROUND THE CORNER, IF EVER THERE WAS A TIME FOR CANDOR, IT IS NOW.
PRIME, I SEE ENEMIES GATHERING AT ALL SIDES, FORCES PLOTTING MY DOWNFALL, MY DEATH. I WANT--
I WANT--
NNN. I WANT YOUR HELP, PRIME. MATRIX HELP ME, BUT I'M SCARED.
I DON'T WANT TO DIE!

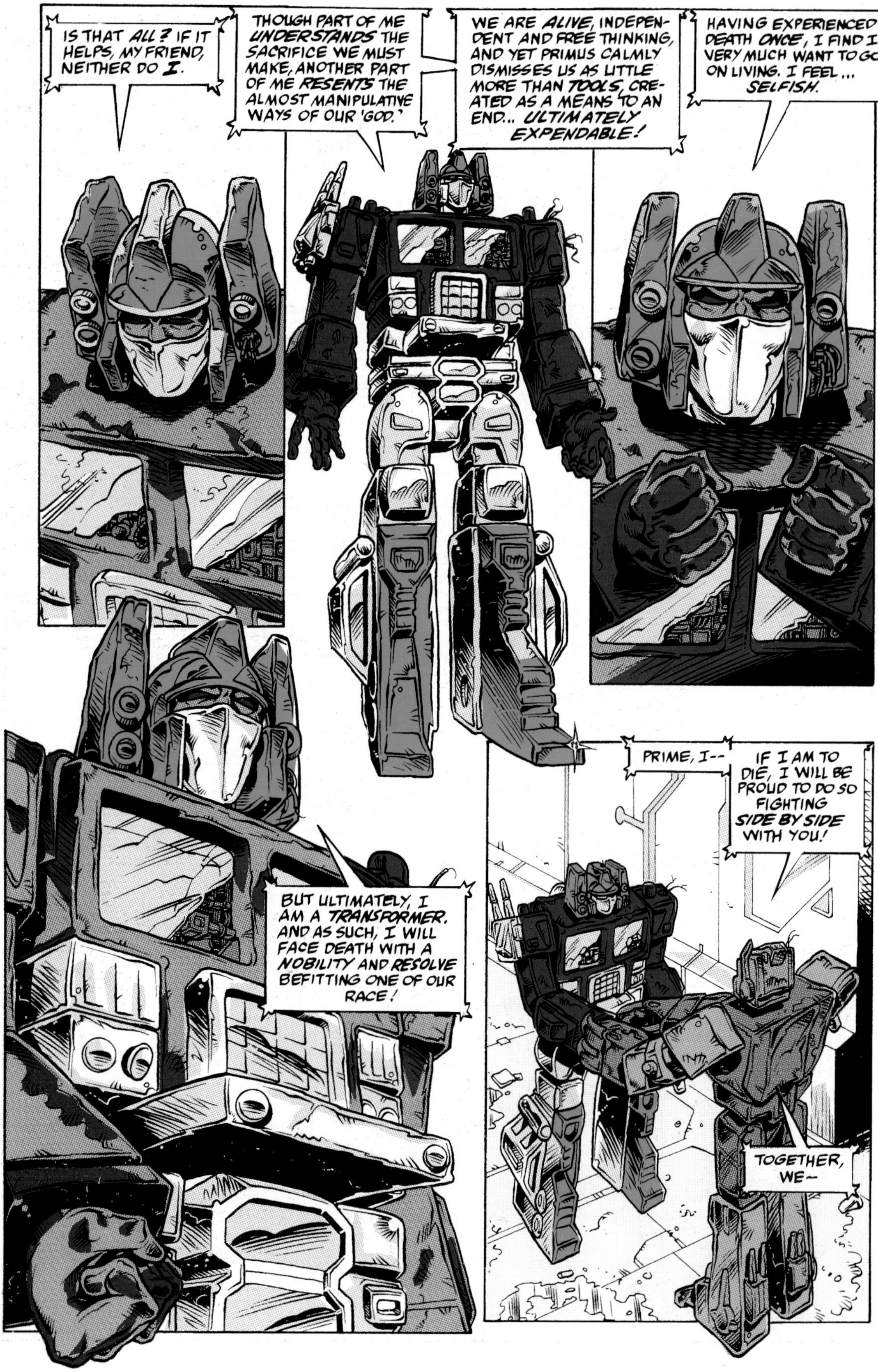
IS THAT ALL? IF IT HELPS, MY FRIEND, NEITHER DO I.
THOUGH PART OF ME UNDERSTANDS THE SACRIFICE WE MUST MAKE, ANOTHER PART OF ME RESENTS THE ALMOST MANIPULATIVE WAYS OF OUR 'GOD.'
WE ARE ALIVE, INDEPENDENT AND FREE THINKING, AND YET PRIMUS CALMLY DISMISSES US AS LITTLE MORE THAN TOOLS, CREATED AS A MEANS TO AN END... ULTIMATELY EXPENDABLE!
HAVING EXPERIENCED DEATH ONCE, I FIND I VERY MUCH WANT TO GO ON LIVING. I FEEL... SELFISH.
BUT ULTIMATELY, I AM A TRANSFORMER. AND AS SUCH, I WILL FACE DEATH WITH A NOBILITY AND RESOLVE BEFITTING ONE OF OUR RACE!
PRIME, I--
IF I AM TO DIE, I WILL BE PROUD TO DO SO FIGHTING SIDE BY SIDE WITH YOU!
TOGETHER, WE--

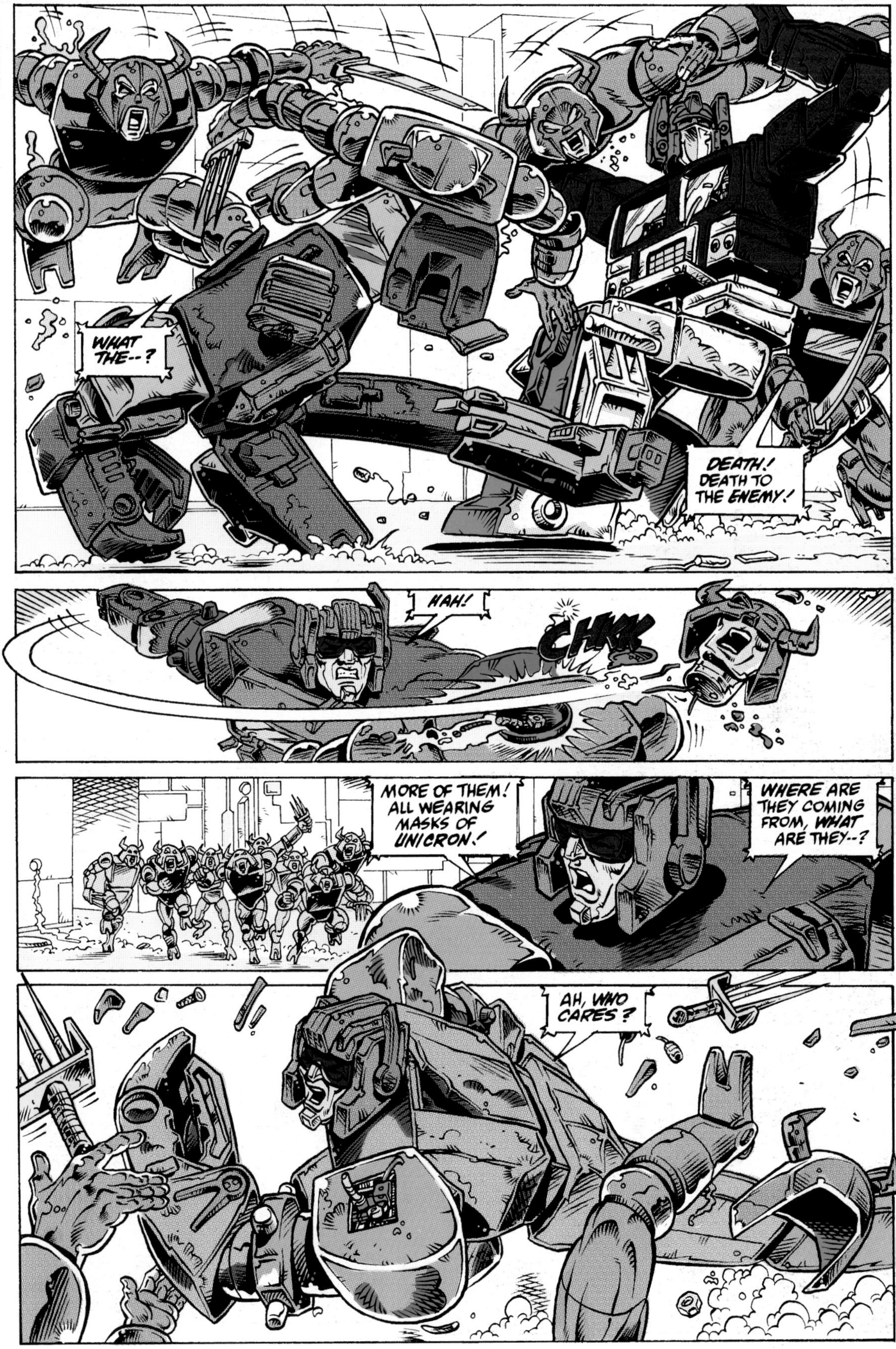

WHAT THE--?
DEATH! DEATH TO THE ENEMY!
HAH!
CHKK
MORE OF THEM! ALL WEARING MASKS OF UNICRON!
WHERE ARE THEY COMING FROM, WHAT ARE THEY--?
AH, WHO CARES?

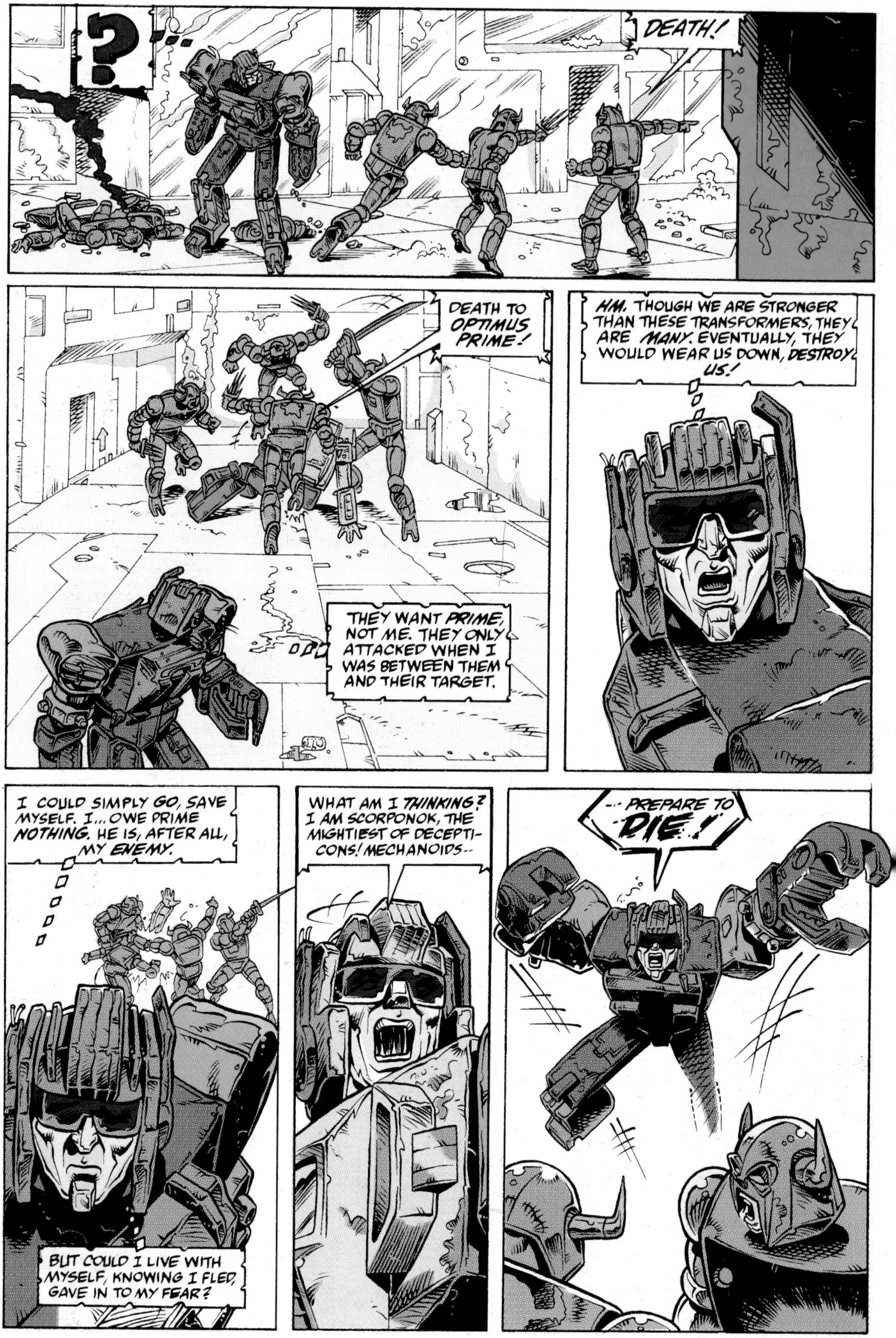
?
DEATH!
DEATH TO OPTIMUS PRIME!
THEY WANT PRIME, NOT ME. THEY ONLY ATTACKED WHEN I WAS BETWEEN THEM AND THEIR TARGET.
HM. THOUGH WE ARE STRONGER THAN THESE TRANSFORMERS, THEY ARE MANY. EVENTUALLY, THEY WOULD WEAR US DOWN, DESTROY US!
I COULD SIMPLY GO, SAVE MYSELF. I... OWE PRIME NOTHING. HE IS, AFTER ALL, MY ENEMY.
BUT COULD I LIVE WITH MYSELF, KNOWING I FLED, GAVE IN TO MY FEAR?
WHAT AM I THINKING? I AM SCORPONOK, THE MIGHTIEST OF DECEPTICONS! MECHANOIDS--
--PREPARE TO DIE!

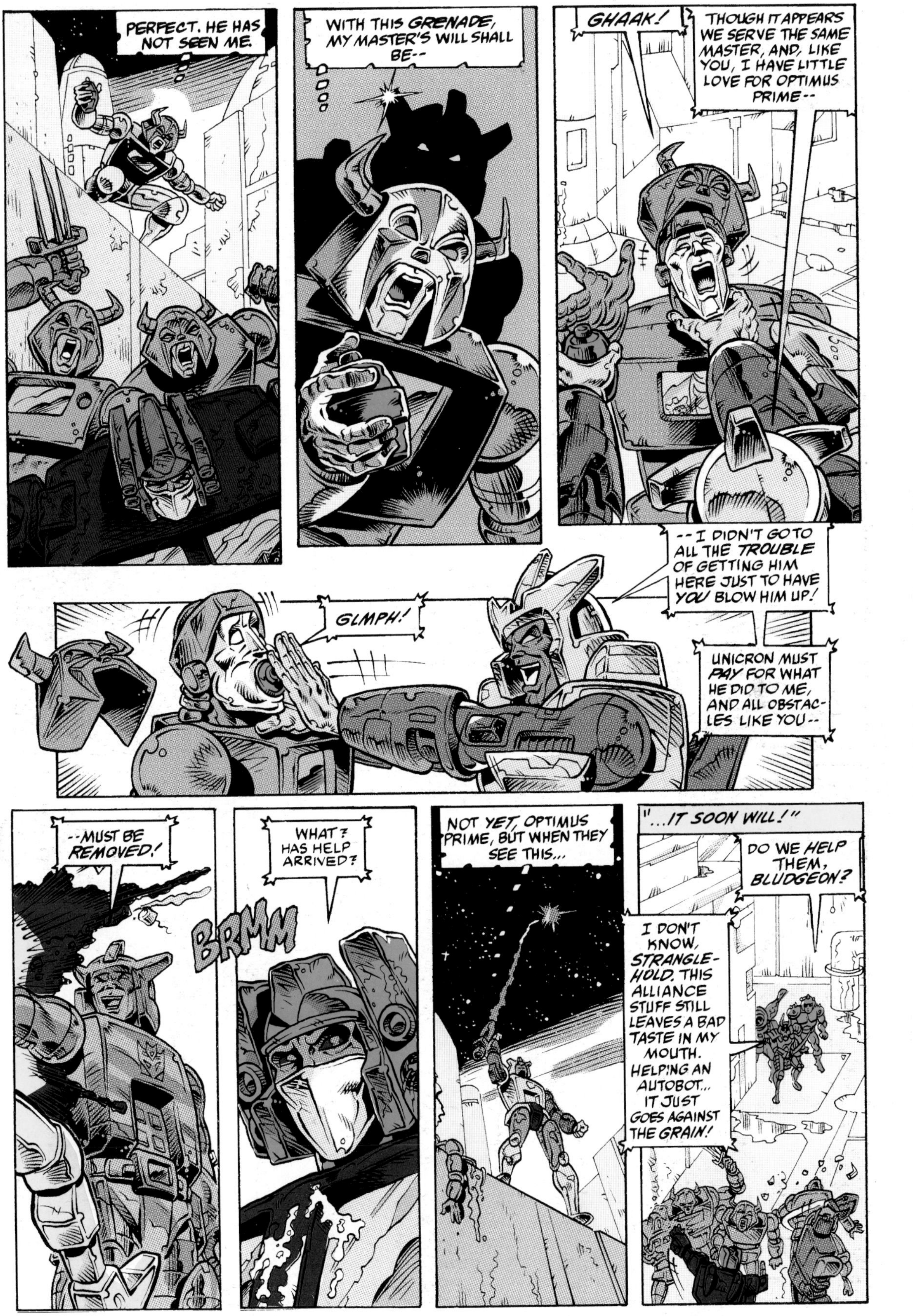
PERFECT. HE HAS NOT SEEN ME.
WITH THIS GRENADE, MY MASTER'S WILL SHALL BE--
GHAAK!
THOUGH IT APPEARS WE SERVE THE SAME MASTER, AND, LIKE YOU, I HAVE LITTLE LOVE FOR OPTIMUS PRIME--
--I DIDN'T GO TO ALL THE TROUBLE OF GETTING HIM HERE JUST TO HAVE YOU BLOW HIM UP!
GLMPH!
UNICRON MUST PAY FOR WHAT HE DID TO ME, AND ALL OBSTACLES LIKE YOU--
--MUST BE REMOVED!
BRMM
WHAT? HAS HELP ARRIVED?
NOT YET, OPTIMUS PRIME, BUT WHEN THEY SEE THIS...
"...IT SOON WILL!"
DO WE HELP THEM, BLUDGEON?
I DON'T KNOW, STRANGLEHOLD. THIS ALLIANCE STUFF STILL LEAVES A BAD TASTE IN MY MOUTH. HELPING AN AUTOBOT... IT JUST GOES AGAINST THE GRAIN!

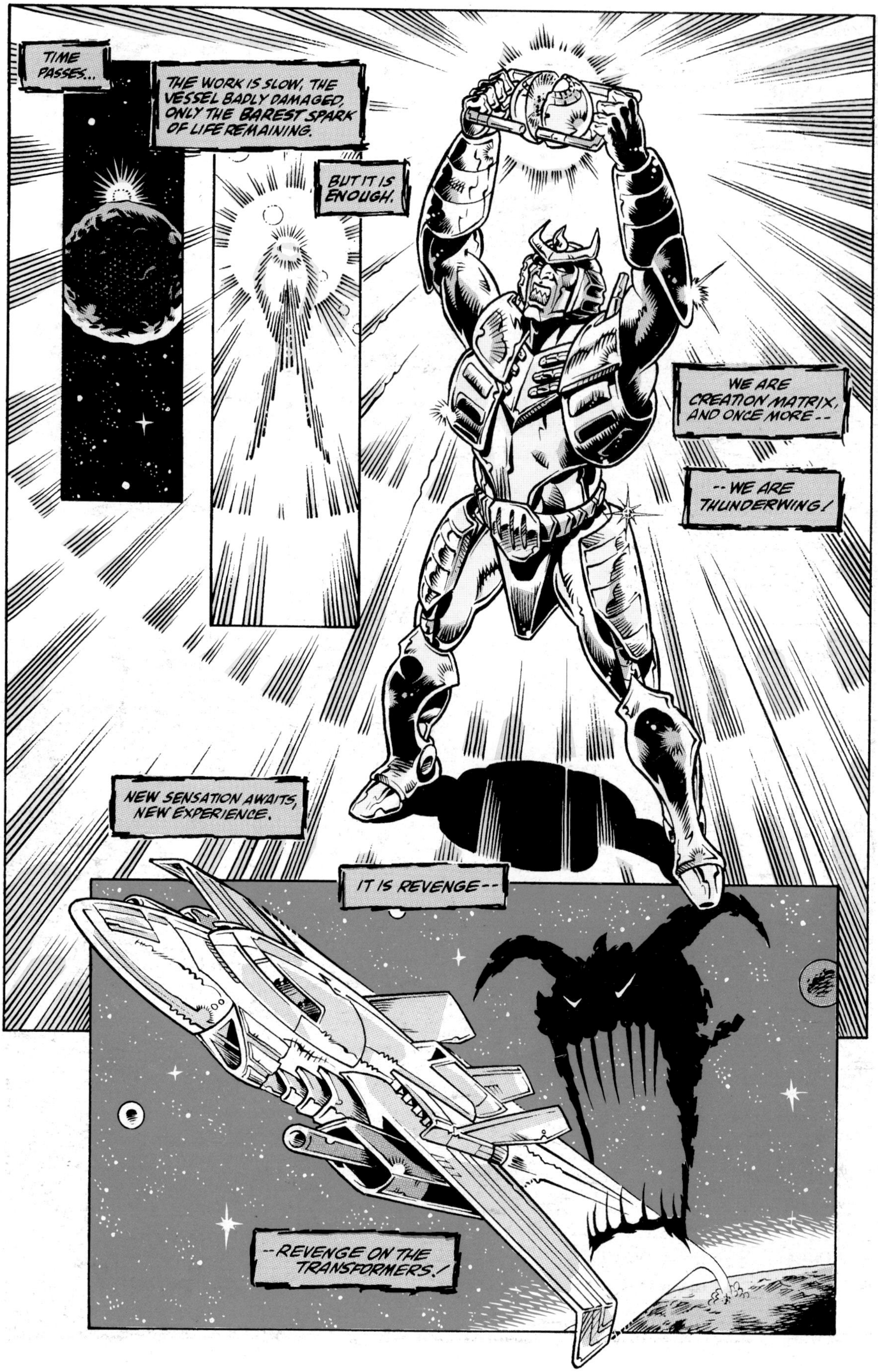
TIME PASSES...
THE WORK IS SLOW, THE VESSEL BADLY DAMAGED, ONLY THE BAREST SPARK OF LIFE REMAINING.
BUT IT IS ENOUGH.
WE ARE CREATION MATRIX, AND ONCE MORE--
--WE ARE THUNDERWING!
NEW SENSATION AWAITS, NEW EXPERIENCE.
IT IS REVENGE--
--REVENGE ON THE TRANSFORMERS!

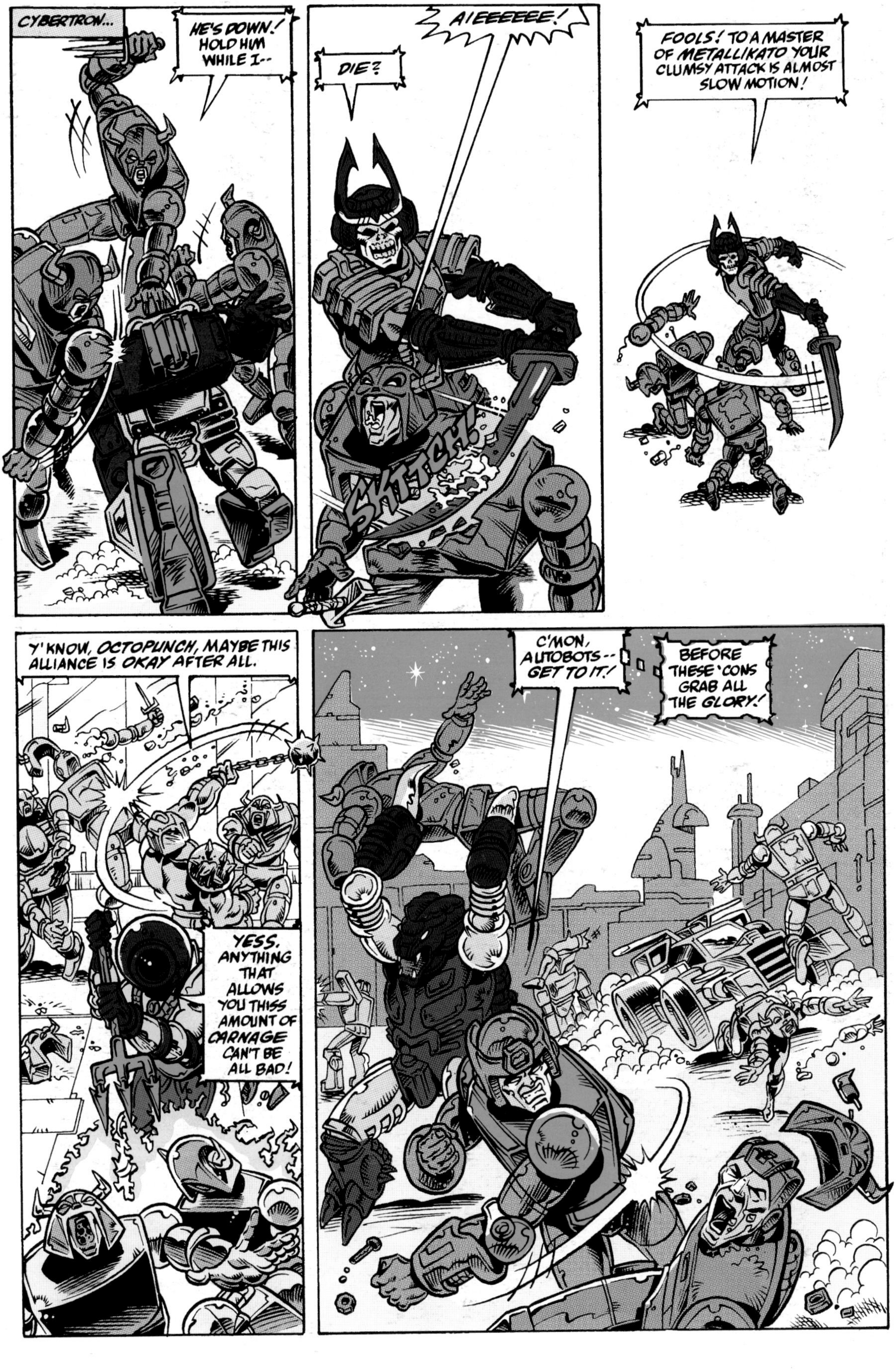
CYBERTRON...
HE'S DOWN! HOLD HIM WHILE I--
DIE?
AIEEEEEEE!
SKTTCH!
FOOLS! TO A MASTER OF METALLIKATO YOUR CLUMSY ATTACK IS ALMOST SLOW MOTION!
Y' KNOW, OCTOPUNCH, MAYBE THIS ALLIANCE IS OKAY AFTER ALL.
YESS. ANYTHING THAT ALLOWS YOU THISS AMOUNT OF CARNAGE CAN'T BE ALL BAD!
C'MON, AUTOBOTS -- GET TO IT!
BEFORE THESE 'CONS GRAB ALL THE GLORY!

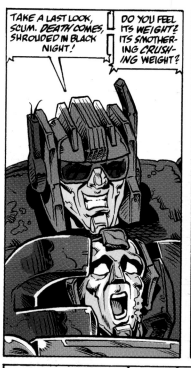

TAKE A LAST LOOK, SCUM. *DEATH* COMES, SHROUDED IN BLACK NIGHT!

DO YOU FEEL ITS *WEIGHT?* ITS SMOTHER- ING *CRUSH- ING* WEIGHT?

ENOUGH! RELEASE HIM, SCORPONOK-- RELEASE HIM *NOW!*

WHAT?

THE BATTLE IS *OVER,* DONE. THE VICTORY, AS SUCH, IS OURS.

NO, NOT UNTIL THE LAST ENEMY HAS BEEN DESTROYED *UTTERLY!*

DO SO AND WE ARE *DOOMED!* IF WHAT I BELIEVE IS TRUE, THESE TRANSFORMERS WERE *POSSESSED,* FORCED TO DO THIS THING. THEY ARE *VICTIMS!*

HERE TODAY, FOR PERHAPS THE FIRST TIME, AUTOBOT AND DECEPTICON FOUGHT SIDE BY SIDE, UNITED AGAINST A COMMON ENEMY. *THAT* IS A *MIRACLE!*

BUT IF WE LET THE BATTLE RAGE BLIND US TO *MERCY* AND COM- PASSION, IT IS ALL FOR *NOTHING!* WHATEVER THE OUTCOME -- WE WILL HAVE *LOST!*

YOU ARE INDEED *WISE,* OPTIMUS PRIME. *POSSESSED* IS EXACTLY WHAT THESE TRANS- FORMERS WERE.

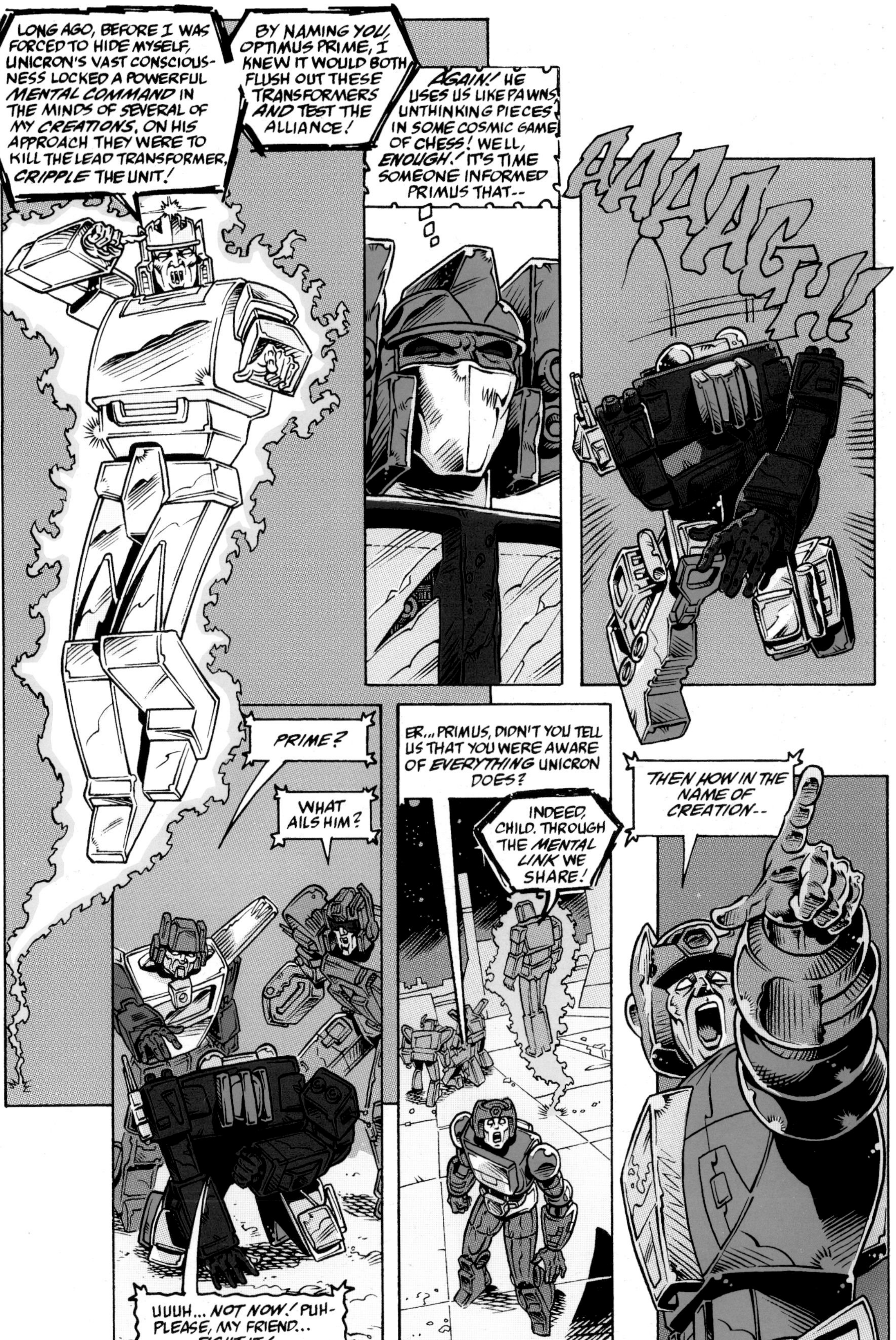
LONG AGO, BEFORE I WAS FORCED TO HIDE MYSELF, UNICRON'S VAST CONSCIOUSNESS LOCKED A POWERFUL MENTAL COMMAND IN THE MINDS OF SEVERAL OF MY CREATIONS. ON HIS APPROACH THEY WERE TO KILL THE LEAD TRANSFORMER, CRIPPLE THE UNIT!
BY NAMING YOU, OPTIMUS PRIME, I KNEW IT WOULD BOTH FLUSH OUT THESE TRANSFORMERS AND TEST THE ALLIANCE!
AGAIN! HE USES US LIKE PAWNS, UNTHINKING PIECES IN SOME COSMIC GAME OF CHESS! WELL, ENOUGH! IT'S TIME SOMEONE INFORMED PRIMUS THAT--
AAAAGH!
PRIME?
WHAT AILS HIM?
UUUH... NOT NOW! PUH-PLEASE, MY FRIEND... FIGHT IT!
ER... PRIMUS, DIDN'T YOU TELL US THAT YOU WERE AWARE OF EVERYTHING UNICRON DOES?
INDEED, CHILD. THROUGH THE MENTAL LINK WE SHARE!
THEN HOW IN THE NAME OF CREATION--

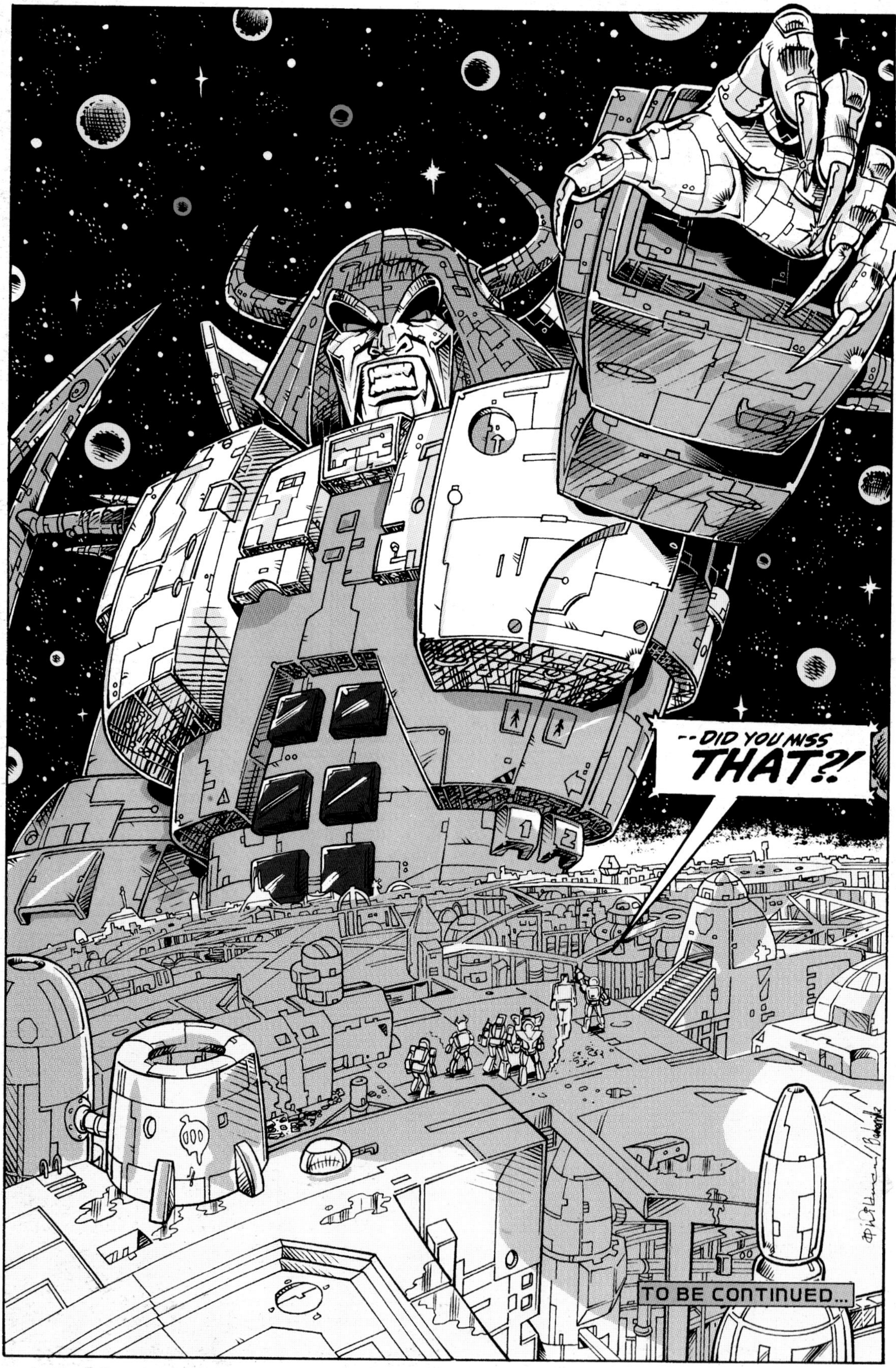

--DID YOU MISS THAT?!
TO BE CONTINUED...

Writer
Simon Furman

Penciller
Andrew Wildman

Inkers
Stephen Baskerville, Harry Candelario & Bob Lewis

Letterer
Rick Parker

Colourist
Nel Yomtov

Original series editors
Rob Tokar & Don Daley

SIMON FURMAN has written too many *Transformers* stories to easily count. His first script work appeared in the kids' horror comic *Scream*, and his long relationship with *Transformers* began with issue #13 of the UK comic. Since then, Furman's comics work has included *Transformers* (US), *Transformers: Generation 2*, *Death's Head*, *Alpha Flight* and *Turok*. Furman now works primarily in animation, and has scripted episodes for *Beast Wars*, *The Roswell Conspiracies*, *Dan Dare* and *X-Men: Evolution*.

ANDREW WILDMAN began his comics career at Marvel UK, where he drew *Galaxy Rangers*, *Thundercats* and, of course, *Transformers*. Following his run on *Transformers* (US) he drew *GI Joe*, *X-Men Adventures*, *Venom*, *Spider-Man 2099* and *Robocop*. Other work includes designs and comic strips for UK hero *Action Man*. Wildman now designs computer games for the UK-based company Rebellion.

#69 "EYE OF THE STORM"

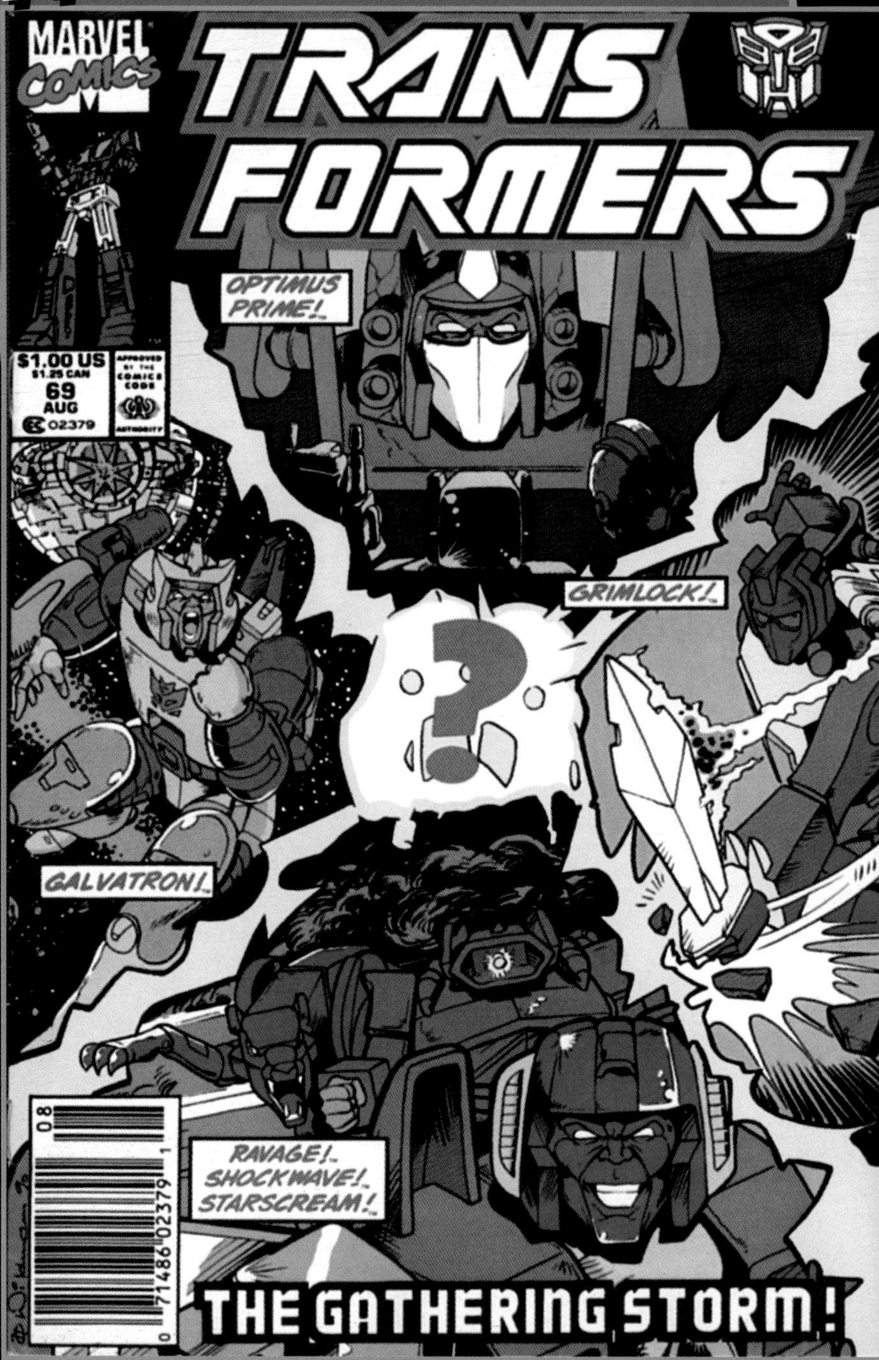

MARVEL COMICS
TRANSFORMERS
OPTIMUS PRIME!
$1.00 US $1.25 CAN 69 AUG
GRIMLOCK!
GALVATRON!
RAVAGE! SHOCKWAVE! STARSCREAM!
THE GATHERING STORM!

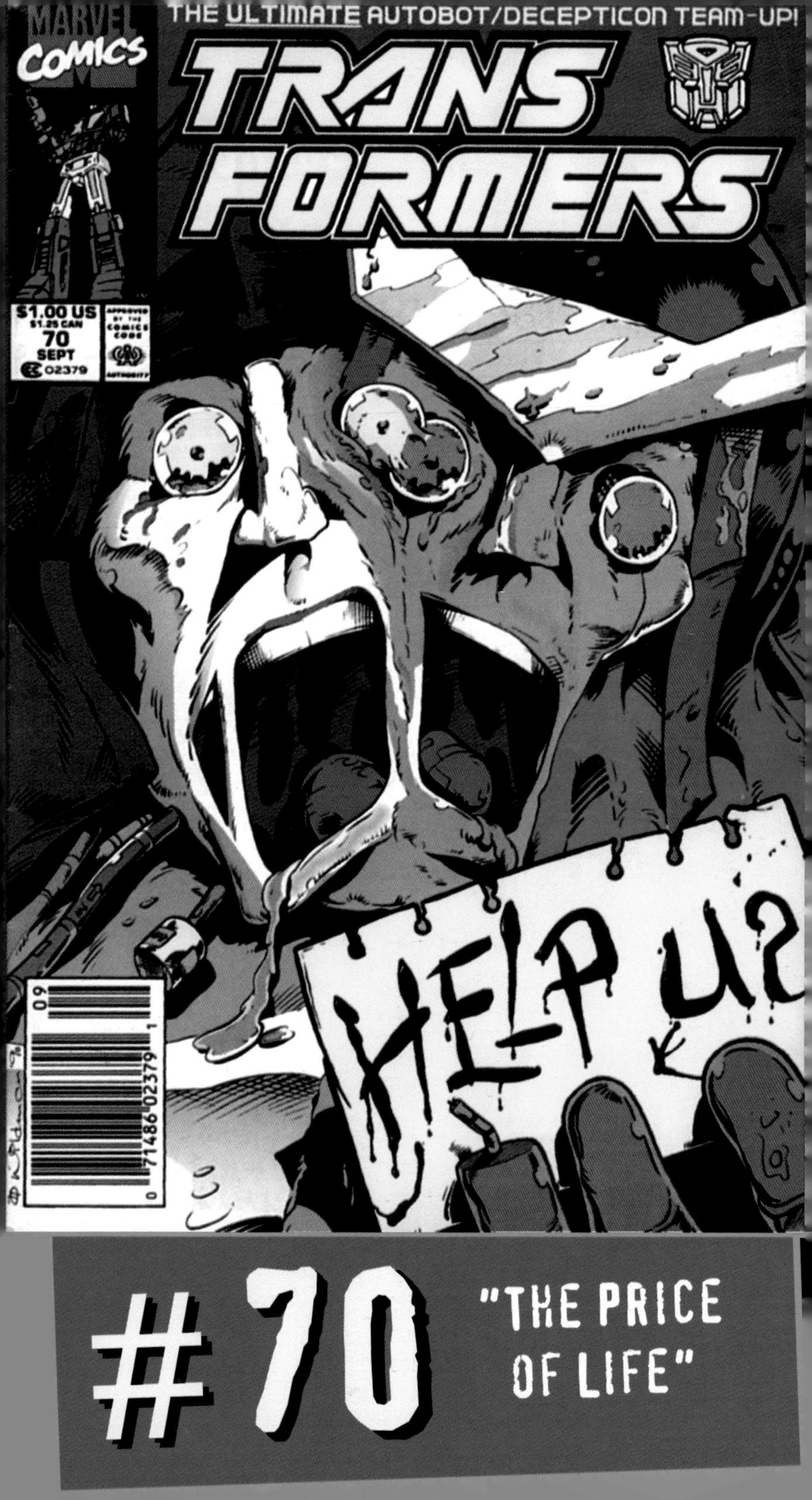
MARVEL COMICS
THE ULTIMATE AUTOBOT/DECEPTICON TEAM-UP!
TRANSFORMERS
$1.00 US
$1.25 CAN
70
SEPT
HELP U

#70 "THE PRICE OF LIFE"

#71 "SURRENDER"

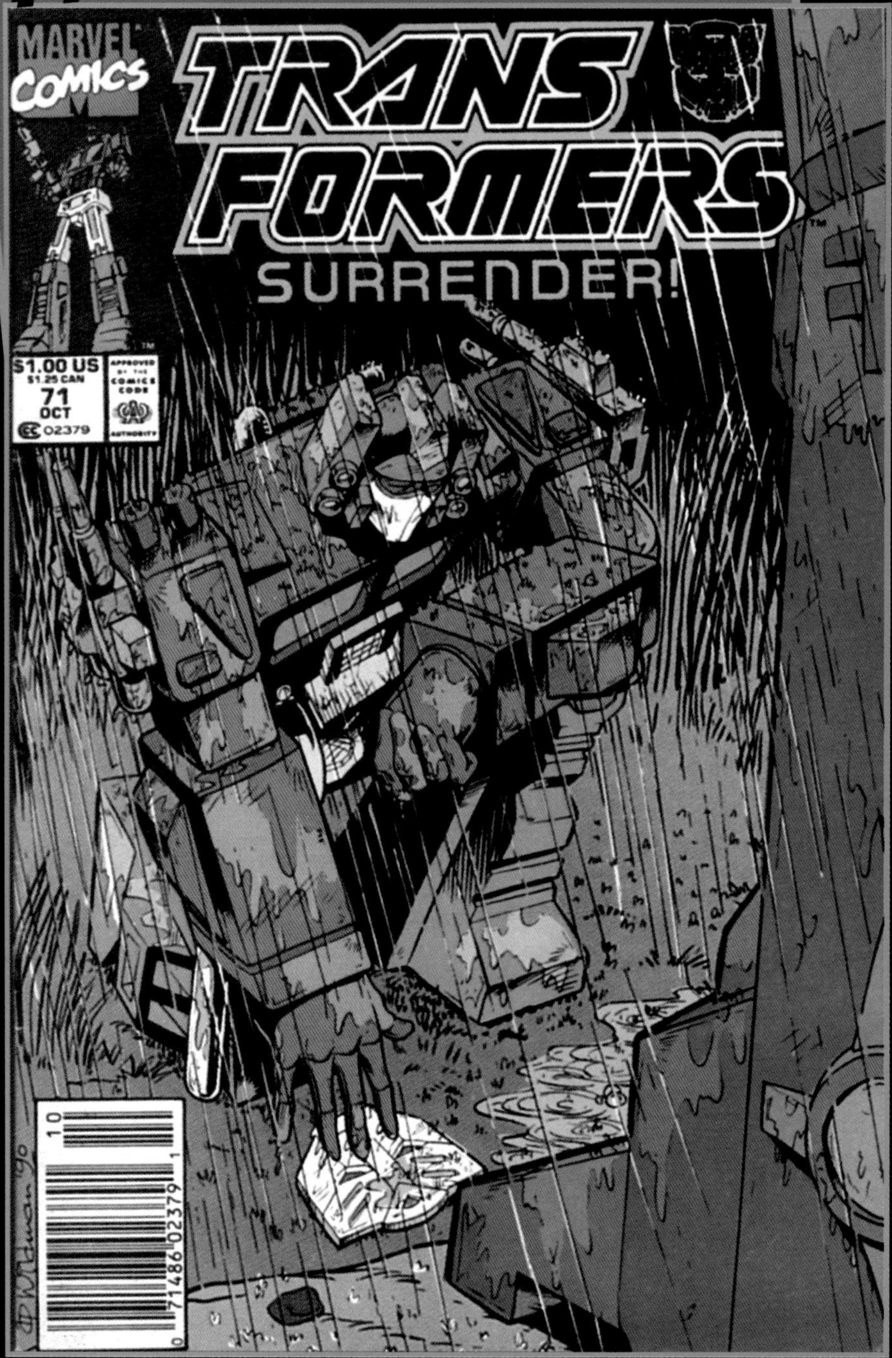
MARVEL COMICS
TRANSFORMERS
SURRENDER!
$1.00 US
$1.25 CAN
71
OCT
02379
APPROVED BY THE COMICS CODE AUTHORITY

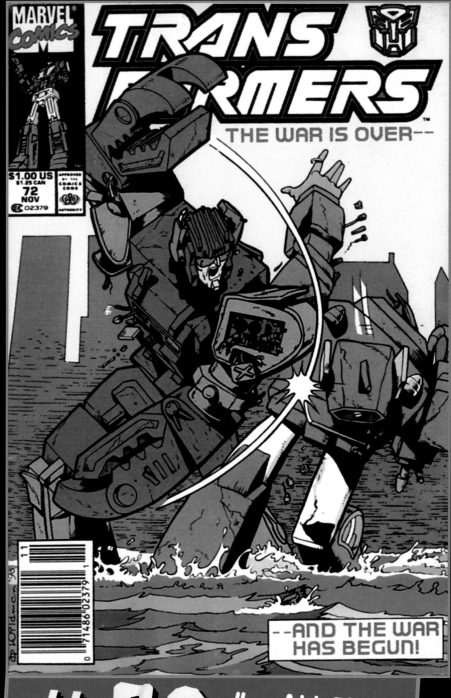

MARVEL COMICS

$1.00 US
$1.25 CAN
72
NOV
02379

TRANSFORMERS

THE WAR IS OVER--

--AND THE WAR HAS BEGUN!

#72

"... ALL THIS AND CIVIL WAR 2"

#73 "OUT OF TIME"

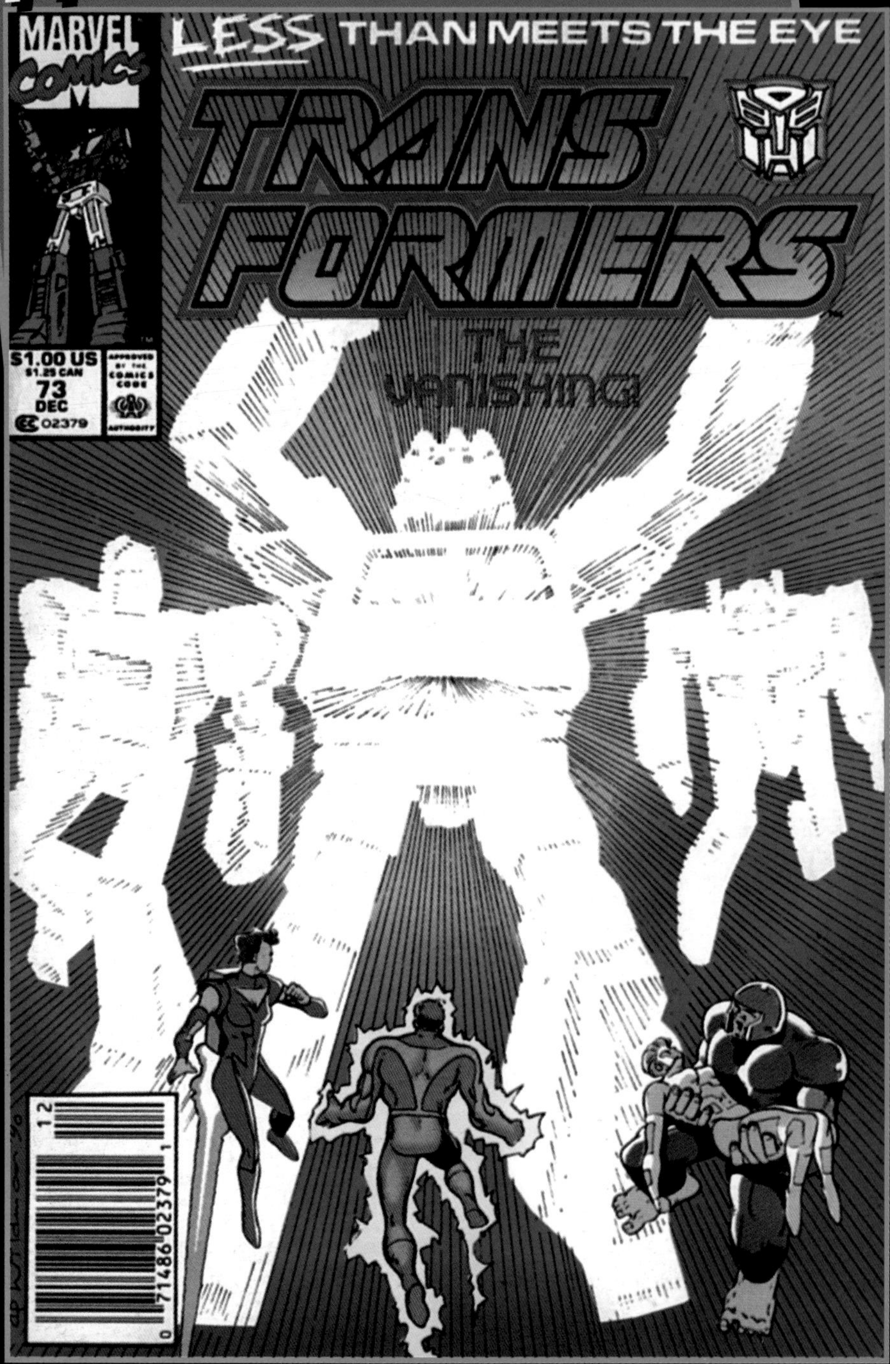
MARVEL COMICS
LESS THAN MEETS THE EYE
TRANSFORMERS
THE VANISHING!
$1.00 US
$1.25 CAN
73
DEC
02379
APPROVED BY THE COMICS CODE AUTHORITY

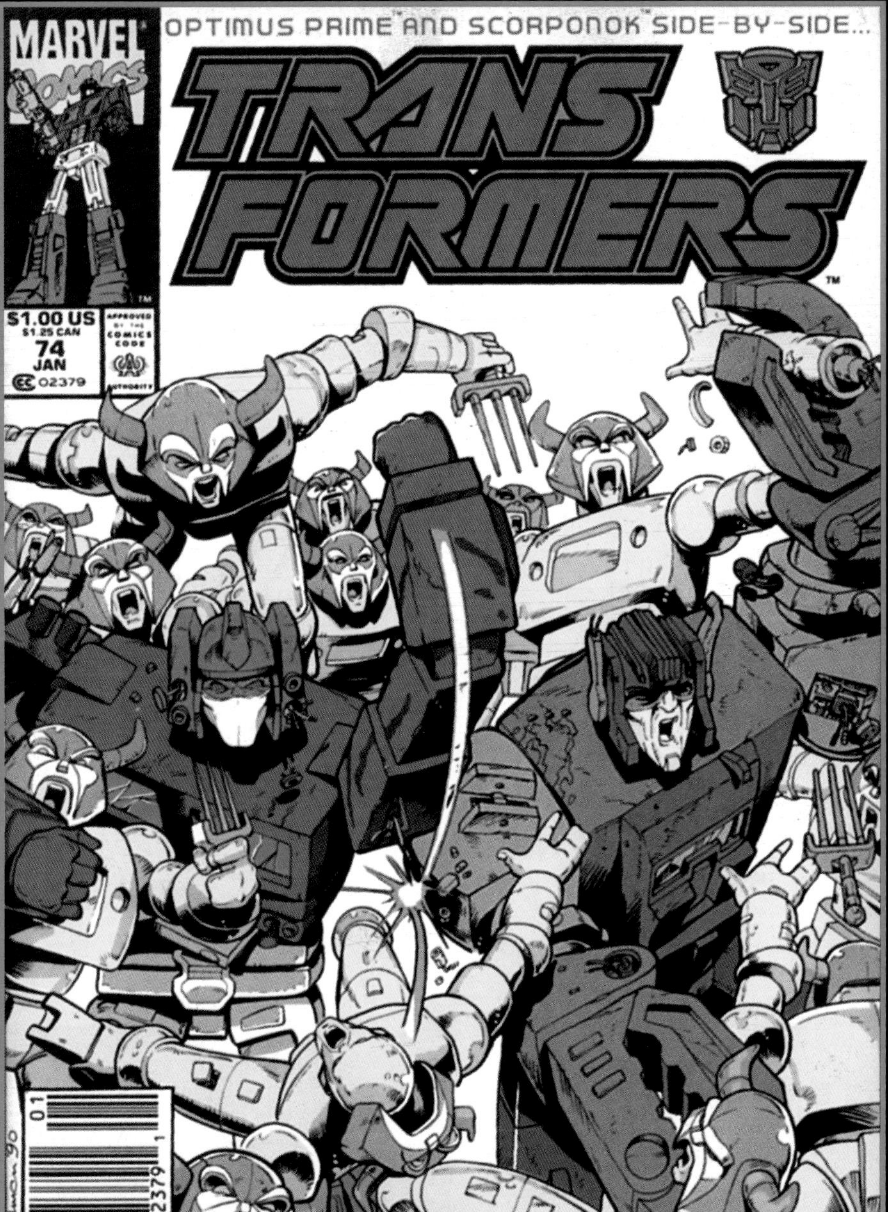
MARVEL COMICS
OPTIMUS PRIME AND SCORPONOK SIDE-BY-SIDE...
TRANSFORMERS
$1.00 US
$1.25 CAN
74
JAN
02379
APPROVED BY THE COMICS CODE AUTHORITY
...AGAINST THE HORDES OF UNICRON!

#74 "THE VOID"

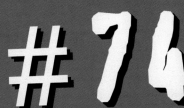

EVOLUTION

Andrew Wildman's incredible double cover (part of which graces this book, part of which can be seen on Transformers: End of the Road… coming in November) was created almost entirely in the computer. Some of the process stages and individual elements are presented here:

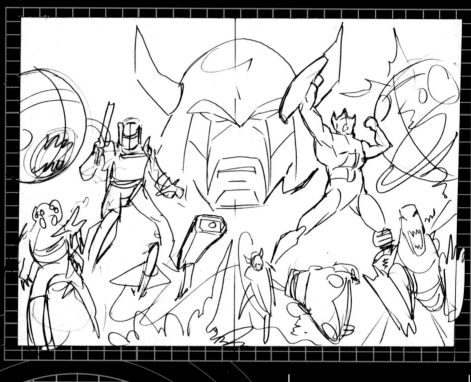

Andrew Wildman's original cover sketch.

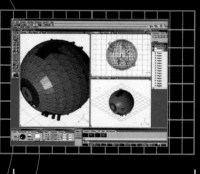

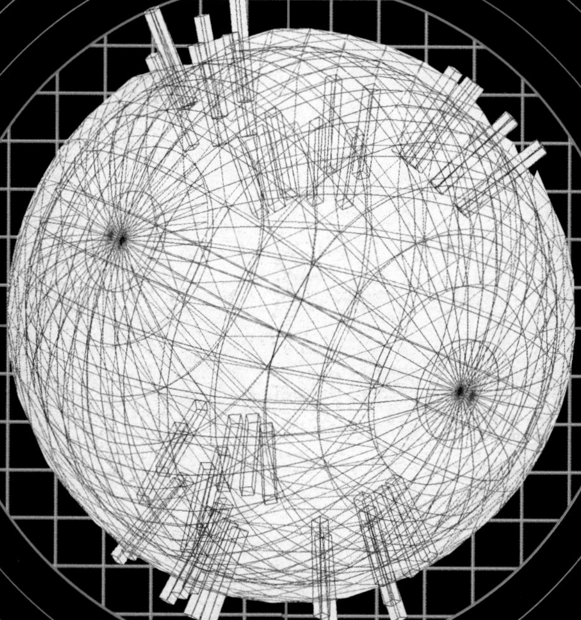

Computer models and wireframes for Unicron.

OF A COVER

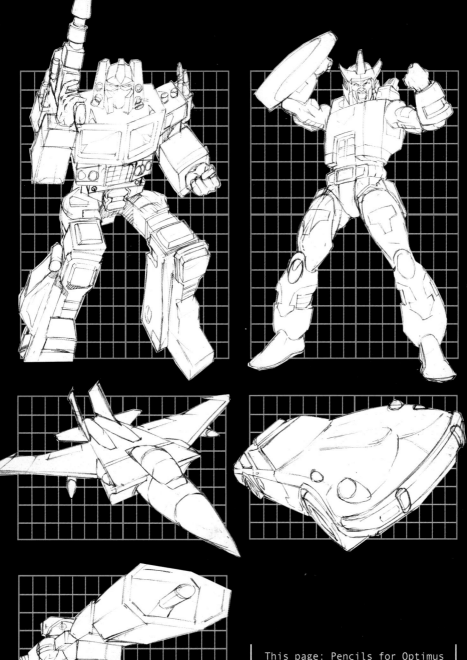

This page: Pencils for Optimus Prime, Galvatron, Starscream, Prowl and Shockwave. Each element was then composited in the computer.

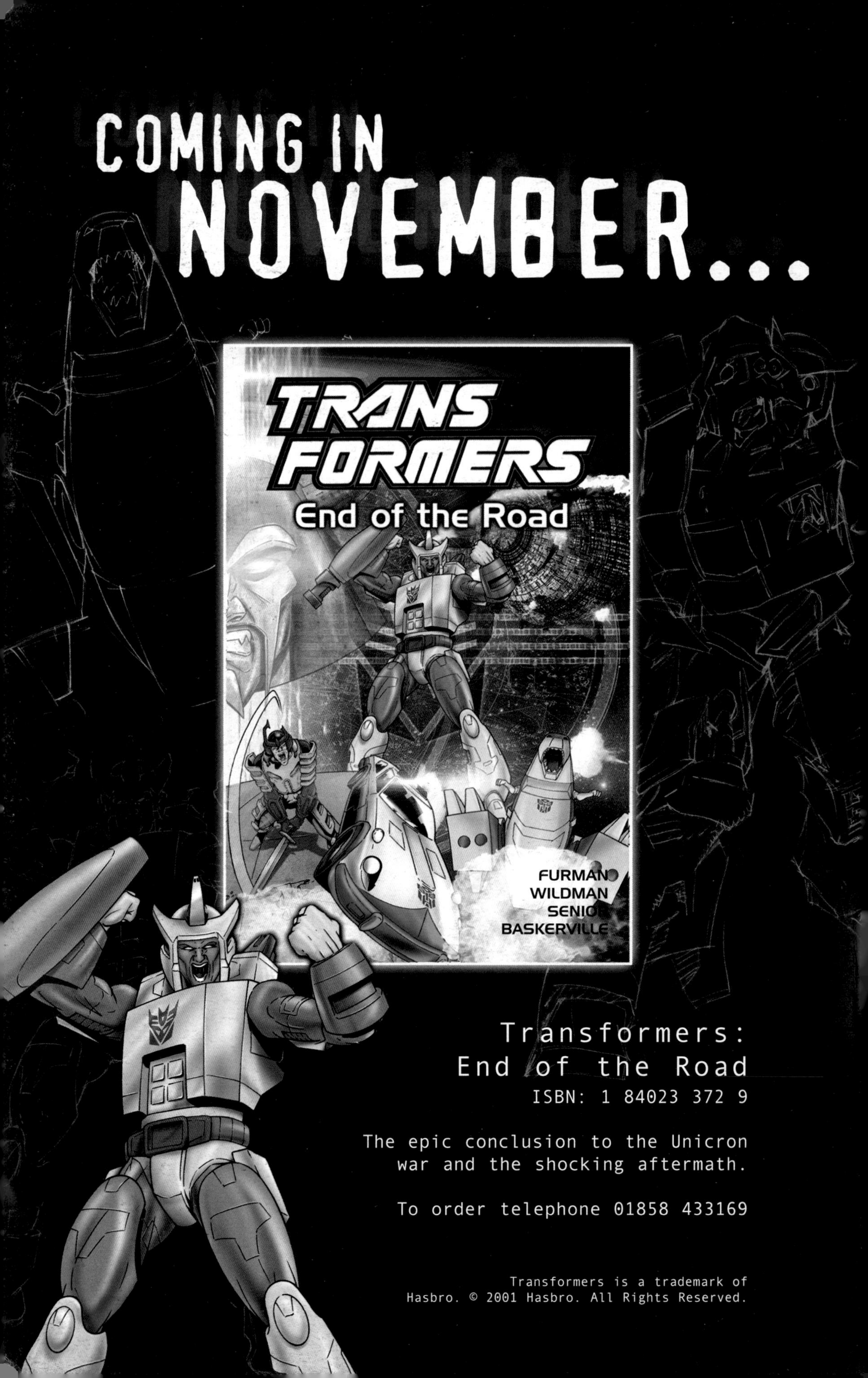
COMING IN
NOVEMBER...
TRANSFORMERS
End of the Road
FURMAN
WILDMAN
SENIOR
BASKERVILLE
Transformers:
End of the Road
ISBN: 1 84023 372 9
The epic conclusion to the Unicron
war and the shocking aftermath.
To order telephone 01858 433169
Transformers is a trademark of
Hasbro. © 2001 Hasbro. All Rights Reserved.